THE CHANGING WORLD
OF CHARLES DICKENS

THE CHANGING WORLD
OF CHARLES DICKENS

edited by
Robert Giddings

VISION
and
BARNES & NOBLE

Vision Press Limited
Fulham Wharf
Townmead Road
London SW6 2SB

and

Barnes & Noble Books
81 Adams Drive
Totowa, NJ 07512

ISBN (UK) 0 85478 325 3
ISBN (US) 0 389 20372 6

**To
the Memory of
Roy Huss**

Printed and bound in Great Britain by
Unwin Brothers Ltd.,
Old Woking, Surrey.
Phototypeset by Galleon Photosetting,
Ipswich, Suffolk.
MCMLXXXIII

Contents

Introduction

by ROBERT GIDDINGS

'My dear Louisa must be careful of that cough,' remarked Miss Tox.

'It's nothing,' returned Mrs. Chick. 'It's merely a change of weather. We must expect change.'

'Of weather?' asked Miss Tox, in her simplicity.

'Of everything,' returned Mrs. Chick. 'Of course we must. It's a world of change. Any one would surprise me very much . . . and would greatly alter my opinion of their understanding, if they attempted to contradict or evade what is so perfectly evident. Change!' exclaimed Mrs. Chick, with severe philosophy. 'Why, my gracious me, what is there that does *not* change! . . .'

—Charles Dickens, *Dombey and Son* (Ch. 29)

1

It is of course true that any moment in history may justly be termed a 'period of transition', although it is certainly the case that the early Victorians were deeply conscious of the fact that they were living at a time of rapid and all-embracing change, aware almost to the extent of believing that they existed in the moment as the past was changing into the future. Sir Henry Holland, writing in the *Edinburgh Quarterly* in 1858, referred to the remarkable period in which 'our lot is cast' and called it 'an age of transition'.[1] Prince Albert, Matthew Arnold, Benjamin Disraeli, Thomas Carlyle, Bulwer Lytton, Frederic Harrison, William Morris, John Morley, Alfred Lord Tennyson all refer specifically to *transition* and the *transitional* age.[2] J. S. Mill found transition to be the leading characteristic of the time; mankind had outgrown old institutions and old doctrines, he believed, and had not yet fully acquired new ones—this had been noticed only recently by the discerning 'a few years ago' and now 'it forces itself upon the most observant'.[3]

The majority of Victorians who could recall an age before the railroad felt that they had lived in two separate worlds: 'It was only yesterday,' Thackeray wrote,

> but what a gulf between now and then! *Then* was the old world. Stage-coaches . . . riding horses, pack-horses, highwaymen, knights in armour, Norman invaders, Roman legions, Druids, Ancient Britons painted blue . . . all these belong to the old period. . . . But your railroad starts the new era, and we of a certain age belong to the new time and the old one. . . . We are of the age of steam.[4]

The very title of Carlyle's *Past and Present* implied a comparison of the modern age and the Middle Ages. For Carlyle, writing in the 1840s, the past was very hard clearly to discern: 'The Past cannot be seen: the Past, looked at through the medium of "Philosophical History" in these times, cannot even be *not* seen: it is misseen; affirmed to have existed. . . .'[5] In a beautiful passage in *Sartor Resartus* he describes the Present as 'an inconsiderable Film dividing the Past and the Future . . .'.[6] Dr. Arnold, on seeing the first train pass through Rugby station, murmured that feudality had gone forever. He noted the fact in his journal for 4 August 1839.[7]

The significant thing realized by those living at the time is that the changes they observe going on around them are not minor, isolated, peripheral changes, but the whole fabric and structure of society was changing—the railway, the mechanical means of industrial production, the steam press, the telegraph—these were only the outward and visible signs of truly radical change. Modern man, Carlyle asserted, lived in a new time, under new conditions: '. . . his course can be the fac-simile of no prior one, but is by its nature original.'[8] The society portrayed in the fiction of Charles Dickens is seen at the period of the beginnings of popular democracy, industrial metamorphosis on a scale unequalled in history, the foundation and preliminary exploitation of a system of transport and communication we may today take for granted, the beginnings of the serious erosion of aristocratic control and the emergence of the ethos of self-help and its consequent effects on the social hierarchy.[9]

In the year of Dickens's birth the news of Napoleon's humiliation at Moscow took days of travel over land and sea to reach the capital cities of Europe. Before he was 40, in 1851, the news of Louis Napoleon's *coup d'état* in December was sent by electric telegraph within an hour of its happening, an immediacy which must have seemed astounding at the time: 'Paris in a state of siege. Dissolution of the Assembly. By electric tele-graph, Paris, Tuesday morning, December 2nd. . . . The President of the Republic accomplished a *coup d'état* this morn-ing. The principal streets in Paris were occupied at an early hour by strong bodies of infantry, cavalry and artillery. . . .'[10]

Fanny Kemble, the actress, describes an early railway journey on 26 August 1830 in terms of equestrian transport:

> We were introduced to the little engine which was to drag us along the rails, she (for they make these curious little fire-horses all mares) consists of a boiler, a stove, a small platform, a bench and behind the bench a barrel containing enough water to prevent her being thirsty for fifteen miles . . . She goes upon two wheels, which are her feet, and these are moved by bright steel legs called pistons. . . . The reigns, bit and bridle of this won-derful beast is a small steel handle. . . . The coals, which are its oats, were under the bench. . . .[11]

The last mail coach from Bath to London ran in 1841, and before Dickens's thirtieth birthday: 'Mr. Weller senior could think about hanging up his whip for good and all.'[12] By 1848 1,800 miles of railways—a third of the whole mileage in use—was already equipped with telegraph wires. In 1846 the Electric Telegraph Company was founded and by 1854 had seventeen offices in London. The arrangements for the candi-dature of the Prince Consort as Chancellor of the University of Cambridge in 1847 were in part conducted by telegram. By the following year *Punch* was predicting the dire effect of the telegraph on

> the operations of everyday life, as it has been proposed to carry an ordinary conversation by means of the Electric Telegraph. . . . We should not be surprised to hear of Her Majesty's having resolved to deliver her Speech by Electric Telegraph . . . and though the dial plate of the machine would not be such a pleasing object as that disc of sunshine, the countenance of Royalty, we think there would be something gained in sparing the Queen the

9

bore of a very tiresome ceremony, in which she is annually obliged to participate.[13]

Contemporary with the development of rail transport was the ascendancy of steam over sail. In 1847, for example, of a total tonnage of 3,000 in the merchant fleet, already 116,000 tons were steamships. In 1842 Dickens and his family sailed for the United States in the steamship *Brittania*. The ocean-going vessels of the mid-century were increasingly steam-propelled and made of iron and, later, of steel. In 1848 Britain produced half the pig-iron of the world, and in the next three decades output was to be trebled. In 1851, Dickens's fortieth year, the Great Exhibition of the Works of Industry of All Nations was staged. In the following year Britain imported 740,000,000 pounds of raw cotton; and exported 1,524,000 yards of cottons; 165,527,000 yards of woollens; 133,193,000 yards of linens; and 1,131,000 pounds of silks. In 1870, the year of his death, the volume of the external trade of Great Britain was worth more than that of France, Germany and Italy put together, and was between three and four times that of the United States. World steel production in this year was 560,000 tons, one half of which was produced in the United Kingdom, and our railway mileage had reached 15,310 miles in use. Over 75% of the 436,000 tons of shipping which used the Suez Canal was British. If Mr. Pickwick's world was 'the world of the fast stage coach and the First Reform Bill',[14] the world of Mr. Dombey was the world of iron and steel, tremendous trade advancement, public agitation for the extension of the franchise, and far-reaching readjustment and upheaval.[15]

2

Dickens's art did not just reflect these momentous changes. To a considerable extent the very nature and quality of his art was shaped, textured and conditioned by these changes. What is really the point is not so much Dickens's effect on history, as history's effect on Dickens.

Dickens's life spanned a period of massive developments in

printing technology and in the means of transport. The steam press meant that thousands of copies could be produced, and the railways created the means of wide distribution. These factors, combined with developments in the cheap production of paper and government legislation which lowered paper costs and reduced tax on advertising revenue, created the popular press and mass-produced journalism. During the same period popular literacy increased, initially as a result of Sunday schools and charity organizations, later in the period by the direct involvement of the government in the schooling of the nation. Forster's Education Act was passed in the year Dickens died.[16] As a youth he was an avid reader of popular crime magazines,[17] and crime was one of the major ingredients of the new mass publications and has remained a staple of the popular press ever since the early Victorian period—the *News of the World* was founded in 1842. He had also been attracted early in life to eighteenth-century periodic literature—Addison, Steele and Goldsmith in particular.[18] These experiences introduced him to violence and melodrama as subjects for writing, and to the idea of literature as a popular, periodically produced artifact. Popular journalism of the sensational sort—with its obsession with 'human interest', with crime, with the unexpected, with sudden reversals of fortune, with wealth and snobbish fantasies—and the mechanics of serial publication are among the most significant conditioning factors of his fiction. The intrusion of violence and crime into the very texture of domestic life is given to us in the description of the Dombey mansion's period of mourning at the death of the lady of the house:

> Mr. Dombey ordered the furniture to be covered up. . . . Accordingly, mysterious shapes were made of tables and chairs . . . covered over with great winding sheets. Bell-handles, window-blinds, and looking-glasses being papered up in journals . . . obtruding fragmentary accounts of deaths and dreadful murders. . . .

At the opening of the century Wordsworth had commented that the effect of city life and factory work was to make people want to read exciting out-of-the-way things. The human mind, he believed, was capable of being moved 'without the application of gross and violent stimulants . . .'. One being, he believed, was elevated above another in proportion as he possessed the capacity to be stimulated without the excitement provided by extremes of passion and sensationalism. Wordsworth perceived it as his duty as a poet to enlarge this capacity among readers of poetry. It is important to note that he believed this situation to be new and recent:

> For a multitude of causes, unknown to former times, are now acting with a combined force to blunt the discriminating powers of the mind, and, unfitting it for all voluntary exertion, to reduce it almost to a state of savage torpor. The most effective of these causes are the great national events which are daily taking place, and the increasing accumulation of men in cities, where the uniformity of their occupations produces a craving for extraordinary incident. . . .[19]

Wordsworth's case has indeed become a familiar one. A character in Jean Anouilh's *The Rehearsal* asks: 'Have you noticed that life, real honest-to-goodness life, with murders and catastrophes and fabulous inheritances, happens almost exclusively in newspapers?'

3

Circumstances combined to produce a revolution in literacy, a marked feature of which was serial publication. This opened up a whole new range of possibilities for the small printer, as well as massive opportunities for the well-capitalized major publishing operator. Eight pages could be printed on one sheet on a hand press and even quite lengthy volumes could be printed with almost no capital, as the income from one issue paid for the next. Unsold weekly parts could be stitched and sold as monthly parts, and then finally bound and sold as a normal volume. In effect, all pockets were appealed to. In order to keep costs down, initially there was an interest in publishing works which carried no copyright. Works were often pirated. Dickens himself was to become a frequent victim of this practice—*Picwick Papers*, as well as the *Post-humorous Notes of the Pickwickian Club*, edited by 'Bos', *The Memoirs of Nicholas Nicklebery*, *Dombey and Daughter*, etc.[20]

The boom in publishing in the first part of the century was

linked with the astonishing developments in transport, as the coming of the railway meant not only that publications could be marketed in areas some way from the place of their production, but that a whole new market was created—the railway bookstall. The figures are impressive: sales of newspapers rose by 33% between 1816 and 1836 and by 70% between 1836 and 1856.[21] The same period saw the serial publication of Limbird's *British Novelists* between 1823 and 1846, and the *Standard Works of Fiction of All Countries* between 1831 and 1832, *Pattie's Pocket Library*, *The Novelist*, *The Novel Newspaper*—all date from this time. One great personal success story here is George Routledge, born the same year as Dickens. He opened his business in Soho Square in 1843 and had branches in New York. By 1854 the *Routledge Railway Library* had over 1,000 titles on offer, at one shilling each. As John William Palmer, printer to Cambridge University who sold his London business to Longmans, commented:

> At the present time books are plentiful, and books are cheap. Formerly books were written for the privileged few; now they are printed for the million. Books of every description, and at almost any price. . . . All tastes are catered for, all opinions find their peculiar expository organ. . . . Everything for a penny. Penny Pulpit—Penny Magazine—Penny Shakespeare—Penny Novelist—Penny Medical Adviser—Penny Educator—Penny Encyclopaedia. . . .[22]

A correspondent wrote to the *New Sporting Magazine* in 1836:

> This is 'the patent age of new inventions' and improvements. Our outward man and our inward man, our senses, all and sundry; everything that we eat, drink, or wear, stand upon, sit upon, walk upon, or ride upon . . . all are partakers of this wondrous march. It annihilates time, confounds space, unsettles rank and distinction. . . . Once upon a time there was your scholar, your traveller, your libertine, and a just and proper distinction amongst mankind. There was no jostling over the lines of demarcation naturally (I may say) drawn between one class and another. But now, Lord save us! since the establishment of the 'general-united-imperial-anti-retrogradation-reading-made-easy society' . . . every barrier which could tend to check the progress of knowledge has been removed. . . .

This was the year of *Pickwick Papers*, the appeal of which, as John Forster commented, cut right across class barriers: 'Judges on the bench and boys in the street, gravity and folly, the young and the old, those who were entering life and those who were quitting it, alike found it to be irresistible.' A witness recorded coming across a group of twenty men and women in a shop who were too poor to be able to afford the shilling to buy the monthly instalment of *Pickwick*. They were renting a copy at two pence a day from a library and one of them was reading it aloud to all the others. The age of the common reader had arrived, and it required a new kind of authorship.

4

Dickens's unique creative gifts were to manifest themselves at this period of increasing popular literacy and the first stages of mass publication. What we recognize as the genius of his fiction is the result of the connection made between genius and the means of production and distribution. All his novels were initially published as serials, and, with the exceptions only of *Hard Times* and *A Tale of Two Cities* and *Great Expectations*, they were published in monthly parts.[23] The relationship between Dickens, his publishers and his public was therefore vital. In order to help the publisher make ends meet, and to make a profit to share with the author—which could only be done provided the publishers were able to offer advertisers useful space to push their goods—Dickens had continually to appeal to a wide readership. In the eighteenth century the five-volume novel was common, sometimes as many as seven volumes. By the time of Scott and Jane Austen the usual number of volumes was cut to three or four. Novel reading was expensive. Each volume might cost as much as half a guinea. Those who could not afford to buy books might read them by getting them from a circulating library. *Pickwick Papers* was published in 1836 in monthly parts at one shilling each. The serial parts of *David Copperfield*, *Nicholas Nickleby*, *Bleak House* and the other masterpieces, were actually consumer products. They carried advertisements for consumer goods—'the Ondina, or Waved Lupon Crinoline' in which the wearer 'may ascend a steep stair, lean against a table, throw herself into an armchair . . . without inconvenience to others or provoking the rude remarks of the observers'. There are plugs for numerous pills, for the 'newly invented swimming gloves' and for the celebrated suits of Mr. Moses:

> Manners and learning, you will all confess,
> Are nought without the supplement of dress;
> Good dress, in fact, will cover sore defects
> While credit on the wearer it reflects.
> The beau ideal which the mind supposes
> Is one who dresses in the clothes of Moses.

This gem of the advertiser's art is from the serial parts of *Dombey and Son*. It is quite true that rising literacy and the sophistication of literary production and distribution offered a writer such as Charles Dickens tremendous opportunities, but on the other hand these very opportunities came with certain conditions. He had to write what the public wanted to read. He had to cast his fictions in particular forms and within certain conventions. His correspondence and other biographical evidence will show his constant battle to write honestly and creatively within the best possible terms to be negotiated between these various requirements, as well as his understandable attempts to get the best price for his efforts. There is something quintessentially Dickensian in the context within which *A Christmas Carol* appeared. Dickens expected great things from this cautionary tale about a man who sold his soul in the ambition to make money. It was to be published by Chapman and Hall on commission. 6,000 copies of the first edition were sold the day it came out in January 1844, and 2,000 copies of the second edition were taken by the trade. Dickens anticipated that he would take at least £1,000! On 10 February Chapmans sent him the accounts which revealed that he was to get only £230 on the first edition. He believed he had been tricked by the publishers: 'I have not the least doubt that they have run the expenses up anyhow purposely . . .' to bring him to heel and cut into his profit.[24] The energies he expended attempting to please the public and trying to maintain good contractual arrangements with his publishers were enormous. Eventually he was to exploit the modern means of transport and communication when he transformed himself into a performer of his own works, touring Britain and the United States from 1858.

The logistics of this amazing series of readings—the travel, correspondence, business management, public relations—were made possible by technical and economic advances, and once again the very nature of the creative artist was redefined. The emotional and physical strain of these performances on Dickens has been well documented. He clearly sensed that public reading added a new dimension to his art. On 15 March 1870 he gave his last reading, at St. James's Hall, a mere three months before he died. As the applause at the conclusion of his reading the trail scene from *Pickwick* died down he addressed the audience and said:

> Ladies and Gentlemen, It would be worse than idle—for it would be hypocritical and unfeeling—if I were to disguise that I close this episode in my life with feelings of very considerable pain. For some fifteen years, in this hall and in many kindred places, I have had the honour of presenting my own cherished ideas before you for your recognition; and, in closely observing your reception of them, have enjoyed an amount of artistic delight and instruction which, perhaps, is given to few men to know. In this task, and in every other which I have ever undertaken, as a faithful servant of the public, always imbued with a sense of duty to them, and always striving to do his best, I have been uniformly cheered by the readiest response, the most generous sympathy, and the most stimulating support. . . .

His stressing the relationship which he felt existed between himself as an artist and the public he served is very striking. He ended with these words: '. . . from these garish lights I vanish now for evermore, with a heartfelt, grateful, respectful and affectionate farewell.'[25] But he was not to disappear. Far from it.

5

Dickens was not immediately to become part of the permanent furniture and fittings of our literary consciousness, in noble eminence 'enthron'd and spher'd', along with Chaucer, Shakespeare, Milton, Pope amid the other luminaries. His reputation has been very much up and down, or rather down and then up, while there has been mutiny, raging of the sea, shaking of earth, commotion in the winds, frights, changes, horrors, as the unity and married calm of academic taste been diverted quite from its fixture. At each change in the estimation of his merits, Dickens has been quite differently perceived. At one time the undisputed master novelist of his day: 'Nothing like it since Shakespeare', said the formidable Lord Jeffrey of *The Old Curiosity Shop*. A decade before his death the tide was already turning. The young Henry James wrote in *The Nation* in 1865 that Dickens had been forcing himself for the past decade—*Bleak House*, *Little Dorrit* showed the strain, and *Our Mutual Friend* was dug out 'as with a spade and pickaxe'. William Samuel Lilley in the 1890s asserted that Dickens was at his best in his earlier works, 'where he makes small pretence to art'. *Pickwick Papers*, he said, was his masterpiece. Later Victorians found Dickens 'unreal'. Apart from a few unusual critics, such as Gissing, Shaw and Chesterton, this view prevailed well into the new century. Even though Middleton Murry was predicting a return of Dickens to favour as early as the 1920s, the novelist's reputation was to reach its all-time low between the wars. But there were the first signs of a major shift in taste. In 1937 T. A. Jackson's *Charles Dickens: The Progress of a Radical* appeared, to be followed two years later by Edmund Wilson's *Dickens: The Two Scrooges*. Both these works, imperfect and tricksy though they might be in some important respects, did show that the art of Charles Dickens was to be taken seriously. This needed saying. The state of play may be gauged from the fact that some ten years after the appearance of these pioneer works of Jackson and Wilson, T. S. Eliot—High Pontiff of the English speaking literary establishment—was able to assert that there 'is no better critic of Dickens living than Mr. Chesterton'.[26] Jackson and Wilson were of singular importance in the developing evaluation of Dickens's genius. They demonstrated the profound effects of two major developments in modern scholarship, the impact of Marxism and Freudianism, of politico-sociological studies and psychology.[27] Even though Dickens was thrust firmly (if politely) out of F. R. Leavis's *The Great Tradition*, he has refused to go away.

Since the centenary of Dickens's death his rehabilitation has been almost completely effected, and it must be stressed that in part it has certainly been helped by the efforts of Dr. Leavis himself and his wife, who published *Dickens the Novelist* in 1971, although it is my view that the real driving force in the Dickens revival was American in origin.[28] But the full and complete apprehension of the staggering power and energy of Dickens's creativity is not just the concern of academic opinion leaders. Our awareness of Dickens is furthered and adjusted by each new film, or musical, or dramatization, or radio serialization or television adaptation or paperback edition. In much the same way as Dickens's creative imagination expressed itself in the dynamic which existed between his genius and the means of literary production and distribution within the social context in the decades 1830 to 1870, so our constantly developing construction of Charles Dickens is assisted and conditioned by modern psychology, historiography, linguistics, social and political science and mass communication. In fact, Dickens's existence in our literature has been, and no doubt will continue to be, similar to that he describes of the Broker's Man in *Sketches by Boz*: '. . . one of a very chequered description: he has undergone transitions. . . .'

NOTES

1. Quoted in Walter E. Houghton, *The Victorian Frame of Mind* (Yale, 1957), p. 1.
2. Ibid., p. 1 and following.
3. J. S. Mill, *The Spirit of the Age* (Chicago, 1942), p. 1.
4. Thackeray, *De Juventute* (1860), reprinted in *Roundabout Papers*.
5. Carlyle, *Past and Present* (1843), Library Edition, Vol. XIII, p. 287.
6. Carlyle, *Sartor Resartus* (1831), Centenary Edition 1896, Vol. I, p. 198.
7. A. P. Stanley, *Life of Thomas Arnold* (1844), Appendix D, p. 723.
8. Carlyle, *Sartor Resartus*, op. cit., pp. 96–7.
9. R. J. Morris, *The History of Self Help*, in *New Society* (3 December 1970), 992–95 and Pauline Gregg, *A Social And Economic History of Britain 1790–1960* (1962), pp. 314–21.
10. *Annual Register*, Vol. 93 (1851), pp. 193–94. Dickens was very impressed with the possibilities of the electric telegraph, cf. *Dombey and Son*. He wrote in a letter in 1856 how excited he had been by a play which had made dramatic use of the electric telegraph: 'It was impossible not to be moved and excited by the telegraph part of it.' *Dombey and Son* (Penguin English Library edition, 1970), p. 985.

11. Frances Ann Kemble, *Record of a Girlhood*, in *Victorian Prose*, edited by Kenneth and Mirium Allot (1956), pp. 1–4.
12. Robin Atthill, *Dickens and the Railway*, in *Magazine of the English Association*, Vol. XIII (Spring 1961), pp. 131–35.
13. *Punch*, Vol. XV (1849), 94.
14. G. M. Trevelyan, *English Social History* (1948), p. 535.
15. See the opening sections of George Kitson Clark, *An Expanding Society— Britain 1830–1900* (1967); and H. Parkin, *The Origins of Modern English Society 1780–1880* (1969); and Humphry House, *The Dickens World* (1969), pp. 113–69.
16. See Louis James, *Fiction for the Working Man* (1974), pp. 1–14.
17. Angus Wilson, *The World of Charles Dickens* (1970), p. 62.
18. Sylvere Monod, *Dickens the Novelist* (Oklahoma, 1968), pp. 30–1.
19. Wordsworth, *Preface to the Lyrical Ballads* in *English Critical Texts*, edited Enright and de Chickera (1965), p. 166.
20. Victor E. Neuburg, *Popular Literature* (1976), pp. 171–72.
21. Raymond Williams, *Communications* (1975), p. 15.
22. J. William Palmer, *Meliora*, 2nd. series (1853), p. 72.
23. See John Butt and Kathleen Tillotson, *Dickens at Work* (1970).
24. Edgar Johnson, *Charles Dickens: His Tragedy and Triumph* (Boston, 1952), pp. 466–67, 490 and following.
25. *The Speeches of Charles Dickens*, edited by K. J. Fielding (1960), p. 413.
26. T. S. Eliot, *Selected Essays* (1952), p. 461.
27. See Robert Giddings, *A Cockney in the Court of Uncle Sam*, in the *Dickens Studies Newsletter* (Southern Illinois University Press, Carbondale, June 1975).
28. See Robert Giddings, review article on John Carey's *The Violent Effigy: A Study of Dickens's Imagination*, in *Dickens Studies Newsletter* (Southern Illinois University Press, Carbondale, June 1976).

1

Literature's 'Eternal Duties': Dickens's Professional Creed

by DAVID PAROISSIEN

I know you would have been full of sympathy and approval if
you had been present at Birmingham [where Dickens accepted
on 6 January 1853 a silver ring and salver presented to him by
the people of the city in recognition of his contribution to
literature], and that you would have concurred in the tone I
tried to take about the eternal duties of the arts to the people. I
took the liberty of putting the court and that kind of thing out of
the question, and recognising nothing *but* the arts and the
people. The more we see of life and its brevity, and the world
and its varieties, the more we know that no exercise of our
abilities in any art, but the addressing of it to the great ocean of
humanity in which we are drops, and not to bye-ponds (very
stagnant) here and there, ever can or ever will lay the foundations of an endurable retrospect. Is it not so?
—Dickens to W. C. Macready, 14 January 1853

1

Generally critics have conceded Dickens's enduring popularity
as one of Britain's most widely read novelists, but many refused
to grant him the status of a serious writer of fiction until
recently. The period between 1939 and Dickens's Centenary

saw a major reappraisal of his contribution to the novel and the growth of a new critical orthodoxy. Dickens is now ranked foremost among the Victorian novelists and included among the great figures of English literature.[1]

Critical reassessment of Dickens's achievement might have come more quickly had he left a body of critical writing. Something comparable, say, to Henry James's Prefaces or Notebooks, or a private record of creative labours similar to the chronicle Flaubert left describing his attempts to perfect *Madame Bovary*, might have saved Dickens from those who saw art and popularity as mutually exclusive activities. A man who writes to explain his writing, however, 'makes a weak case', Dickens believed, because a work 'should explain itself; rest manfully and calmly on its knowledge of itself; and express whatever intention and purpose' are in the author.[2] Holding such views, Dickens wrote very brief prefaces and made few public statements about his art, one result of which was to foster the view of him as a brilliant but undisciplined autodidact. This misconception of Dickens remained unchallenged until the publication of The Nonesuch Letters in 1938 and important essays by Edmund Wilson and George Orwell.[3] These landmarks, recent writers agree, represent the turn of the critical tide and the beginning of the modern practice of taking Dickens seriously as a writer whose world-view merits attention and whose contribution to the art of fiction commands respect.

The three-volume collection of letters assembled by Walter Dexter demonstrates a continuous concern with the art of the novel in several important ways. For example, the letters attest to Dickens's preoccupation with the novelist's craft, and specific comments to young authors reveal some of his views about the purpose of character, the handling of plot, and the use of background and description. The letters also provide the raw material from which we can infer Dickens's opinion about literature's purpose and the gravity with which he saw his professional obligations. The letters do not furnish a complete aesthetic credo, but taken together they illustrate the major principles that guided Dickens throughout his career as a novelist and journal editor.

As a young writer who quickly took his place in what he called 'the procession of Fame' (*P*, II, 156), Dickens frequently found himself called upon to dispense advice to others eager to follow the same path. This role was later reinforced when Dickens added to his achievements the successful editorship of *Household Words* and *All the Year Round*, where for a twenty-year period he exercised considerable influence upon the numerous contributors to both journals. Throughout his 'conductorship' and stretching back to his early days, Dickens gave writers consistent advice: master the form you choose, he told aspiring poets, dramatists, novelists, and all 'Voluntary Correspondents', who threw their thoughts upon paper, hoping vainly that their productions would merit publication in one of his journals (*Household Words*, 16 April 1853).[4] Do not rush to print, Dickens advised, but hold yourself only to the most professional standards in self-appraisal. Most sobering to young writers was Dickens's plain-speaking about the personal sacrifice writing demanded. If time was spent 'at the cost of any bitterness of heart', the novice was wrong to make writing his vocation; if he did his duty cheerfully, and made 'these toils a relaxation and solace', he did right. One also needed the strength to take rejection notices without falling into 'vexation and disappointment'. But if failure made the writer wretched and if he pursued a career in literature with neither the talent nor the calling, Dickens did not spare the aspirant the necessary truth. '[L]ock up your papers, burn your pen, and thank Heaven you are not obliged to live by it' (*P*, II, 157).

The patient and informative letters Dickens wrote to those submitting stories to *Household Words* and *All the Year Round* make more specific points about the nature of fiction and are of interest for that reason. Turning to Dickens's letter to Wilkie Collins about the 1867 Christmas Story, *No Thoroughfare*, we see him stating succinctly the importance of generating narrative interest and the means by which the author provides 'a very Avalanche of power' to engage the reader. A flight and a pursuit, horrors and dangers, 'Ghostly interest, picturesque interest, breathless interest of time and circumstance'—all are basic ingredients used by Dickens to force the design, irrespective of length, to a powerful climax (*NL*, III, 542).

By contrast, other letters concern those aspects of the craft of fiction about which earlier critics pronounced Dickens ignorant. Dickens frequently reminded less experienced of the importance of not intruding upon the narrator in their own persons, and of showing characters working out their purpose through dialogue and dramatic action in the manner of the novelist, who should not tell about his characters or talk of them discursively, in the manner of the essayist (*NL*, III, 138). Do not cry, ' "Lo here! Lo there! See where it comes!" ' Dickens told Constance Cross. Rather, try to present characters unaffectedly, with the art of seeming to leave them to present themselves (*NL*, III, 774). To help readers see people or places, much could be done through the addition of 'little subtle touches of description' to give an 'attendant atmosphere of truth' and 'an air of reality'. Without that, Dickens thought, passionate characters ran the danger of glaring, wheeling, and hissing like great fireworks, which went out and lighted nothing (*NL*, II, 850).

Other letters forcefully demonstrate the inaccuracy of the clichés about the supposed ease of serial composition, which enabled the writer to toss off his weekly or monthly quota to an undiscerning audience. Writing in 'detached portions' required a particular and exacting skill, one calling for an eye to be kept on the novel as a whole while attending to the serial parts. You cannot take a story and cut it up into the instalment into which it would have to be divided for a month's supply, Dickens wrote to Mrs. Brookfield, without discovering the impossibility of such a procedure. Rather 'that specially trying mode of publication' by the week or by the month required 'a special design', in which the scheme of the chapters, the manner of introducing the people, and the plotting of the story's progress and principal scenes were all completely integrated into the serial's double focus of the instalment and the whole (*NL*, III, 461).

Dickens is equally perceptive about the basic choices facing a novelist in the use of form. If the writer chooses to anatomize 'the souls of the actors', slowness, care, and 'a longer space of time' are necessary (*NL*, II, 849). Otherwise, if restricted to a more limited compass, the novelist must limit himself to whatever can be accomplished within the bounds of length. And at all times, the writer must face the crucial question: what truly belongs to this ideal character under these particular imagined circumstances? 'When one is impelled to write this or that, one still has to consider,' Dickens wrote to Emily Jolly, '. . . "How much of it is my own wild emotion and superfluous energy" ', and how much of the subject matter is dictated by the intellectual logic of the fiction itself? Not surprisingly, Dickens offers no simple formula by which to judge the extent personal experience should or should not manifest itself in any work. Instead, he emphasized the importance of the writer's adjusting his original experience of persons, places, and emotions to the new imaginative context of the fiction. 'It is in the laborious struggle to make this distinction, and in the determination to try for it, that the road to the correction of faults lies' (*NL*, II, 850).

As Dickens admitted to Emily Jolly in support of the sincerity of his advice, his own tendency towards impatience and impulsiveness when writing made him all the more aware of the need for the control he urged upon others. '[I]t has been for many years the constant effort of my life to practise at my desk what I preach to you', he explained to this talented contributor to *Household Words* (*NL*, II, 850). Indeed, Dickens's injunction to self-discipline, seriousness, and the need to master one's craft represents the distillation of experience and the expression of the iron professional will that won him so outstanding a position among his contemporaries. When he fell hard at work on a book, Dickens usually put in a full day, routinely writing from nine to two in the afternoon throughout the period of the book's composition. Although Dickens was no word-counter like Trollope, who imprisoned himself at his desk and mercilessly produced '250 words every quarter of an hour',[5] he found that the demands of serial fiction superseded almost every aspect of his attention, including even emotional upsets and turmoil. 'Every Artist, be he writer, painter, musician, or actor, must bear his private sorrows as best he can, and must separate them from the exercise of his public pursuit', Dickens wrote in an obituary notice for Clarkson Stanfield in *All the Year Round*.[6] On this occasion the 'private loss of a dear friend' also represented 'a loss on the part of the whole community', which justified Dickens's stepping forth 'to lay his little wreath' for the painter he affectionately called 'Stanny'. Only once in Dickens's career did private sorrow become so overwhelming as to interrupt his work. As a young

man, grief over Mary Hogarth's death on 7 May 1837 compelled him to break off the overlapping serial instalments of
The Pickwick Papers and *Oliver Twist* for a month.[7]

Although Dickens appears to have taken the view that
literary creation owed more to perspiration than inspiration,
he recognized the importance of getting excited and having the
afflatus upon him, as William Godwin characterized his state
of mind while writing *Things As They Are; or, The Adventures of
Caleb Williams*.[8] 'You know that I have frequently told you that
my composition is peculiar', Dickens wrote to Catherine
Hogarth, breaking an appointment to spend an evening with
her during their courtship. 'I never can write with effect—
especially in the serious way—until I have got my steam up,
or in other words until I have become so excited with my
subject that I cannot leave off' (*P*, I, 97).

Perhaps getting started on a book caused Dickens more
anxiety than the actual composition, which, once the initial
agonies of plotting and contriving were over, usually went along
with the minimum of 'frowning horribly' at 'a blank quire of
paper' (*P*, V, 419; *NL*, II, 235). Some sense of the relish with
which Dickens went about writing scenes is conveyed by his
description of himself during the final stages of *Barnaby Rudge*.
September 1841 found him burning into Newgate gaol, tearing
'the prisoners out by the hair of their heads', and showing the
convicts playing 'the very devil' as they sacked Lord Mansfield's
house. 'I feel quite smoky when I am at work', he repoted to
John Forster (*P*, II, 377; 385). On an earlier occasion, an eye-
witness described Dickens intently at work on *Oliver Twist*, his
facial muscles playing, his mouth set, and his tongue tightly
pressed against closed lips as the feather of his pen moved
rapidly across the paper.[9] Later, when Dickens was writing
David Copperfield, his eldest daughter Mary saw another idiosyncrasy. Watching her father at work from the couch in his
study, where she lay convalescing from a serious illness, Mary
noted how he would write quietly for a period, and then jump
up and rush to a mirror. Peering into it, he would pull a
variety of faces, study each intently, and then return excitedly
to his writing table, where he would resume the narrative.[10]

Although on one occasion Dickens told Forster that 'Invention, thank God, seems the easiest thing in the world' (*P*,

IV, 612), he could not get on 'FAST' or sustain a rapid pace of composition without the presence of streets and numbers of figures. London—that 'magic lantern'—was indispensable both to his imagination and to his physical need to walk extensively while working on a novel. Without streets and crowds, as he discovered in Italy in 1844, his ideas 'seemed disposed to stagnate', after a day spent toiling at his desk when no prospect of theatres, crowds, and accessible streets beckoned. Neither Genoa nor Lausanne substituted adequately for London, but when Dickens and his family moved to Paris in November 1847, he found that city—'wicked and detestable'—a 'wonderfully attractive' stimulus to his work on *Dombey and Son* (*P*, IV, 669).

After Dickens bought Gad's Hill and established himself there in the 1860s, France and Paris became increasingly important to him as outlets for his restlessness. Once separated from his wife in 1859 and after selling their family home, Tavistock House, Dickens turned away from London as a source of excitement, preferring to avoid the city, except for weekly visits to the office of *All the Year Round*, and went abroad for recreation and a change. 'My being on the Dover line, and my being very fond of France, occasion me to cross the Channel perpetually', he wrote to his friend W. J. Cerjat in 1864 of his new life after settling into Gad's Hill.

> Whenever I feel that I have worked too much, or am on the eve of overdoing it, and want a change, away I go by the mail-train, and turn up in Paris or anywhere else that suits my humour, next morning. So I come back as fresh as a daisy. (*NL*, III, 403)

Of the letters referring to a single novel, those Dickens sent Forster during the composition of *Dombey and Son* stand out for the copiousness and detail with which Dickens charted his progress. Two reasons account for this. During the early stages of the book, Dickens was abroad and was therefore unable to talk over the plot with Forster as it unfolded. Secondly, the ten years between 1840 and the founding of *Household Words* mark the period during which Dickens and Forster were most intimate. Accordingly the letters relating to *Dombey and Son* reveal Dickens's increased concern with a need to explore the painful experiences of the past he had hitherto avoided. The letters also document Dickens's growing wish to impart greater structural unity to his novels and show how he exercised tight control over the illustrations. Nevertheless, the care taken with this novel did not preclude the possibility of last minute changes and sudden revisions. After receiving a note from Francis Jeffrey, in which the critic noted his refusal to believe that Mrs. Dombey would become Carker's mistress, Dickens got the idea for 'a tremendous scene'. Edith Dombey would undeceive Carker at their trysting place in Lyons and tell him that she never meant to submit to his advances at all. Jeffrey's objection—an astute guess based on his reading of the serial parts—prompted Dickens to reconsider his original plan and to work out a different solution (*P*, V, 211). If the novel could be improved—and in this case Dickens concurred with Jeffrey—he adapted suggestions that merited attention.

2

When Dickens urged upon his fellow writers the seriousness and dignity of the profession of letters and exhorted them to enter authorship alert to the public responsibilities writing involved, he spoke with conviction. Primarily, Dickens believed that literature should enlarge the mind and improve the understanding by portraying the different varieties and shades of the human character and by showing, as his first protagonist learns, that there is more to life than business and the pursuit of wealth. Since Mr. Pickwick could afford to retire comfortably and gracefully 'to some quiet pretty neighbourhood in the vicinity of London', his decision was obviously one borne of privilege. At the same time, his retirement illustrates a more general truth in that he chooses to devote his remaining years to something other than commerce by voluntarily holding himself accountable to a moral code of decency and humility that does not presuppose financial success. ' "If I have done but little good," ' Mr. Pickwick exclaims as he surveys his recent travels, ' "I trust I have done less harm" ' (*The Pickwick Papers*, Ch. 57).

The significance of Mr. Pickwick's resolution at the novel's opening to go in search of adventures that would provide him with amusing and pleasant recollections in his 'decline of life' is further reinforced by the narrator. Taking leave of 'our old friend', he reminds readers that there are ever some experiences 'to cheer our transitory existence here', provided that we look for them. Seeking them out, we learn, depends less on one's wealth than on one's outlook. There are 'dark shadows on the earth', but we need not act like bats or owls, the narrator reminds us, by preferring the night.[11] Rather we ought to shift our view at will and fill some of our solitary hours with a sense of 'the brief sunshine of the world' conveyed by the novel.

Dickens took seriously the need to counterbalance darkness with sunshine, and he consistently stressed throughout his career the importance of uniting 'notices of all bad [things]' with 'all good [ones]'. Cheerful views, he thought, should combine with the 'sharp anatomization of humbug', and writers should ennoble human life, not denigrate it (*P*, IV, 328). To do so, authors need not deny 'the darkest side of the picture'; rather, in treating evil, they should also treat good and do their best, as Dickens outlined his programme for *Household Words* in 1850, to encourage people to persevere individually, to retain their faith 'in the progress of mankind', and to inspire thankfulness 'for the privilege of living in the summer-dawn of time' ('A Preliminary Word', *Household Words*, 30 March 1850).

In a significant but neglected essay published in *The Examiner* in 1848, Dickens spoke authoritatively of the artist's role in similar terms. 'The Rising Generation', a series of twelve drawings by John Leech, prompted his remarks, which were broad enough to apply to literature as well as to art. Praising Leech as the first English caricaturist 'who has considered beauty as being perfectly compatible with his art', Dickens elaborated on the aesthetic implications of introducing beautiful faces and agreeable forms. What impressed Dickens was Leech's refusal to make his pictures wearisome by introducing 'a vast amount of personal ugliness'. A satirical point about a character could be made, Dickens wrote, without making the individual unappealing, a strategy Dickens defended not because he objected in principle to the portrayal of ugliness but because he saw no artistic reason for producing an unnecessarily disagreeable result. To the contrary, he argued, the audience is more likely to respond and to take an interest in a pleasant object than an unpleasant one. Besides, Dickens added, with reference to 'the old caricature' of the farmer's daughter 'squalling at the harpsichord', the satire on the manner of the girl's education 'would be just as good if she were pretty'. Furthermore, he contended,

> The average of farmers' daughters in England are [sic] not impossible lumps of fat. One is quite as likely to find a pretty girl in a farmhouse as to find an ugly one.[12]

No one can justly question Dickens's willingness in his novels to admit that life's sombre hues exist, or infer from his comments on Leech's drawings that he recommended turning one's back upon the world's harsh realities. Treating unpleasant subjects, however, called for tact and for the 'becoming sense of responsibility and self-restraint' of the kind shown by Leech. His good nature, Dickens thought, was 'always improving' and Leech imparts 'some pleasant air of his own to things not pleasant in themselves'.[13] Leech, like Dickens's Uncommercial Traveller, was on the side of 'the great House of Human Interest Brothers', whose business was served by trying to improve life and afford amusement by showing 'rather a large connection in the fancy goods way' ('His General Line of Business', *The Uncommercial Traveller*).

The artist's role, in Dickens's view, is clearly linked with a conception of the nature and purpose of literature firmly rooted in a historical position similar to the Horatian formula that art should edify and combine instruction with pleasure. Amplifying Horace's *utile* and *dulce*, we might extend the terms along the lines suggested by Wellek and Warren, who include 'Useful' to mean not wasting time and deserving serious attention, while 'Sweet', they suggest, is equivalent to ' "not a bore", "not a duty", "its own reward" '.[14] If we narrow the context further, we can also see how such assumptions about literature's purpose merged with the reform tradition of the Victorian novel, in which novelists committed themselves to trying to improve nineteenth-century society. Regardless of how improvement could or should be implemented as a matter of social and political policy, the novelists agreed that fiction should provide a paradigm to show people how to behave more decently in the future and offer what Dickens called 'an occasional refuge to men busily engaged in the toils of life' (*P*, V, 570).

The Victorian novelists' confidence in the educational role of letters and literature's ability to improve society was further reinforced by the optimism with which they saw the growth of literacy in nineteenth-century England. The 'educational metamorphosis',[15] in which the middle classes became more literary and the lower classes learned to read, was seen by both reformers and writers as the foundation for all political and social progress. Writing in *England and the English* in 1833, Bulwer Lytton perceptively recognized that with the demise of the British aristocracy signalled by the Reform Act of 1832, a new national effort must be made to create a better society. In Bulwer's opinion, writers were indispensable to that goal. They bore the responsibility for renewing the country's energy and mobilizing a progressive and directive government because 'reformed legislation', he thought, was impossible without 'reformed opinion'. 'Now is the day for writers and advisers', he declared; '*they* prepare the path for true lawgivers; they are the pioneers of good; no reform is final, save the reform of mind.'[16] By teaching the population to read and by providing people with morally improving books, his argument ran, social benefits would follow.

If the writer is committed to teaching and creating the '*new moral standard of opinion*' Bulwer called for, how do we distinguish the artist who approached life, in Orwell's phrase, 'always along the moral plane', from the propagandist?[17] Bulwer showed little interest in this issue in *England and the English*, but Dickens, less of a cultural historian than his friend, raised the question in *The Examiner* several months after the essay he published on Leech. On this occasion, Dickens wrote critically of 'The Drunkard's Children', a series of sketches by George Cruikshank which provoked a 'gentle protest' from the novelist about moral art that crossed the line between views expressed with sincerity and responsibility and those deliberately simplified and dogmatic.[18] Cruikshank's design in 'The Drunkard's Children' was to provide a definitive statement about the dangers of alcohol, to which Dickens objected not because Cruikshank presumed to instruct but because 'teaching, to last, must be fairly conducted. It must not be all on one side.' A partisan commitment to temperance, Dickens understood, encouraged his former illustrator to reduce the problem of drunkenness to an inflexible proposition: it was either an inborn vice or the fault of the gin-shops. 'Drunkenness', Dickens responded, cannot be confined to a single interpretation because it is

> the effect of many causes. Foul smells, disgusting habitations, bad workshops and workshop customs, want of light, air, and water, the absence of all means of decency and health, are the commonest among its common, everyday, physical causes.

And among its moral causes Dickens listed the mental weariness induced by unremitting labour, the lack of 'wholesome relaxation', ignorance, and the need for 'reasonable, rational training'. What the poor did not want was 'the mere parrot education' they were offered by the well-meaning but unimaginative philanthropists of the kind Dickens attacked in *Bleak House*.

Cruikshank's motives in 'The Drunkard's Children' and 'The Bottle', the first of his attacks on the evils of alcohol, Dickens granted, deserved the highest respect; but if the moralist is to strike at all, Dickens argued, he 'must strike deep and spare not'. By placing the blame solely upon those who indulged in the vice and by not bringing the deeper and more pervasive causes of drinking 'fairly and justly into the light', Cruikshank compromised the 'very serious and pressing truth' of the national origins of the problem. He also ran the danger, Dickens thought, of defeating the end the pictures were supposed to bring about. 'There is no class of society so certain to find out' the weakness of Cruikshank's argument 'as the class to which . . . [the pictures] are addressed.' If art were to be affective, Dickens concluded, it must do more than propound a theorizer's doctrinaire solution. Rather the artist should be subversive in the sense that he should discourage complacency among his readers by moving them to look for explanations in the inadequacies of the status quo. Responsibly and imaginatively directed, good art could persuade readers or viewers to understand the problem more deeply by showing how drinking began 'in sorrow, or poverty, or ignorance—the three things in which, in its awful aspect, it *does* begin'. The design then, Dickens confided to Forster, would have been 'a double-handed sword' and 'too "radical" for good old George, I suppose' (*P*, V, 156).

3

Art's persuasiveness should not be limited to exploring the inadequacies of Victorian Britain and awakening readers to social and political injustice. A second assumption about literature's function to which Dickens subscribed with equal vigour was that fiction should supply readers with a satisfying emotional and imaginative experience. In this manner books had served Dickens during his impoverished childhood, so effectively keeping alive his fancy, as he wrote of the 'glorious host' of protagonists from eighteenth-century fiction, that the therapeutic influence of their company proved to him a lasting model of literature's ability to remedy unhappiness (*David Copperfield*, Ch. 4).[19] Fiction, Dickens always maintained, should provide a balm, confer happiness, and function as a counterweight to external gloom by creating romance from the realities of life. Indeed, Dickens's conviction that literature should furnish an antidote to 'facts' and soften everyday existence by transforming it with the imagination was one of his most characteristic attitudes.

Dickens's comments to Forster about the latter's biography of Goldsmith articulate similar views from a different perspective. A good biographer, Dickens thought, should always make the period to which his subject belonged as fresh and lively as if it were presented 'by the real actors come out of their graves on purpose'. At the same time, the biographer should choose someone whose life was worth the effort, an individual whom the reader could love and admire. On every page, Dickens wrote to Forster after reading his life of Goldsmith, he found reason to praise 'the sense, calmness, and moderation' with which Forster had achieved this end. As a result, the reader strengthened 'with his [Goldsmith's] strength—and weakness too, which is better still' (*P*, V, 289). Dickens did not suggest that Goldsmith's 'discouraging imprudences' should be avoided; in treating them, the responsible biographer took care not to make his subject's achievements any less impressive than they were. Following this formula, the biographer was free to acknowledge his subject's faults provided that he did not dwell on his failures, thereby reducing a great man's accomplishments and failing to present his character so as to elicit from others the goodness and courage evident in the life he records.

Dickens's contention that biographers should inspire is a variation of his position that fiction fulfilled its purpose by arousing cheerfulness and by burning with the bright light of fancy. Fancy, as critics have noted, is a variable term in Dickens's vocabulary, synonymous sometimes with the imagination and ranging at others to include an escape from the world of facts as well as the creative and contemplative power by which an artist transformed life. Yet for all its nuances, the notion of fancy as the imaginative re-creation of real life in romantic terms best illuminates Dickens's idea of the writer's function. The novelist should deal with 'real' life by looking on his mind as 'a sort of capitally prepared and highly sensitive plate' which received impressions of people and places from all walks of life, and then stored the information for later use. As Dickens described this process to W. H. Wills while on a reading tour in the north of England in 1858, his mind 'made ... little fanciful photographs[s]' of everything that impressed him. Scenes from a walk—in this case through the squalid coal-mining villages of the Pit country between Durham and Sunderland—clearly provided glimpses of 'real' life, which would be useful, Dickens thought, when he returned home. In fact they might 'come well into *H[ousehold] W[ords]* one day', but only after the impressions taken on the spot had been modified by fancy (*NL*, III, 58). As Dickens observed on another occasion, it was not enough 'to say of any description that it is the exact truth. The exact truth must be there,' he wrote to Forster in one of his most explicit comments about his practice, 'but the merit or art in the narrator, is the manner of stating the truth' (*F*, IX, i, 279).[20]

Dickens stuck tenaciously to his self-imposed injunction to dwell 'upon the romantic side of familiar things' (Preface, *Bleak House*) and not to be 'frightfully literal and catalogue-like' because he thought the very success of popular literature 'in a kind of popular dark age' depended on 'such fanciful treatment' (*F*, IX, i, 279). He also regarded his books as a personal communication, social acts between himself and his readers, which called for authorial delicacy and tact.[21] Care was particularly important in this relationship because, as he stated in the 1850 prospectus describing the editorial principles of *Household Words*, he was ambitious 'to be admitted into many homes with affection and confidence'. Neither was guaranteed unless readers accepted Dickens's editorial presence, which they were unlikely to do without knowing what to expect. By 1850 Dickens had of course won a large measure of trust; but at the beginning of an experimental enterprise, he saw the importance of reaffirming the values he stood for. Old readers would be assured, he reasoned; and new ones might be attracted by the promise to portray 'many social wonders', provide knowledge of 'good and evil', and to treat life's hopes, triumphs, joys, and sorrows ('A Preliminary Word', 30 March 1850, *Household Words*).

Dickens's regard for his audience and his resolve to avoid anything that might give offence by encouraging unproductive self-scrutiny and unhappiness among readers appear throughout his correspondence with contributors to the journals he ran between 1850 and 1870. In several letters he acknowledged his perception of the duties of the 'Editor of a periodical of large circulation' (*NL*, III, 510), and discussed the conflicts that arose between an editor and an author. A work may well have artistic integrity, Dickens thought, and be the product of an accomplished writer who is a good man or woman, but it may nevertheless contain passages or scenes requiring cutting or modification, if the editor were to pass them as suitable to a mass of readers.

Modern readers will quickly equate Dickens's unwillingness to 'offend the ear', as he wrote in the 1841 Preface to *Oliver Twist*, with a nineteenth-century reticence about sex. In the case of Dickens's response to Charles Reade's *Griffith Gaunt* (1866), they are correct. The novel depicted among other scenes Gaunt's going drunkenly to his wife's bed and fathering a child, as well as a passage where Kate, his wife, and Mary, his mistress, have Gaunt's 'illegitimate child upon their laps and look over its little points together'. On the basis of such incidents, Dickens wrote to Wilkie Collins, that if, hypothetically, he were under cross-examination and reminded that he was an editor, he would not pass them because they were capable of perversion 'by inferior minds' (*NL*, III, 510).

Yet for all the predictability of Dickens's response, we oversimplify his reaction by portraying it solely in terms of Victorian prudery about sex. The more important observation in the letter to Collins is the weight Dickens placed on his responding as an editor. Were he free to speak as a writer or critic with a less specific family audience in mind, Dickens could express his appreciation of the novel's obvious artistic merits. *Griffith Gaunt*, Dickens thought, was the work of 'a highly accomplished writer and a good man'. This remark suggests that Dickens recognized the complexity of the issue. A work by a serious author could legitimately include material that did not always coincide with his definition of editorial responsibility.

The letters Dickens wrote to Emily Jolly and Harriet Parr raise a similar problem. As a critic Dickens responded to stories by both writers with strong emotions and generous praise, admiring Emily Jolly's 'surprising knowledge of one dark phase of human nature' in her 'A Wife's Story' (*NL*, II, 679), and marvelling at the power Harriet Parr displayed in *Gilbert Massenger* (1855). The novel moved me, Dickens informed the author, 'more than I can express to you. . . . I felt the highest respect for the mind that produced it' (*NL*, II, 684). As an editor, however, Dickens had to consider how such fiction would affect a large audience. There was no point in causing unnecessary pain, he wrote to Miss Jolly, whose story closed with 'so tremendous a piece of severity' that Dickens judged the ending would defeat her purpose. The catastrophe, as it stands, Dickens objected, 'will throw off numbers of persons who would otherwise read it, and who . . . will be deterred by hearsay from doing so' (*NL*, II, 679). Similarly, while moved and impressed by *Gilbert Massenger*, Dickens told Harriet Parr that he was not sure

> whether I could have prevailed upon myself to present to a large audience the terrible consideration of hereditary madness, when it was reasonably probable that there must be many—or some— among them whom it would awfully, because personally address.

With a palpable sigh of relief, Dickens ducked further discussion about publication by telling the author that the length of her story rendered it 'unavailable for *Household Words*' (*NL*, II, 684).

Censorship or silences of the kind Dickens advocated are thought intolerable today. Perhaps sharing Virginia Woolf's observation that 'If you do not tell the truth about yourself you cannot tell it about other people', a contemporary editor or publisher would endorse her contention that Victorian writers crippled themselves, diminished their nature, and falsified their object. 'What books Dickens could have written had he been permitted! Think of Thackeray as unfettered as Flaubert or Balzac!' wrote Virginia Woolf, sympathetically quoting R. L. Stevenson's lament that writers in the late nineteenth century were condemned to avoid ' "half the life" ' that passed them by.[22]

These remarks deserve comment because they are misleading without some qualification. First, Victorian standards of the acceptable were perhaps less uniform and more flexible than a modern writer like Woolf might assume. Even in the case of Dickens, who readily agreed to write novels and edit journals suitable for 'family fare', the most cursory glance at his work reveals a catalogue of illegitimate children, prostitutes, seducers, and individuals with perverse sexual appetites, to mention the topics most likely to bring a blush to the cheek of 'the young person'. Secondly, as this list suggests, the issue was perhaps less a matter of avoiding the forbidden and more one of the manner in which controversial subjects were treated. Moreover, the rationale for the kind of revisions Dickens frequently recommended rested upon aesthetic principles rather than a simple-minded commitment to bowdlerizing. When advising Emily Jolly to alter the ending of 'A Wife's Story' by sparing the life of the husband and one of the children, Dickens justified the change in this way: 'So [with the revisions he suggested] will you soften the reader whom you now as it were harden, and so you will bring tears from many eyes, which can only have their spring in affectionately and gently touched hearts. I am perfectly certain', he added, curiously foreshadowing the argument Bulwer Lytton later used to persuade Dickens to alter the ending of *Great Expectations*, 'that with this change, all the previous part of your tale will tell for twenty times as much as it can in its present condition' (*NL*, II, 680).

The 'good reasons' Bulwer urged upon Dickens to alter the original ending of *Great Expectations*, in which Pip and Estella are kept definitely apart by her remarrying 'a Shropshire doctor', do not exist in Bulwer's words. We can, however, infer from the essays Bulwer wrote about the aesthetics of narrative art, and from Dickens's general practice, that Bulwer's argument rested on a definition of the novel that certainly included the need for credible human beings but did not advocate a total commitment to realism or naturalism. Dickens and Bulwer both saw the novel more in terms of a Romance, in which the writer typically claimed 'a certain lattitude', if we paraphrase Hawthorne's Preface to *The House of the Seven Gables*, to deviate from 'a very minute fidelity' not merely to 'the possible, but to the probable and ordinary course of man's experience'.[23] Rather than concern themselves with propositional truth about a character or situation, Dickens and Bulwer preferred to deal with truth to human nature. In the former, *truth about* presents assertions capable of verification; in the latter, *truth to*[24] is something in which the reader becomes persuaded when the writer convinces by making the reader willingly substitute his belief in the probable for a possible 'marvellous truthfulness' arising from the situation depicted. 'Those critics who . . . have the most thoughtfully analysed the laws of aesthetic beauty', wrote Bulwer in 1863, 'concur in maintaining that the real truthfulness of all works of imagination—sculpture, painting, written fiction—is so purely in the imagination, *that the artist never seeks to represent the positive truth, but the idealized image of a truth*. As HEGEL well observes "That which exists in nature is a something purely individual and particular. Art, on the contrary, is essentially destined to manifest the general." '[25]

We might consider Bulwer's argument for revising the end of *Great Expectations* as an illustration of this theoretical point. In less abstract language, the possibility of Pip's coming across Estella eleven years after he last saw her is not the real critical issue as Bulwer and Dickens perceived it. Accepting without question the appropriateness of their meeting—the convincing atmosphere and medium of the narrative cleverly discourage our calculating the probability of their coming across each other that particular evening in December—we are moved in our hearts by Pip's obvious happiness and by the inference we draw from his final words. His seeing no shadow of another parting suggests that indeed one does not fall. Admittedly the text allows a different semantic interpretation—because Pip cannot see the shadow of Estella's departure does not preclude her going away again—but since Dickens made Estella a widow in the revised version, presumably so she was eligible to marry Pip, her rejecting him is possible though hardly likely if Dickens wanted to affect our hearts and feelings. There is therefore considerable latitude for an author despite the requirement that he or she idealize truth in the manner favoured by Dickens and Bulwer. As Dickens emphasized to Emily Jolly, the revisions he suggested were concerned with the manner in which positive attitudes should be conveyed. 'I would leave her new and altered life to be inferred', Dickens said of the heroine in 'A Wife's Story'. 'It does not appear to me either necessary or practicable (within such limits) to do more than that' (*NL*, II, 681).

4

While the novelist legitimately concerned himself with an idealized truth about human experience and with the thoughts and feelings that arose from the world of the author's imagination, he should not neglect the everyday reality to which his readers belonged. Dickens took as self-evident the view that art had four reference points—the universe, the work, the author, and the audience—and that the novelist wrote not to test the reader's interpretive ingenuity in the way that, say, Robbe-Grillet does but to be understood. While the text allowed a certain degree of interpretive freedom, it was designed to have a core of fixed or clearly defined meanings accessible to any competent reader familiar with the language and form employed by the author. Communication between the author and his readers therefore meant that the novelist passed along his knowledge of the world—religious, social, political, and psychological—and that he tried to ensure that his readers understood the correspondence between the text and external reality.

Any view of art based upon these assumptions also recognizes the need of the writer to operate within what Fielding called 'the Bounds of Possibility'. We must believe in the characters as people resembling those in life; the events that unfold around them must be credible; and the places characters visit and the homes they live in must be based on actuality. Dickens shared Fielding's call for 'Possibility', and both his theorizing about fiction and his practice confirm how he strove to create characters, scenes, and plots that fell within his interpretation of Fielding's definition of 'the Compass of human Agency'.[26]

One way to ensure a sense of authenticity and verisimilitude, as several letters attest, was to draw on the manners, speech, and appearance of individuals known to the author. As the letters make clear, Dickens went to considerable length to observe people in action and gather the details which imparted a convincing air to his fiction. Requiring a magistrate 'whose harshness and insolence' would render him a fit subject for satirical presentation in *Oliver Twist*, Dickens arranged to be smuggled into London's Hatton Garden Court to watch the notoriously severe Mr. Laing at work (*P*, I, 267). He undertook an arduous winter journey to north Yorkshire, falsely presenting himself as the agent of a widow anxious to place her boys at a Yorkshire school in order to observe a local master whose infamy had spread as far as London (*P*, I, 481–83). Similarly, Dickens spent a morning in August 1840 wandering about Bevis Marks 'to look at a house for Sampson Brass' (*P*, II, 118). He directed his illustrator to study the face of a particular City merchant, whom Dickens thought resembled Mr. Dombey 'to a T', when Phiz was making sketches for the protagonist of the novel (*P*, IV, 586), and he included among his other works fictional versions of real people so accurately observed as to cause pain to those who found the portraits unflattering.

Upon one occasion, Dickens's artistic process even worked the other way. Instead of his going to real people for corroborative details and the specifics which conferred a palpable reality, someone so compellingly fascinating presented himself that Dickens added a new character to a work already carefully plotted and under way. Mr. Venus in *Our Mutual Friend*— ' "Preserver of Animals and Birds" ' and ' "Articulator of human bones" ' —was 'discovered' by Marcus Stone, the

illustrator, after the first two monthly numbers of the manuscript had been written (*NL*, III, 380). Regardless of the
sequence of events governing the creative process, however,
Dickens's commitment to mimetic art—the representation of
real life in a recognizable form—remained a paramount
assumption throughout his career. Making the reader see the
'awful reality' of people and things around was one of the
artist's major functions and the indispensable component of
any masterpiece. Even Cruikshank's dogmatic moralizing in
'The Drunkard's Children', Dickens thought, compelled
respect because of its mimetic achievement. The power of the
closing scene, he wrote, 'is extraordinary', conveying the
reality of a death-bed scene in the hulks and the presence of
the surrounding figures with a fidelity 'worthy of the greatest
painter'. The Old Bailey Trial scene also impressed Dickens
because the eye could 'wander round the court, and observe
everything that is a part of the place'. The very light, atmosphere, and reality, he believed, were reproduced with 'astonishing truth'. 'So in the gin-shop and the beer-shop; no
fragment of the fact is indicated and slurred over, but every
shred of it is honestly made out.'[27]

Yet portraying 'reality' was not without problems, as
Dickens quickly learned, especially for the writer interested in
'these melancholy shades of life' where poverty and misery
dwelt.[28] Anyone seriously concerned with the portrayal of
those who skulked uneasily through the 'great black world of
Crime and Shame'[29] ran the danger of pushing *de facto* limits
governing the treatment of low life to their extreme. No
publisher or public censor ruled that thieves, housebreakers,
or prostitutes were forbidden subjects; but reviewers of *Oliver
Twist* raised objections, especially to Nancy and her love for
Bill Sikes.[30] In an aggressive Preface written in 1841 to counter
his critics, Dickens assumed a rhetorical posture later adopted
by Zola, similarly harassed, in his volume of essays entitled *Le
Roman expérimental* of 1880. Why waste time, both argued,
railing at novelists for presenting things that really happened?
'It is useless to discuss whether the conduct and character of
the girl seems [sic] natural or unnatural, probable or
improbable, right or wrong', Dickens asserted in 1841. 'IT IS
TRUE.' Thirty-nine years later, Zola claimed much greater

licence with the same principle for the Rougon-Macquart series, invoking the truth as a justification for writing freely about sexuality, the laws of heredity, and 'the overflow of appetite'.[31] Dickens of course was unwilling to pursue the argument as far as Zola, but he did not shy from following truth through 'profligate and noisome ways' to the 'bottom of the weed-choked well'. The novelist must be free, he believed, to look at 'the best and worst shades of our nature', including its 'ugliest hues'. Where Dickens differed from Zola was in his manner of stating the truth: one could treat the lives of licentious wretches without overstepping commonly held definitions of decency and acceptability.

Perhaps one of the best illustrations of how truthful but disturbing material can be introduced in a non-offensive way is John Peerybingle's fireside nightmare in *The Cricket on the Hearth* (1845). Designed as a Christmas story with a seasonal song of comfort, the narrative also shows that shadows can fall upon even the most domestic and blissful of hearths. The cloud in this instance is a wife's supposed infidelity, which the protagonist and the reader are manipulated into temporarily believing when Dot Peerybingle is portrayed as the apparent accomplice of the mysterious stranger whom her husband unexpectedly brought home one day. Dot's affectionate behaviour and her complicity in the stranger's disguise are grossly misinterpreted by Tackleton, the story's merchant-villain, as he asks the carrier to look through the window of his warehouse. Sitting alone that evening by his own hearth, 'now cold and dark', John Peerybingle broods over the spectacle of Dot whispering and joking with the stranger, whose transformation from the deaf, old, white-haired man he befriended to the young gallant he had recently witnessed from Tackleton's counting house. Back in his disguise, the stranger now lies asleep beneath Peerybingle's 'outraged roof', happy in the knowledge, the carrier imagines, that he has won the heart that '*he* had never touched'. Grief stricken, the carrier sits alone until 'fiercer thoughts' arise in his usually generous and warm breast. A loaded gun on the wall inspires a dark, ill-timed thought, which dilates in his mind like 'a monstrous demon', and takes complete possession of him: 'it was just to shoot this man like a Wild Beast.' But just as love is turning into hate and gentleness into blind ferocity, the moralist in the form of the chirping crickets steps in with his supernatural aids. The fairies of destruction are banished and pain and doubt are exorcised and transformed by the suggestion of a more noble response. In a paradigm of behaviour obviously offered to the reader for emulation, John remembers the happiness he and his wife have formerly enjoyed. In turn, these memories awaken his better nature, under whose influence he proposes a rather extraordinary solution for a Victorian husband. He will make his wife the best reparation in his power and do her the greatest possible kindness by releasing her ' "from the daily pain of an unequal marriage, and the struggle to conceal it. She shall be as free as I can render her" ' (Chirp the Third).

Nineteenth-century readers likely to question the heterodoxy of the carrier's proposal are quickly reassured by later events. The deaf old man was not Dot's lover in disguise of course but her friend May Fielding's *fiancé*, who had come back dressed unlike himself in order to observe May and to judge whether or not she still loved him after he had heard that May was to bestow herself upon another and a richer man. Thus what John Peerybingle saw from the counting-house was not his wife's plotting with the stranger to supplant him but Dot's spontaneous joy upon learning that the arranged marriage between Tackleton and Mrs. Fielding's daughter could be averted by the timely appearance of May's true lover, who also turns out to be Caleb Plummer's long-lost son.

As a summary of the plot suggests, the predominant mood is one of romance and festivity, and the darker side of life's problems—present in the delicate hint of the difficulties surrounding matrimony—is resolved by the narrator's clearing up the misunderstandings among the characters and unravelling the mysteries. Such authorial manipulation was perfectly legitimate according to Dickens, who saw no objection to comforting people with a moving tale of happiness and generosity, especially at Christmas. No time was more singularly appropriate to remind readers of the importance of not making coffins of their hearts and sealing up forever their best affections.

This same Christmas story also includes Caleb Plummer, whose work as a toymaker can serve as a useful metaphor for the artist intent on providing delight by making artifacts which are drawn from life. Stories, like the toys and dolls' houses crafted by Caleb and his blind daughter Bertha, are designed for pleasure; they also, like the playthings, represent 'all stations in life'. Just as there were 'Suburban tenements for Dolls of moderate means; kitchens and single apartments for Dolls of the lower classes; [and] capital town residences for Dolls of high estate', so stories, we can infer, should be based upon a similar fidelity to life. But in denoting social degrees and in confining dolls to their respective stations, the makers of the toys, like the writers, were nevertheless free to improve on Nature, who 'is often froward and perverse'. The narrator makes this point lightly, joking that Caleb and Bertha substitute 'wax limbs of perfect symmetry' for the 'Doll-lady of Distinction' and her compeers, but the comment contains a serious assumption. Nature—whether in the form of people, house, or dogs, whose tails Caleb attempts to pinch because he wants 'To go as close to Natur' ' as he can to fill the order he has received for barking dogs—provides the subject matter to be transformed by the artist's 'bold poetical licence' (Chirp the Second; Chirp the First).

The importance of transforming reality becomes clearer if we look at Caleb's activities on a domestic level too. To his own life and his blind daughter's he brings the same kind of magic or art that he imparts to the toys. The cracked and ugly ceiling, the four bare walls of the room they share, Caleb's sack-cloth coat, and their cold, harsh, and exacting employer Tackleton are all appropriately altered. Respectively, the 'blotched' and peeling walls become 'an enchanted home of Caleb's furnishing, where scarcity and shabbiness were not', the coat a 'beautiful new great-coat', and Tackleton 'an eccentric humourist who loved to have his jest with them'. Bertha of course cannot see what is really there; what she 'sees' nevertheless is true in the sense that hers is a transcendental vision of how things could be. And that such a change is possible is dramatized by the events of the narrative: Caleb's son returns rich from South America and Tackleton is converted into a compassionate and generous human being. The blind girl therefore was right because she trusted the eyes given to her by the artist. Caleb, the narrator reminds us, is no sorcerer, but he has mastered the only magic that remains to us: 'the magic of devoted, deathless love: Nature has been the mistress of his study; and from her teaching, all the wonder came' (Chirp the Second).

5

Dickens's view of literature's 'eternal duties' is closely integrated with his social and political beliefs. As one who walked London's shelterless midnight streets and prowled the city's 'foul and frowsy dens',[32] he did not shy from presenting what he knew of vice and hunger or from using every fictional resource he commanded to persuade readers to sympathize with society's outcasts. Among those most crucially in need of help were the young children, who grew up, as Jaggers puts the case in *Great Expectations*, 'as so much spawn', to be 'imprisoned, whipped, transported, neglected, cast out, [and] qualified in all ways for the hangman' (Ch. 51). The catalogue is a long one, but Dickens knew perhaps more intimately than most of his contemporaries just how extensive the threat was to all who existed beyond the pale of middle-class life.

The picture of nineteenth-century society one can construct from Dickens's later novels is a bleak one, showing little hope for the children Jaggers described as living in 'an atmosphere of evil' and only limited opportunities for adult happiness in an urban environment where hostile forces appeared to prevail. But such an interpretation, I think, requires qualification, particularly in view of the novels' implicit optimism and Dickens's equally unshaken faith in the moral authority of the artist to encourage hope. The novelist, Dickens believed, had a duty to present his readers with valid models of human behaviour and to provide a vision of life capable of urging people to virtue and goodness. As John Gardner argues in his essay on 'Moral Fiction', societies are created or destroyed by the myths or fiction to which they subscribe because art affects society.

> To put it another way, mankind has always lived by myth, religious or poetic. By myth we shape our understanding of ourselves, and lay the foundation of the future. By bad myths . . . [portraying man as innately evil, doomed, irrational, and depraved] we plant the future in land mines.[33]

If the best fiction is to humanize, what are the implications for the novelist? Essentially this view, as Gardner suggests, commits the writer to portraying protagonists who are useful models of human behaviour, characters whose struggle against confusion, error, and evil gives support to our own battle with similar problems. Such an obligation does not preclude the importance of delight—the sense that in Sleary's words, 'People mutht be amuthed.' Nor does it mean that the writer should sacrifice his concern with form. At the same time, aesthetic scrupulousness cannot suffice for any novelist holding the view that fiction should focus upon the importance of finding honourable responses to contemporary problems and encouraging in readers a love of life as an end in itself.

Dickens's confidence in the ability of art to affect people positively by providing models of good behaviour drew strength from his Christian vision of life and his faith that somewhere in the world order and intelligibility exist. Although his characters might not fully perceive this, there is a fundamentally Christian sense emanating from the novels, especially in the belief that repentance is genuinely possible for all except those who will their destruction by refusing to change their hearts. Even in the later novels, where Dickens is most obviously pessimistic, the works nevertheless provide a counter to the sense of a universe devoid of moral absolutes and inured to misery and destruction. Painful though Esther Summerson's reconstruction of an authentic self is, she does manage to attain a degree of confidence and stability to make her a mature individual; bewildering though readers find Victorian London, Bucket's rational (and, at times, humane) intelligence shows us how the fragments of urban life can be put together. Arthur Clennam, a male version of Esther, goes from moral and mental stasis to an eventually modest and fulfilled life. And even in *Our Mutual Friend*, the nadir of Dickens's despair for many critics, such middle-class values as belief in the past and the future, the capacity to sublimate one's own needs to those of others or to values outside the self, and the conception of love as self-sacrifice instead of self-fulfilment miraculously survive in the daughter of a Thames water-rat, a bad idle dog called Wrayburn, the spoilt, mercenary Bella, John Harmon, a lonely orphan, and in the misshapen but beautiful Jenny

Wren. Lack of personal esteem, profound dissatisfaction, intense ennui—certainly each of the characters, in varying degrees, is subject to these torments; but their dilemmas are neither permanent nor incapable of resolution.

Change for the better in these novels is of course limited to individuals and not to the whole of society. But that is an important distinction to a writer like Dickens, who was steeped in the Protestant tradition with its emphasis on the convertion of the inner man or woman as the precondition of change in the world. The roots of this belief, as Eugene Goodheart suggests, are based not upon political ideology but upon a religious idea inspired by England's experience of Protestantism.[34] To improve society was a matter of individual responsibility and of exerting one's 'best self'. Any art therefore that tried to bring about a change in readers, and by extension the society they lived in, was exercising its highest moral authority. Such a view of literature's function, Goodheart contends, was abetted by the persistent strain of Pelagian belief in England—evident at its most secular in the Victorian idea of self-help—that accomplishing one's salvation was a personal responsibility. And people, Dickens believed in his broadly Unitarian way, had the means to perfect or corrupt themselves by the exercise of their free will.

The enduring theme in Dickens's fiction that it is never too late for penitence and atonement embodies this optimistic faith. Given the encouragement that moral fiction ought to provide, people can and will opt for good. The price of maintaining this essentially progressive view of history in the face of circumstances offering unsettling evidence to the contrary doubtless exacted its toll on Dickens's emotional and imaginative resources. Yet however conjectural any final assessment of his personality must remain, consensus on one issue is surely possible. Dickens's novels testify to his belief that literature could never be 'too faithful to the people' by advocating their happiness, advancement, and prosperity[35] just as certainly as his untiring dedication to amusing and delighting readers accounts for his pre-eminence and popularity today.

NOTES

1. See Ada Nisbet, 'Charles Dickens', *Victorian Fiction: A Guide to Research*, ed. Lionel Stevenson (Cambridge, Mass.: Harvard University Press, 1966), pp. 44–153; 'Dickens & Fame 1870–1970: Essays on the Author's Reputation', *D*, 66 (May 1970), 83–185; and Philip Collins, 'Charles Dickens', *Victorian Fiction: A Second Guide to Research*, ed. George H. Ford (New York: MLA, 1978), pp. 34–113.

2. *The Letters of Charles Dickens*, ed. Walter Dexter (Bloomsbury: The Nonesuch Press, 1938), II, p. 385. Hereafter references to the three-volume Nonesuch Dickens letters will be cited in the text as (*NL*), with the appropriate volume and page number to that edition. For the years covered by the definitive Pilgrim Edition of *The Letters of Charles Dickens*, i.e., to 1849, I shall cite that edition as (*P*), with the appropriate volume and page reference to the letters edited by Madeline House, Kathleen Tillotson, and Graham Storey. When Dickens's novels are quoted, I have inserted the chapter reference in the text, with chapters numbered continuously, as in most accessible editions.

3. Edmund Wilson, 'Dickens: The Two Scrooges', *The Wound and the Bow* (1941); George Orwell, 'Charles Dickens', *Inside the Whale* (1940).

4. Dickens with Henry Morley, 'H.W.', 16 April 1853. Harry Stone includes this essay in his *Charles Dickens's Uncollected Writings from Household Words 1850–1859* (Bloomington, Indiana: Indiana University Press, 1968), II, pp. 467–75.

5. Anthony Trollope, *An Autobiography* (1838; rpt. London: Oxford University Press, 1923), Ch. XV, p. 249.

6. Dickens, 'The Late Mr. Stanfield', *All the Year Round*, 1 June 1867. See also *Miscellaneous Papers*, ed. B. W. Matz (New York: Charles Scribner's, 1911), II, p. 240. References to this collection of Dickens's periodical contributions will also appear in other footnotes, where I provide parenthetical references to the volumes as (*MP*) as well as the date and original source of the essay.

7. The serial publication of *Oliver Twist* in *Bentley's Miscellany* (February 1837–March 1839) was also interrupted on two further occasions, partly as a result of Dickens's quarrels with the journal's owner and publisher, Richard Bentley, and partly as a publication strategy. By delaying the serial publication of the novel's dramatic ending, Dickens thought, he would improve the sales of the book's publication as a three-volume novel in November 1838.

8. William Godwin, Preface to the Standard Novels Edition of *Fleetwood* (1832) and Appendix II, *Caleb Williams*, ed. David McCracken (London: Oxford University Press, 1970), p. 338.

9. Frederic G. Kitton, citing Henry Burnett's description of his visit one night to Doughty Street, in *The Novels of Charles Dickens* (London: E. Stock, 1897), p. 29.

10. Turning towards her, Dickens also 'began talking rapidly in a low voice' after his 'extraordinary facial contortions'. Mary notes that she found the experience 'most curious' and did not fully appreciate its significance

until she recognized the natural intensity with which Dickens threw himself into the characters he created. Mamie Dickens, *My Father as I Recall Him* (New York: E. P. Dutton, n.d.), pp. 46–8.

11. *The Pickwick Papers*, Ch. 57. Cf. the narrator's observation in *Oliver Twist*, Ch. 34: 'Men who look on nature, and their fellow-men, and cry that all is dark and gloomy, are in the right; but the sombre colours are reflections from their own jaundiced eyes and hearts. The real hues are delicate, and need a clearer vision.' Dickens later spoke of his 'invincible repugnance to that mole-eyed philosophy which loves the darkness, and winks and scowls in the light' in Boston on 1 February 1842. See *The Speeches of Charles Dickens*, ed. K. J. Fielding (Oxford: Clarendon Press), p. 19. And in *Nicholas Nickleby*, Ch. 53, the narrator reflects: 'But youth is not prone to contemplate the darkest side of a picture it can shift at will.'

12. 'Leech's "The Rising Generation",' *The Examiner*, 30 December 1848 (also *MP*, I, 148).

13. *MP*, I, 150.

14. René Wellek and Austin Warren, *Theory of Literature* (1949; rpt. Harmondsworth: Penguin, 1963), p. 30.

15. E. E. Kellet, 'The Press', *Early Victorian England 1830–1865*, ed. G. M. Young (London: Oxford University Press, 1934), II, p. 3.

16. Edward Bulwer Lytton, *England and the English*, ed. Standish Meacham (1833; rpt. Chicago, University of Chicago Press, 1970), pp. 381–82.

17. George Orwell, 'Charles Dickens', *The Collected Essays, Journalism and Letters of George Orwell*, ed. Sonia Orwell and Ian Angus (London: Secker & Warburg, 1968), I, p. 427.

18. 'Cruikshank's "The Drunkard's Children"', *The Examiner*, 8 July 1848 (*MP*, I, 113–17). In his own essay 'The Drunkard's Death', *Sketches by Boz*, Second Series, Dickens writes not to show how the bottle leads to ruin but to present a study of an irrational state of mind in which drunkenness becomes equated with madness, not sin. For a useful discussion of the term 'propaganda' and the extent to which the term might be stretched to mean 'effort, whether conscious or not, to influence readers to share one's attitude towards life', see Wellek and Warren, *Theory of Literature*, pp. 35–6.

19. Kathleen Tillotson comments perceptively on Dickens's habits: 'He is perhaps chiefly a re-reader—going back and back to that shelf of boyhood favourites lovingly enumerated in *David Copperfield*.' See, 'Writers and Readers in 1851', *Mid-Victorian Studies*, Geoffrey and Kathleen Tillotson (London: Athlone Press, 1965), p. 309.

20. Quoted by Forster in his *Life of Charles Dickens*, ed. A. J. Hoppé (London: Dent, 1969), II, p. 279. Future references to this edition will appear in the essay, where I cite Forster's divisions by Book and Chapter, together with the page reference to the Everyman text.

21. See for example Dickens's 1841 Preface to the first book edition of *The Old Curiosity Shop*, in which he quotes with approval from Henry Fielding's Preface to *Tom Jones*. An author should view himself, wrote Fielding, 'as one who keeps a public ordinary, at which all persons are welcome for their money'. And to prevent giving offence or disappointing

his customers Fielding argued that the writer, like 'the honest and well meaning host', should provide 'a bill of fare'. Later, Dickens wrote to a prospective contributor to the 1852 Christmas number of *Household Words* telling him how the issue should have 'some fireside name' and consist of stories supposed to be told 'by a family sitting round the fire' (*NL*, II, 422).

22. Virginia Woolf, quoted by Tillie Olsen in her *Silences* (New York: Dell, 1978), pp. 142–43. Readers should note that Dickens's acceptance of the restraints forced upon him by his large audience was not always freely given. Writing to Forster from Boulogne on 15 August 1856, Dickens spoke strongly of his resentment at the moralistic expectations he was compelled to adopt in the interests of his readership. See *NL*, II, 797.

23. Nathaniel Hawthorne, Preface, *The House of the Seven Gables* (1851).
24. For a useful discussion and comments on how artistic truth differs from propositional truth, see John Hospers, *Meaning and Truth in the Arts* (Chapel Hill: University of North Carolina Press, 1946), Chs. V and VI.

25. Bulwer Lytton, 'On Certain Principles of Art in Works of Imagination', *Caxtonia: A Series of Essays on Life, Literature, and Manners* (1863; rpt. New York: Harper and Row, 1864), p. 312.

26. Henry Fielding, *Tom Jones*, Bk. VIII, Ch. i, 'Concerning the Marvellous' in fiction.

27. *MP*, I, 116.

28. 1841 Preface, *Oliver Twist*.

29. Dickens to Miss Coutts, 4 January 1854, *The Heart of Charles Dickens*, ed. Edgar Johnson (New York: Duell, Sloan and Pierce, 1952), p. 252.

30. W. M. Thackeray made this point in 'Going to See a Man Hanged', *Fraser's Magazine*, 22 (August 1840), 154–55; 'Horae Catnachiane', *Fraser's Magazine*, 19 (April 1839), 408–9; and *Catherine: A Story* (1839–40), Ch. 3 and the final paragraphs. For a list of other attacks on *Oliver Twist*, see Kathleen Tillotson (ed.), The Clarendon Dickens (Oxford: Clarendon Press, 1966), Appendix F, p. 399.

31. Émile Zola, Preface, *The Fortunes of the Rougon Family* (1871) in *Documents of Modern Literary Realism*, ed. George J. Becker (Princeton: Princeton University Press, 1963), p. 161. Becker also provides the text of Zola's 'Experimental Novel' (1880), pp. 162–96.

32. 1841 Preface, *OT*.

33. John Gardner, 'Moral Fiction', *The Hudson Review*, 29 (Winter 1976–77), 497–98.

34. Eugene Goodheart, *The Failure of Criticism* (Cambridge, Mass.: Harvard University Press, 1978), p. 28. Ch. 2 of Goodheart's book, 'English Social Criticism and the Spirit of Reformation', provides a stimulating analysis of the moral basis of the criticism of Carlyle, Ruskin, and Arnold.

35. *Speeches*, ed. K. J. Fielding, p. 157.

2

The Politics of
Barnaby Rudge

by THOMAS J. RICE

'By Jove, how radical I am getting!' wrote Charles Dickens, in August 1841, as *Barnaby Rudge* neared its completion.[1] Forster glosses this letter with the picture of Dickens, 'in moments of sudden indignation at the political outlook, [talking] of carrying off himself and his household goods, like Coriolanus, to a world elsewhere'.[2] His facetious resolve to move his family to 'Van Dieman's Land' reflects a genuine distress over the recent fall of Melbourne's Whig ministry in the July 1841 elections. To Dickens, Peel's new Tory coalition was indistinguishable, despite the change in name to 'Conservative', from the reactionary faction of the Ultra-Tories:

> The bright old day now dawns again, the cry runs through the land,
> In England there shall be—dear bread; in Ireland sword and brand!
> And poverty and ignorance, shall swell the rich and grand,
> So rally round the rulers with the gentle iron hand,
> Of the fine old English Tory days;
> Hail to the coming time![3]

Although Dickens's suspicions of the Conservatives were shared by his fellow liberals,[4] the alarm voiced in this political 'squib' was that of a man who sensed a *personal* threat in the new ministry. In the years 1837–41 Dickens had become

51

increasingly involved in contemporary politics, supporting the Anti-Corn Law League, the establishment of a humane pro-gramme for governing Ireland, the continued maintenance of some provision for the poor (although he attacked the New Poor Law in *Oliver Twist*), and the agitation for National Education, policies and movements threatened by the new ministry. A deeper and more personal cause for Dickens's distress at the fall of the Melbourne ministry was the refuta-tion of his implicit political message in *Barnaby Rudge*, his current publication which, too, had become deeply involved with, in fact dependent on, contemporary party politics. The results of the July 1841 elections had subverted Dickens's political message in *Barnaby Rudge*, and the frustrations attend-ant on completing a politically 'lame duck' novel certainly convinced Dickens to turn his political attention in his future writing, in Humphrey House's words, towards matters of 'administration', rather than towards 'politics proper'.[5]

The bulk of the commentary on *Barnaby Rudge* skims very lightly over the surface of its political subject matter, pre-ferring to discuss the book either as a novel *per se* or as an historical novel.[6] Indeed, one of *Barnaby*'s greatest liabilities is the extent to which its purposes are enmeshed with con-temporary political issues which have been obscured by time (a liability inherent in the political novel genre). My chief objective here, then, is to review the political context of *Barnaby Rudge*, to demonstrate how closely the novel reflects its contemporary situation, comments directly on the condition of England, and expresses the worst fears of liberal politicians. This novel should not be read solely as political propaganda, to the exclusion of other concerns. Yet several important features of *Barnaby Rudge*, as well as Dickens's powers of 'political understanding and vision',[7] can be clarified by this emphasis. The history of *Barnaby*'s composition can only be fully understood in terms of its political intentions. And, since its narrative embodies a fully articulated political allegory, several of its uniquely 'un-Dickensian' characteristics can only be justified in light of its political context. This reconstruction of the political milieu of the late 1830s would be a thankless task, however, if the reader profits only in an increased knowledge of *Barnaby Rudge*'s topicality. I shall argue that

Dickens was, in fact, a particularly astute observer of the political process and the 'message' of his novel bears on more than its immediate frame of reference. His warning that political extremism of the left or right insures social instability is of enduring validity. Furthermore *Barnaby Rudge* illustrates the most explosive of all political situations: an *alliance* between the two political extremes, radical and reactionary, the direst threat imaginable to Dickens and his middle-class audience.

The second Melbourne ministry (Whig, 1835–41) was able to rule only by maintaining a precarious alliance with various Radical factions, as buffers against the assaults of the extreme left, and a tacit alliance with the more moderate elements of the fragmented Tory Opposition, similarly as a protection against the extreme right.[8] The apparently ideal political synthesis of this coalition provided a less than ideal, indeed a virtually inactive, government. Decisive action in any direction would have destroyed the equilibrium. The ministry's efforts to maintain the balance by conciliating both the Radicals and Conservatives progressively eroded its liberal support. Ultimately the alliance dissolved.

One illustration of the internal divisions which insured a constant tension within this coalition is provided by a closer examination of the Radical section. The Radicals were far from a political 'party' in the modern sense. There were, in fact, four identifiable types of 'Radical', ranging from the moderate to the extreme: the 'sentimental' or 'humanitarian' Radical (Dickens clearly identified with this faction[9]), the 'philosophic' or 'Benthamite' Radical, O'Connell's Radical Irish Party (the 'Liberator' was a professed follower of Bentham[10]), and the Ultra-Radical Chartists. The first three of these factions held Parliamentary seats and generally supported the ministry. The Chartists, who were campaigning for Parliamentary representation, were restrained from anti-ministerial agitation by sympathetic Radicals who sponsored their cause within the government. These Radicals who championed the Charter in Parliament did so solely to distract the Ultra-Radicals from the highly emotional anti-Poor Law agitation which was being directed against the Melbourne ministry. The eventual break between the Radicals and the

Chartists was occasioned by this feared merger of the anti-Poor Law and universal suffrage movements.

Although passed in 1834 during Melbourne's first ministry (Peel assumed office very briefly in 1834–35), the New Poor Law remained the most significant political achievement of the Whig ascendancy. The Law had originated in the Benthamite Radical section, so neither the humanitarian nor the Ultra-Radicals felt restrained from attacking the legislation by any sense of 'party'. In *Oliver Twist* Dickens had himself harshly criticized the inhumane workhouse system and the 'bumbling' Poor Law Commissioners. He did not aim at discrediting the philosophic Radicals who had framed the law,[11] yet the novel painfully embarrassed the architects of the bill and the ministry that supported it. In this respect Elie Halévy has credited the workhouse chapters of *Oliver Twist* with encouraging the anti-ministerial agitation by introducing the anti-Poor Law propaganda into the homes of the middle class.[12]

Any embarrassment of their political foes certainly delighted the Ultra-Tories, especially when its impact was strongly felt by the traditionally Whig middle class. What was particularly gratifying to these reactionaries, however, was the knowledge that the anti-Poor Law agitation was inspired and organized from within their own party. While ardently supported by the lower-class victims of the workhouse system, the campaign against the law was promoted by the likes of James Rayner Stevens and Richard Oastler, both 'doctrinal "reactionaries" '.[13]

In this light Dickens's advertisement of the anti-Poor Law propaganda earned him an enthusiastic following in the Ultra-Radical camp and the silent gratitude of those reactionary forces he most despised, both at the expense of a ministry he supported. To borrow a phrase from Elie Halévy's discussion of Feargus O'Connor, the notorious leader of the anti-Poor Law movement, Charles Dickens was a 'most serviceable tool of the Tory demogogues'.[14] As I have discussed elsewhere, Dickens's writing of *Barnaby Rudge* was in part an atonement for this unintended impact of *Oliver Twist*.[15] The realization that this reparation came too late to prevent the fall of the Melbourne ministry would have aggravated Dickens's alarm at the political situation, but it seems clear that the greater reason for Dickens's concern in August 1841 was his fear of the approaching recurrence of the political nightmare he was in the midst of recreating in *Barnaby Rudge* (the 7 August 1841 issue of *Master Humphrey's Clock* contained the first chapter of his masterful, twenty-four chapter narrative of the Riots (Chapters LI–LXXIV)). A study of the novel's conception and composition confirms that Dickens had come progressively to see the political conditions leading to the Gordon Riots as precisely analogous to the political situation in England, in 1839–1841.

Dickens initially conceived *Barnaby Rudge* as early as 1834 as an historical novel, based on the Gordon Riots of 1780. The novel's prototype, *Gabriel Vardon, The Locksmith of London,* was definitely being planned by May of 1836.[16] The first number of the new work, however, did not appear until February 1841, making *Barnaby* his fifth novel. Although the most persuasive explanation for this long gestation period is Dickens's dissatisfaction with his contracts, my chief concern here is to account for the forces which compelled him to complete the proposed work. When Dickens first considered a novel on the subject of the Gordon Riots, his material would have had little promise as a vehicle for political commentary. At that time the nascent Chartist agitation hardly resembled the Gordon Riots. The two phenomena, separated by a span of nearly sixty years, differed in both motive and scope. While the Gordon Riots were inspired chiefly by religious bigotry, with no particular social grievance, the Chartist agitation was basically an economic phenomenon, increasing and decreasing in strength according to variations in the trade cycle.[17] Although many of the most vociferous Chartist orators were clerics, Chartism was simply the 'blind revolt of hunger', bearing no religious overtones.[18] As a further contrast, the riot of 1780 was a single episode of short duration, whereas the Chartist agitation persisted for several years. At the time Dickens was first projecting his novel (*c.* 1836), moreover, the Charter had yet to be written and the localized discontent which grew into the national movement, as yet, had offered no threat to English society.

Dickens's interest in the Gordon Riots may have been stimulated by any number of factors, including the periodic anti-Catholicism which punctuated public opinion during his youth, especially whenever the Catholic Emancipation Act was debated in Parliament. Yet, a survey of the Parliamentary debates and the Press, over the period 1820–42, reveals remarkably little mention of the Riots. Those few references which do appear find two principal lessons in the Gordon Riots: the ignorance of the masses and the viciousness of religious intolerance.

For the Tories the Gordon Riots served as a useful metaphor in their attacks on the Whigs' lower middle-class constituency. The 'Riots of 'Eighty' were an apt illustration of mob-rule demonstrating the dangers in widening the electorate to include the lower classes.[19] The Tories hesitated to employ this allusion extensively, however, because the Gordon Riots represented more than popular tumult in the minds of the public. The 'no-Popery' theme of the Riots was inseparable from the memory of mob-violence. The uprising was one of the last prominent outbursts of English anti-Catholicism, an outpouring of religious bigotry from the predominantly Nonconformist middle and lower classes directed against 'Papist' tendencies in the government.[20] The Whig party, with its political base in these sectarian classes, had always led the agitation against the 'Romist' Tories. Sir George Savile's Act of 1778 was construed as a demonstration of official sympathy for Catholics by a Tory ministry, if not a first step towards political Emancipation. Nonconformists had received no such consideration from the government. The fact that the Act was intended only to provide Lord North with Catholic manpower for the North American Army, to continue the war against the American revolutionaries, had no effect on the discontent.[21] Although the Whig party was innocent of any implication in the Gordon Riots, they were vulnerable to attack for having led the initial political opposition which paralleled the popular agitation.

After 1800 the issue of religion increasingly became involved with the questions of the Anglican Church Establishment and the government of Ireland. Hence, the respective programmes of the Whig and Tory parties caused a reversal in their attitudes towards Catholicism. To disestablish the Church of England, the Whigs, who had the interests of the oppressed Nonconformists at heart, realized that the emancipation of and an alliance with the Irish Catholics was necessary. 'From 1807 to 1812, in opposition, the Whigs more and more became "the party favouring the Catholics".'[22] Until the outbreak of an anti-Catholic reaction in the 1840s, precipitated by the Oxford Movement, the Whig party maintained the unaccustomed role of the pro-Catholic faction.[23] The Tories, on the other hand, to protect their interests in the continuance of both the Church Establishment and the Orange government of Ireland, resurrected the emotion-filled 'no-Popery' cry of their adversaries.

With this realignment in mind, it should come as no surprise that neither the Tories nor the Whigs were eager to allude to the Gordon Riots. The popular identification of the 'no-Popery' theme with the Riots was likely to reflect on the Tories, even though they might stress the aspect of mob-violence. As a result, the Tories preferred to use the French Revolution as an illustration of the mob's incapacity for self-government. Likewise, Whig politicians would be reluctant to cite the example of the Gordon Riots to bait the Tories for their anti-Catholicism. The Whigs' association with the Radical 'democrats' had preserved their traditional constituency and their reputation as the party of the lower-class rabble. The Radicals, who considered themselves neither Whig nor Tory, could have alluded to the Gordon Riots at the expense of the Tories; however, they refrained rather than risk embarrassing their Whig allies.

This moratorium on the memory of the Gordon Riots lasted until the late 1830s when the alignments of the major parties shifted again. As the politically moderate Whigs and liberals sought to dissociate themselves from the Ultra-Radical Chartists and to differentiate themselves from the anti-Catholic Ultra-Tories, they resorted more frequently to the metaphor of the Gordon Riots as the occasion, and the target of their attack, suited. Charles Dickens was exceptional, however, in recognizing early the full appropriateness of the Gordon Riots as a political metaphor for the contemporary situation and among the first to alert the public to the most unlikely alliance that was developing between the Ultra-Tories and the Ultra-Radicals. The 'no-Popery' faction and the mob were linked together again. The development of this alliance through 1840 parallels Dickens's renewing interest in *Barnaby Rudge*. In fact, it could be argued that his periodic return to his projected novel was related as closely to the new-found appropriateness of his subject matter as to the pressure of his publisher.

A brief review of Dickens's various starts on the novel aptly illustrates their relationship to contemporary events. A false start in January 1839 was contemporaneous to the most impressive show of Chartist strength, the National Convention. The dissimilarity between the mob of the Gordon Riots and the unexpectedly tame political display of the Convention may have added to the frustration of Dickens's early attempt at composition. By the autumn of 1839 the Convention had dissipated itself and localized violent demonstrations had begun to break out. Furthermore, in some quarters the common goals of the Ultra-Tories and the militant Chartists had been recognized, along with the possibility of a future alliance. In August, Daniel O'Connell had employed the Gordon Riots as a parallel to the contemporary situation.[24] In September, Dickens resumed his novel, completing two chapters.

In November 1839 London was stunned by the news of an incendiary uprising which had taken place in Newport. Its leaders, Frost and Williams, were tried for treason early in 1840. Both the riot and the defence of its leaders provoked continued reference to the Gordon Riots. During the following year the Ultra-Radicals consolidated their forces and, despite the imprisonment of several of their leaders, continued to threaten violence. It appeared that a more serious uprising was inevitable. Furthermore, during this period the Ultra-Tories were openly encouraging the Chartists to join their ranks against the government. Simultaneously, the reactionaries' anti-Catholic campaign was at its height. Even the equanimity of Greville was disturbed by this state of affairs. On 31 December 1839, he reflected the general uneasiness that would characterize the coming year in his journal entry: 'Parties are violent, Government weak, everybody wondering what will happen, nobody seeing their way clearly before them.'[25] Dickens's sinister depiction of a crowd of the 'unemployed', in Chapter XLV of *The Old Curiosity Shop*, written in the autumn of 1840, further reflects the temper of the times. It was against this background of general foreboding that Dickens resumed *Barnaby Rudge* early in 1841.

Bentley's advertisements for *Barnaby Rudge* were linked with Dickens's false starts on the novel, for obvious reasons. Nevertheless, their content is illuminating. In December 1838 the subject of the novel was unspecified. In December 1839, after the Newport Riots, the advertisement identified the novel as a 'Story of the Great Riots'. A third announcement, in February 1840, was quite clearly a case of opportunism. Bentley, at this time, had no reason to expect the novel at all. Yet, he took advantage of the interest in the treason trials to announce the novel and repeat the identification of its subject.[26] The history of *Barnaby Rudge*'s advertisements, therefore, suggests more than Dickens's unhappy relationship with his publisher. The contemporary relevance of a tale of the Gordon Riots was as obvious to Bentley as it would have been to the public.

By 1839, therefore, Dickens's planned novel on the 'Riots of 'Eighty' would have had sufficient topicality to make its composition attractive, as the false starts of January and September attest. In publishing the work at this time, he would have had the added opportunity of attacking the Ultra-Radicals and Ultra-Tories together, thus emphatically reversing the political impact of *Oliver Twist*. In fact, this is what Dickens does in *Barnaby Rudge* in his presentation of the unequal alliance between the depraved Hugh of the Maypole, who confuses 'no-Popery' with the Chartist cry of 'no-property', and Sir John Chester, the type of the decadent, reactionary aristocrat. Chester emerges as the arch-villain of the piece, a manipulator in his public and private affairs who is charged with the full responsibility for the riots. In provoking the uprising, Chester epitomizes Dickens's conception of the Machiavellian Tory demagogue:

> Now really, to foment his [Gordon's] disturbances in secret, through the medium of such a very apt instrument as my savage friend here [Hugh], may further our real ends; and to express at all becoming seasons, in moderate and polite terms, a disapprobation of his proceedings, though we agree with him in principle, will certainly be to gain a character for honesty and uprightness of purpose, which cannot fail to do us infinite service, and to raise us into some importance. (XL, 306)[27]

Yet *Barnaby Rudge* did not appear in 1839, but early in 1841. The final impetus for the composition, then, was not simply the opportunity to 'kill two birds with one stone'. The novel was ultimately written in response to the actual formation of an alliance between the two extremist factions, the militant Chartists and the anti-Catholic Ultra-Tories.[28] Thus, the figurative topicality of the Gordon Riots metaphor was transformed by contemporary events. By late 1840 the Riots had become a literal and totally appropriate metaphor for the English political situation. History had indeed repeated itself with extraordinary fidelity. As Dickens hastened to point out, the 'Hughs' and 'Chesters' were combining to remove the Melbourne ministry from power.

Once this political allegory in *Barnaby Rudge* is recognized, Chester's multiple relations with his illegitimate son Hugh, as well as with his legitimate son Edward and with the conspirators can be seen as projections of the Ultra-Tories' duplicity and violations of trust in their positions of political and potentially moral leadership. Chester's treacheries are doubled by the betrayals of John Gashford, the manipulative secretary of Lord Gordon. The various domestic rebellions in the Haredale, Willet and Varden households, likewise, modify and refine the parallels to the Ultra-Radicals in the contemporary political situation. However, rather than attempt to delineate Dickens's allegory fully, in the limited space of this essay, I would prefer to focus on two prominent and unique features of Dickens's political attitudes evident in *Barnaby Rudge*: his unexpectedly sympathetic treatment both of Lord George Gordon, leader of the 'no-Popery' movement, and, incongruously, of Roman Catholicism itself. These two arresting and apparently inconsistent dimensions of *Barnaby Rudge* are direct and representative reflections of Dickens's ambivalent responses to the extremes of Chartism and Toryism, democracy and autocracy, chaos and order, from his 'middle' social and political position.[29]

Dickens portrays the leader of the Gordon Riots, Lord George Gordon, as deluded and, in fact, himself misled, thus relieving him of full responsibility for the ensuing chaos. Whether Dickens willingly distorted the actual historical figure of Gordon, or unwittingly based his characterization on overly sympathetic biographies, does not concern me in this place. The fact remains that in the novel there is a great distance between the leader of the 'no-Popery' faction and his supporters. Responsibility for the riots is diverted from Gordon, the fanatical ideologist of the Protestant Association, and attributed to self-seeking subordinates. Gashford, a lapsed Catholic, acts out of sheer hostility towards his former co-religionists, especially Haredale. Dennis, the hangman, is intent on increasing his supply of prisoners to be 'worked off' and Sim Tappertit is revolting against his 'enslavement' as an apprentice. Hugh of the Maypole seeks total revenge on the society that rejects him.

Dickens's distinction between Gordon and the prime movers of the riots is an important corollary to one of his central themes in the novel: the individual's responsibility for his deeds.[30] However, Dickens's ambivalence towards the figure of Gordon also reflects his equivocal attitude towards both the Chartist leaders and the People's Charter itself. Rather than present Gordon as a typical arch-villain, Dickens deliberately tempered his characterization, strengthening the parallel with the contemporary political situation. The moral leadership of the Chartists was separated from its following and, as with Dickens's Gordon, the question of its responsibility for the violent agitation is problematic.

Dickens would also have been largely sympathetic to many of the ideals of the People's Charter. The six points of the Charter, briefly, were: universal manhood suffrage, the ballot, payment of members of Parliament, abolition of the property qualification for members, equal constituencies, and annual elections. Four of these demands would have alleviated specific abuses and would have gained Dickens's immediate support.[31] The ballot would have provided the privacy for free electoral choice, salaried members would have lessened the temptation of bribery, reapportionment would have provided equal representation, and regular elections would have made members more responsive to popular opinion. Only conditionally could Dickens support the two remaining points of the Charter. The widening of the electorate to include all classes and the removal of property qualifications to allow anyone to enter Parliament, while indispensable for the democratization of England, presupposed that the people would govern themselves wisely, an assumption Dickens distrusted. He clearly believed that the people, first, had to be *educated* to appreciate their responsibilities as self-governors. Very likely such thinking led him to make education a significant social theme in *Barnaby Rudge*, as a proposed remedy for English society in response to the Charter.[32]

Dickens's reservations were shared by many of his fellow liberals.[33] The course of the Chartist agitation further reinforced this popular impression of the people's incapacity for self-rule. The Chartists rapidly abandoned the ideology of the Charter, advocated the use of physical force, aggravated class animosities, and defeated themselves in their service to the Ultra-Tories.[34] Dickens's fear of the ignorant masses suffuses his descriptions of the riots in *Barnaby Rudge*, which are permeated with the horror for the mindless mob's reign of terror. While produced by valid contemporary fears of social upheaval, in retrospect Dickens's visions of chaos can be seen as misrepresenting the bulk of the Chartist agitation. Most Chartists 'were guilty of no disorderly conduct or looting. They were content to force their poverty upon the notice of the rich. They did not intimidate, they merely asked for pity.'[35] However, Dickens does accurately reflect the excessive contemporary fear of the Chartists as a whole and of the social threat they might come to be, which had been stimulated by a small number of the agitators, the so-called 'physical force' faction. This group of rabid revolutionaries, under the direction of Feargus O'Connor and Rev. James Rayner Stephens, had succeeded in diverting the Chartist agitation away from the People's Charter after assuming the leadership of the movement following the failure of the National Chartist Convention in 1839.[36] Their hold on the popular imagination, while disproportionate to the real power at their command, was an important influence on both the mob scenes and the sympathetic portrait of Gordon, the displaced leader in *Barnaby Rudge*.[37]

The most serious of the revolutionary Chartist outbreaks occurred at Newport in November of 1839, several months after the break-up of the Convention. Up to this time the government had controlled the militants with a minimum of interference. The Whigs wished to avoid the Tory blunder of the Six Acts of 1819, special measures limiting the right of free assembly, which had served only to provoke further Luddite agitation. The ministry had finally reacted with some severity during the Birmingham Riots in mid-August 1839, making numerous arrests. The Newport Riots, the most ambitious and carefully planned uprising, were repressed harshly. Twenty-four Chartists were killed and fourteen were tried for high treason.[38]

Viewed objectively the riots were a 'feeble affair'. The mayor of Newport and a small detachment of soldiers effectively routed the mob. Nevertheless, the government wished to make a demonstration of the case to forestall further Tory criticisms for leniency. The Press reported the repression of the riot and the subsequent trials in detail.[39] The impact of the Newport uprising on the public imagination is directly attributable to the suddenness of the event, after a three-month period of apparent calm. The incendiarism and the daring attempt of the rioters to release Chartist prisoners provoked immediate comparison to the Gordon Riots.[40]

Yet, showing a detachment born of political insight, Dickens exempts Gordon from full responsibility for the 'Riots of 'Eighty' as he would acquit the displaced, moderate Chartist leaders William Lovett and Thomas Attwood who, while they were responsible for the National Chartist Convention of 1839 (a potentially revolutionary action, inviting, by name, a comparison with the French Convention of 1793), found their 'moral force' control superseded by the 'physical force' policies of O'Connor, Stephens, and Oastler, and were not implicated in either the Birmingham or the Newport uprisings.[41] In the same fashion, Lord Gordon surrenders control of the Protestant Association to his incendiary secretary Gashford and Gashford's henchmen, Hugh, Dennis, and Sim.

The second intriguing political feature of *Barnaby Rudge* is Dickens's uncharacteristically sympathetic treatment of the Catholic victims of the Gordon Rioters. Of course we might expect Dickens to sympathize with the victims of any such kind of injustice, yet it seems clear that it was not the facts of his historical source alone that placed him in a position supporting members of a religion he considered, along with the vast majority of his contemporaries, benighted, superstitious, morally debilitating, and, perhaps, politically threatening.[42] That the

Haredales are *English* as well as Catholic might relieve them of some of Dickens's suspicions (this discrimination of Catholicisms is important), yet Catholics owing allegiance to a foreign 'political' entity, the Pope, they remain. With the possible exception of Daniel O'Connel who, as a Catholic, was understandably sensitive to drifts in opinion, Dickens was probably the first important observer of contemporary events to recognize, late in 1840, that the militant Chartists were assimilating the anti-Catholic programme of the Ultra-Tories, in effect combining with the Ultra-Tories in a potentially catastrophic alliance. Dickens's realization that this maturing political merger of mass agitation and anti-Catholicism precisely duplicated the situation of the Gordon Riots provided the final impetus for his return to *Barnaby Rudge*, at the beginning of 1841, and gave him his political message.[43] The allegory of the 'Riots of 'Eighty' was complete. *Barnaby Rudge* was going to prevent disaster by alerting its middle-class readership to the emerging political situation. Unfortunately, its political message, though recognized,[44] did not prevent the fall of the Melbourne ministry; fortunately, things thereafter did not turn out precisely as envisioned by Dickens or the most hopeful of the Ultra-Tories and Ultra-Radicals, who did not gain by Peel's ministry. The threat of violent religious persecution, nevertheless, was genuine.

Although the Chartist agitation through 1840 was remarkably free from religious bias, the seeds had been sown for an outbreak of 'no-Popery' within the movement.[45] The Irish Catholics had scrupulously avoided any contact with the Chartists, and were to remain outside their numbers until after the death of O'Connell. When the violent agitation was at its height, Irish immigrants actively co-operated with municipal authorities in restraining the Chartists. The average Chartist would have little love for the Irish Catholics, in any event, since the Ultra-Tories were actively encouraging his belief that the influx of cheap Irish labour had created the recession in the economy.[46] The Irish Catholic seemed destined to be the next scapegoat for public indignation. Certainly to O'Connell and Dickens an outbreak of 'no-Popery' outrages seemed imminent. It is equally certain that the Ultra-Tories tried their utmost to bring this about, in a manner which invited further comparison with the Gordon Riots.[47]

To a contemporary of Dickens, the Protestant Association in

Barnaby Rudge would have provoked immediate comparison to the Protestant Association of the Ultra-Tories, reconstituted in 1839. The Press had followed the activities of this organization closely, especially during the season of the Newport Riots. Several editorials on the Association and transcripts of their meetings stand in juxtaposition to the reports of the riots and trials. The Association's activities were particularly emphasized in the liberal journals, in part to divert popular comparisons to the Gordon Riots away from the Newport uprising and towards the Ultra-Tory 'no-Popery' faction.[48] Similarly, Dickens diverts responsibility for the Gordon Riots away from the Association and towards the vindictive and hypocritical manipulators of its members, Gashford and Chester, both allegorical representatives of contemporary Tory demagogues. As Haredale observes of these two: 'You are the essence of your great Association, in yourselves' (XLIII, 327).

An ex-Catholic, Gashford's only conceivable motive for his vindictiveness towards his former brethren is his own political advancement. By abandoning his Catholic faith, he has gained the political freedoms that the rioters wish to deny to the Catholics. In Gordon he has found the vehicle for his advancement. Gashford 'wore the aspect of a man who was always lying in wait for something that *wouldn't* come to pass; but he looked patient—very patient—and fawned like a spaniel dog' (XXXV, 267). He attaches himself to Gordon in the hope of rising to a position of power as the 'great' man's secretary. To attain his goal he has no scruples about persecuting his former co-religionists.

Gashford's Catholic background reinforces his kinship with the Ultra-Tories. This right-wing faction was composed, in great part, of high-Churchmen. Their authoritarianism, doctrines, and liturgy traditionally invited comparison to the Church of Rome. The Tory party had been associated with the Catholics in the popular mind since the days of the 'Popish Plot'. Despite their active campaign against 'Popery' in the late 1830s, members of their own ranks were demonstrating further Papist leanings. Long before the publication of Tract 90 the English public had been informed of the Catholic tendencies of the Oxford Puseyites.[49] Part of the attack on the Ultra-Tory 'no-Popery' fanaticism pivoted on this irony. While Gashford's ex-Catholicism reflects the traditional identification of the Ultra-Tories with the Catholics, Dickens further capitalized on this irony of Catholics persecuting Catholics in his description of the mob: 'It was a most exquisite satire upon the false religious cry which had led to so much misery, that some of these [dying rioters] owned themselves to be Catholics, and begged to be attended by their own priests' (LXXVII, 597).

For the most part, the liberal attacks on the Ultra-Tories for their equivocal attitude towards Catholicism were subsumed under the general charge of 'hypocrisy', religious and political, emphasizing the traditional Papist leanings of the reactionaries. Later, as the alliance with the Ultra-Radicals became increasingly obvious, the attacks centred on their political equivocation.[50]

These themes of hypocrisy and equivocation dominating the liberal reaction to the resurrected 'no-Popery' cry are strongly paralleled in Dickens's creation of his central political character in *Barnaby Rudge*, Sir John Chester. A rival to Pecksniff as Dickens's consummate hypocrite, Chester assumes allegorical dimensions in *Barnaby Rudge*, embodying the political chicanery and hypocrisy of the Ultra-Tories. His relationship with his illegitimate son Hugh, noted earlier, becomes Dickens's implicit commentary on the political relations between the reactionaries and the 'physical force' Chartists. There is a striking similarity between the depiction of the alliance between the Ultra-Tories and the Ultra-Radicals in the liberal Press and Dickens's presentations of the Chester-Hugh relation. The following editorial from the *Morning Chronicle* could serve as a description of the unequal relationship between father and illegitimate son in *Barnaby Rudge*, if the names Chester and Hugh were to replace the labels 'Tory' and 'Chartist':

> The Tory and Chartist alliance has disgusted all honest men as a monstrous portent. It implies on the one side so much of hypocrisy and corruption, and on the other of base motive or blind passion, and on both sides so much flagrant disregard for even the semblance of political integrity, that only the demonstration of glaring facts could render it credible. The *Times*, however, which often differs in its morale from the other journals of its own party as well as from those of all other parties, regards this union with singular complacency. . . . Chartism may be a

fanaticism, but it is not a corruption. When the Chartist does the dirty work of Toryism and monopoly, his Chartist principle is gone. He is *ipso facto*, a renegade as well as a hireling.[51]

Dickens reinforces the inequality of this alliance by emphasizing Chester's fastidious disgust with Hugh's brutality and bestial odour. Hugh is too pointed a reminder that he is performing his father's 'dirty work'.

During the height of the Chartist agitation the Ultra-Tories, with duplicity that makes Dickens's Chester seem hardly an exaggeration, castigated the ministry for its policy of non-interference, while unhesitatingly provoking further agitation against the New Poor Law and inviting anti-Catholic demonstrations. They publicly voiced their alarm at the social upheaval but privately offered to defend the rioters in court. They saw the Chartists as effective tools to provoke the political reaction they desired. Like Chester, the Ultra-Tories believed that they had nothing to lose and everything to gain from the agitation. In Halévy's words: 'If the Tories were so successful in exploiting the fear of Chartism, it was because they were not very afraid of it themselves.'[52]

Sir John Chester, though reminiscent of Lord Chesterfield (for whom he professes admiration (XXIII, 173)), is not based on any comparable figure from the time of the Gordon Riots. Gashford's sinister manipulation of Gordon and the Protestant Association similarly has no historical source. Dickens thus violates one of the major 'rules' for historical fiction, established by Scott, by allowing his fictional characters to influence events to the extent Chester and Gashford do. The most persuasive explanation for this is that he was more interested in commenting on contemporary politics than in adhering faithfully to the facts of history or the canons for historical novels. By elevating Chester to the House of Lords, making him a politically prominent figure in *Barnaby Rudge*, and by giving him an active role in precipitating the riots, Dickens accentuates Chester's allegorical role as a representative of the Ultra-Tories in the early 1840s. By doubling Chester's behaviour with Gashford's, and giving Gordon's secretary a Roman Catholic heritage, Dickens makes the representation complete.

The political allegory of *Barnaby Rudge* is much fuller and more finely detailed than can possibly be described in this brief essay. Most of the novel's remaining characters and situations too have their representative political significance, from the 'insubordinates' Joe Willet, Miggs, Mrs. Varden, Sim Tappertit, and Edward Chester, and the 'mediator' Gabriel Varden, to the 'insurrectionists' Rudge, Barnaby, Dennis, Hugh, and Sim. Even Dickens's descriptions in the book assume political significance (elsewhere I have identified Varden's house as a metaphor for the English 'Constitution'[53]). Yet the chief importance in recognizing the political allegory in *Barnaby Rudge* is not to show Dickens's narrative ingenuity, which hardly needs to be argued, but to correct the prevalent misconception that he 'was not a man of great political understanding and vision'.[54] Dickens was and could be an astute observer of party politics. However, having been victimized by the notoriously unreliable and unpredictable shifts in political alignments, during a time of considerable instability, Dickens evidently learned from his experience in writing *Barnaby Rudge* to direct his political concerns, thereafter, towards the more stationary 'targets' of political institutions, from the Court of Chancery (*Bleak House*) to the Circumlocution Office (*Little Dorrit*). That they would not 'move' was both a major point of his satire and a virtue for his method.

NOTES

1. *The Letters of Charles Dickens*, Vol. 2, ed. Madeline House and Graham Storey (Oxford: Clarendon, 1970), p. 357.
2. John Forster, *The Life of Charles Dickens*, ed. J. W. T. Ley (London: Palmer, 1928), p. 191.
3. Quoted by Forster, p. 192. Dickens wrote several such anti-Tory political squibs, after the fall of the Melbourne ministry, and sent them to Forster in August 1841 as anonymous contributions to the partisan cause.
4. The liberal *Morning Chronicle*, a newspaper Dickens had formerly worked for and continued to read, remarked in a leading editorial: 'Should Robert Peel return to power, it must be as the repealer of the Catholic Emancipation act' (18 December 1839). The Irish 'Liberator', Daniel O'Connell expressed fears of a popular revolt if the Tories were to return to power; see *The Correspondence of Daniel O'Connell*, Vol. 2, ed. W. J. Fitzpatrick (London, 1888), pp. 203–4, 218–20, 264–65.

5. Humphrey House's otherwise excellent summary of Dickens's political attitudes, in *The Dickens World*, 2nd edn. (London: Oxford University Press, 1942), pp. 170–214, while legitimately stressing Dickens's generally sceptical view of the political processes and institutions of his time, discusses *Barnaby Rudge* only peripherally and misses the practical political intent of the novel. House's assessment of Dickens's limited grasp of contemporary politics, however, has continued to discourage study of the political dimensions of his fiction: 'He was not a man of great political understanding and vision, not a prophet: his imagination worked on the data society gave him. . . . Dickens, as we have seen, was an exceedingly practical person, who thought in terms of money and getting things done: in other words, he was more concerned with administration than with politics proper' (p. 182).

6. For the most important discussions of *Barnaby Rudge*, see: A. E. Dyson, '*Barnaby Rudge*: The Genesis of Violence', *Critical Quarterly*, 9 (1967), 142–60; Avrom Fleishman, *The English Historical Novel* (Baltimore: Johns Hopkins, 1971), pp. 102–14; Harold F. Folland, 'The Doer and the Deed: Theme and Pattern in *Barnaby Rudge*', *PMLA*, 74 (1959), 406–17; James K. Gottshall, 'Devils Abroad: The Unity and Significance of *Barnaby Rudge*', *Nineteenth-Century Fiction*, 16 (1961), 133–46; Jack Lindsay, '*Barnaby Rudge*', *Dickens and the Twentieth Century*, ed. John Gross and Gabriel Pearson (London: Routledge, 1962), pp. 91–106; John Lucas, *The Melancholy Man: A Study of Dickens's Novels* (London: Methuen, 1970), pp. 92–112; Steven Marcus, 'Sons and Fathers', *Dickens, From Pickwick to Dombey* (New York: Simon and Schuster, 1965), pp. 169–212; Sylvère Monod, '*Barnaby Rudge*', *Dickens the Novelist* (Norman: University of Oklahoma Press, 1968), pp. 186–99 and 'Rebel with a Cause: Hugh of the Maypole', *Dickens Studies*, 1 (1965), 4–26; S. J. Newman, '*Barnaby Rudge*: Dickens and Scott', *Literature of the Romantic Period, 1750–1850*, ed. R. T. Davies and B. G. Beatty (New York; Barnes and Noble, 1976), pp. 171–88; Anthony O'Brien, 'Benevolence and Insurrection: The Conflicts of Form and Purpose in *Barnaby Rudge*', *Dickens Studies*, 5 (1969), 26–44; Thomas Jackson Rice, '*Barnaby Rudge*: A Vade Mecum for the Theme of Domestic Government in Dickens', *Dickens Studies Annual*, 7 (1978), 81–102 and 'The End of Dickens's Apprenticeship: Variable Focus in *Barnaby Rudge*', *Nineteenth-Century Fiction*, 30 (1975), 172–84; and Paul Stigant and Peter Widdowson, '*Barnaby Rudge*: A Historical Novel?', *Literature & History*, No. 2 (October 1975), 2–44.

7. House, p. 182.

8. Elie Halévy, *The Triumph of Reform: 1830–1841*, trans. E. I. Watkin (New York: Barnes and Noble, 1961), pp. 190–99. Halévy writes: 'Thus a curious spectacle was witnessed in the House; the three leaders of the Commons, Lord John Russell, Peel, and O'Connell, all parading as moderates. Protected by Peel against the Ultra-Tories and by O'Connell against the Ultra-Radicals the Government survived' (p. 198).

9. See House, pp. 170–72.

10. Halévy, p. 136.

11. House, pp. 92–3.

12. Halévy, p. 288.
13. Halévy, p. 287.
14. Halévy, p. 301.
15. See my '*Oliver Twist* and the Genesis of *Barnaby Rudge*', *Dickens Studies Newsletter*, 4 (March 1973), 10–15.
16. The date of 1834 is suggested by John Butt and Kathleen Tillotson, *Dickens at Work* (London: Methuen, 1957), p. 63. The first positive reference to the novel is the contract with Macrone for *Gabriel Vardon, the Locksmith of London*, in 1836. For a concise summary of the contractual negotiations for *Barnaby Rudge*, see Edgar Johnson, 'Dickens Clashes with His Publishers', *The Dickensian*, 45 (1949–50), 10–17, 76–83.
17. See George Rudé, *The Crowd in History, 1730–1848* (New York: Wiley, 1964), pp. 52, 62, and R. C. O. Matthews, *A Study in Trade Cycle History: Economic Fluctuations in Great Britain, 1833–1842* (New York: Cambridge University Press, 1954).
18. Halévy, p. 323.
19. As in George Canning's speech on the subject of Parliamentary Reform, in 1820, cited by John Holloway in 'Logic, Feeling, and Structure in Political Oratory: A Primer of Analysis', *The Art of Victorian Prose*, ed. George Levine and William Madden (New York: Oxford University Press, 1968), pp. 251–54. Simon Maccoby maintains that the Gordon Riots provided 'one of the strongest arguments against radical reform for decades', in *The English Radical Tradition, 1763–1914* (London: Black, 1966), p. 4. Also see Llewellyn Woodward, *The Age of Reform, 1815–1870*, 2nd edn. (Oxford: Clarendon, 1962), p. 20.
20. Rudé, p. 61, and E. R. Norman, *Anti-Catholicism in Victorian England* (New York: Barnes and Noble, 1968), p. 19.
21. J. P. deCastro, *The Gordon Riots* (London: Oxford University Press, 1926), pp. 4–5.
22. Asa Briggs, *The Making of Modern England, 1783–1867* (New York: Harper, 1959), pp. 197–98.
23. See Briggs, p. 284. Butt and Tillotson note that 'Early in 1842 Dickens's friends in *Punch* were attacking the "Puseyites"' (p. 84). Also see Edgar Johnson's comments on Dickens's reaction to the Oxford Movement in his *Charles Dickens: His Tragedy and Triumph* (New York: Simon and Schuster, 1952), p. 1133 and passim.
24. Although Daniel O'Connell had compared the growing Chartist and Ultra-Tory collusion to the Gordon Riots in an untraced public letter as early as August 1839 (see the angry rebuttal of George Cubitt, printed in the *Morning Chronicle*, 5 September 1839), and the *Morning Chronicle* itself began suspecting an alliance in August 1840 ('A number of Tory gentlemen have been secretly communing with some of the leading Chartists, for the purpose of inducing them . . . to aid them in turning out the present ministry' (10 August 1840)), only in the late spring of 1841 did the liberals generally sense the advanced state of the anti-ministerial coalition.
25. Charles Cavendish Fulke Greville, *The Greville Memoirs, 1814–1860*, ed. Lytton Strachey and Roger Fulford (London: Macmillan, 1938), IV, 222. Cited by Halévy, p. 299, n. 2.

26. These announcements appeared in the *Morning Chronicle* for 13 December 1838, 14 December 1839, and 20 February 1840, respectively.

27. This and all subsequent references to *Barnaby Rudge* are to the *New Oxford Illustrated Dickens* (London: Oxford University Press, 1954).

28. See Halévy's discussion of this emerging alliance, p. 191ff.

29. For discussion of *Barnaby Rudge*'s unique form, which owes more to Dickens's developing narrative technique than to his political intentions, see my essay on 'The End of Dickens's Apprenticeship: Variable Focus in *Barnaby Rudge*', *Nineteenth-Century Fiction*, 30 (1975), 172–84.

30. See Harold F. Folland, 'The Doer and the Deed: Theme and Pattern in *Barnaby Rudge*', *P.M.L.A.*, 74 (1959), 406–17.

31. See Halévy, p. 295 and n. 3. The *Morning Chronicle* announced similarly partial support for the Charter in editorials for 25 and 28 March 1839. Woodward asserts that 'there is hardly a point in the chartist political programme which did not find some support among the middle-class political parties' (p. 127). A useful recent summary of Dickens's responses to Chartism is found in Patrick Brantlinger's *The Spirit of Reform: British Literature and Politics, 1832–1867* (Cambridge, Mass.: Harvard University Press, 1977), pp. 83–96.

32. For a full analysis of Dickens's theme of education in the novel, see my '*Barnaby Rudge*: A Vade Mecum for the Theme of Domestic Government in Dickens', *Dickens Studies Annual*, 7 (1978), 81–102.

33. See Maccoby, p. 33ff., and Woodward, p. 96.

34. Contemporary to the Birmingham Riots and the resurfacing anti-Poor Law agitation, in the lead editorial for 23 July 1839, the *Morning Chronicle* observed that 'the reasons why the middle classes do not join the ranks of the Chartists are tolerably obvious; and they also apply to a large proportion of the working and of other classes. One is, that the disposition of the more prominent orators to excite the multitude to violence has long been observed, and has caused alienation, disgust, and apprehension. Another is, that the Charter itself is a crude and incongruous composition, not carrying out the principles it professes, and less tending to union than to the intolerance of political sectarianism. And a third reason is that Chartism exists as a class badge, not truly identified even with the class (of working men) whose badge it claims to be, and with the effect of deepening the "class animosities", the obliteration of which is so justly represented as desirable. These reasons will, we apprehend, continue to operate so long as the facts exist on which they are founded.'

35. Halévy, p. 324. Also see F. C. Mather, *Public Order in the Age of the Chartists* (Manchester: Manchester University Press, 1959), p. 12.

36. The popular fears of insurrection are amply reflected in the rumours of Chartists arming themselves with pikes and drilling in the countryside, which punctuate the *Morning Chronicle*'s reports in the spring of 1839 (e.g., 6–14 May 1839, passim.). Maccoby (pp. 173–85) and Woodward (pp. 132–37) describe the displacement of the 'moral force' leaders of the Chartists, William Lovett of the London Working Men's Association and Thomas Attwood of the Birmingham Political

Union, by the revolutionary, 'physical force' leadership.

37. Maccoby describes the magnitude of the popular alarm in many quarters at the apparent threat of the Chartist agitation: 'It became early associated in the public mind with incendiary oratory, mob processions and threats of "Physical Force" . . . far outdistanc[ing] those of the Jacobins' (p. 116).

38. See Halévy, pp. 311–28, and F. C. Mather, 'Government and the Chartists', *Chartist Studies*, ed. Asa Briggs (London: Macmillan, 1959), pp. 372–78.

39. See the *London Times*, 12 February 1839, and the reactions of the *Morning Chronicle*, 16–22 July 1839.

40. Butt and Tillotson, p. 82.

41. See Halévy, pp. 296–301, and Maccoby, 173–85.

42. See E. R. Norman, *Anti-Catholicism in Victorian England*, pp. 13–16.

43. Only Kathleen Tillotson seems to have noted the influence of the contemporary Tory anti-Catholic campaign on *Barnaby Rudge*, and that only in passing (Butt and Tillotson, p. 83). The topicality of Dickens's concern for popular upheaval, of course, has been frequently noted.

44. Y. V. Kovalev cites early reviews of *Barnaby Rudge* as a political document, in 'The Literature of Chartism', *Victorian Studies*, 2 (1958), 117–38. Also see N. C. Peyrouton, 'Dickens and the Chartists', *Dickensian*, 60 (1964), 72–88, 152–61.

45. The Nonconformist ministers, who were usually outspoken in their hatred of Catholicism (see Norman, *Anti-Catholicism in Victorian England*, p. 17 and passim), actually exerted their considerable influence to prevent an outbreak of no-Popery at this time. Throughout the late 1830s these clerics were 'active supporters of the ruling classes in their struggle with the spirit of revolution' (Halévy, p. 324).

46. For the Irish role in restraining the Newport rioters, see the *Morning Chronicle*, 28 November 1839. This paper also published reports of 'The Protestant Society' meetings which called for the repeal of the Catholic Emancipation Act, *as well as* the harsh restriction of Irish immigration to prevent the further cheapening of labour; see the transcript of a Liverpool meeting of the society, for example, in the *Morning Chronicle*, 8 October 1838.

47. See the *Morning Chronicle*, 28 September 1838, and note 47, below. In a letter to P. V. Fitzpatrick (21 August 1839), Daniel O'Connell discusses the Ultra-Tory efforts to provoke hostility towards the Irish Catholics: 'Indeed, the spirit that binds together the Tory party in this country is the "No-Popery" feeling—the hatred of Catholicity. You can not form an idea of how prevalent this feeling is, nor how much and how vivaciously it is cherished by the English parsons. . . . I have no doubt they would rejoice in a rebellion or any convulsion that enabled them to extirpate Catholicity with the blood of the Catholics. I do not in the slightest degree exaggerate' (*The Correspondence of Daniel O'Connell*, II, 203).

48. The lead editorial of the *Morning Chronicle*, for 27 December 1839, is the

most significant example of the liberals' campaign to discredit the Protestant Association: 'In the *Annual Register*, for 1780, we find a passage descriptive of the Anti-Popish spirit then excited, which might be employed, *verbatim*, to describe the effects of the knavery and fanaticism of the present day. . . . An obstinate disease is thrown off by degrees: the throes and paroxysms of bigotry are waxing fainter and fainter. True—we have Lord George Gordons among our hereditary legislators; and the catalogues of "squires and parsons" present at Orange Protestant meetings, remind us indeed much of the days of Sacheverel; but where are the mobs to rise at their behest, and plunder and destroy? The Rodens, the Winchilseas, the Beresfords, the Phill-potts, have remained impervious to the civilization of the ages; but not so the people of England.' Clearly Dickens, who was to begin *Barnaby Rudge* within two weeks of this editorial, did not share its writer's confidence in the masses (though both writers did, incidentally, turn to the *Annual Register* as a primary reference). Daniel O'Connell had, three months earlier, recognized that the Tories had found 'the mobs to rise at their behest' in the Ultra-Radicals (see note 23, above), and through 1840 Dickens was formulating the novel which was to warn the English people of the dangers of this alliance.

49. See 'The Present Position of Catholicism', *British and Foreign Review*, April 1838, pp. 423–24; 'The Papistical Tendency of the Tracts for the Times', *Church of England Quarterly*, April 1839; and the *Morning Chronicle*, 7 January 1839.

50. The *Morning Chronicle* illustrates both these tactics in its repeated attacks on the reactionaries' 'hypocritical bigotry of the "jolly full bottle"' (14 September 1839), particularly inveighing against the anti-Catholic propaganda appearing in the most influential Tory periodicals, the *Quarterly Review* and the *London Times*. The *Morning Chronicle*'s Guy Fawkes Day (5 November) editorial for 1840 is an appropriate and typical example: 'If the sensitive minds of these theological November-izers be so keenly alive to the evils of Popery, they might find, nearer home, a worse form of it than that exhibited in the parish priests of Ireland. . . . Do the O'Sullivans and Stowells ever travel by Oxford? Do they know anything of the Pusey Popery, conceived in the bosom of the Church of England, and feeding on the womb in which it was engen-dered? Do they read the *Quarterly Review*? . . . We will not advise them to compare this sect with the laborious and compassionate priesthood of papal Ireland of the present day, but with the Catholic plotters of two centuries and a half ago.' Also see 14 September 1839, 11 March 1840, and 20 January 1841. For the *London Times*'s too little recognized partisanship during this period, see Fox Bourne's *English Newspapers* (London, 1887), II, 107–8. Dickens twice alludes to the *London Times*'s service to the Ultra-Tories in *Barnaby Rudge*, citing the 'Thunderer' (a common epithet for the paper) as the bigot's favourite reading (XXXIX, 296; XLI, 312).

51. The *Morning Chronicle*, 5 June 1841. Also see 8 June 1841.

52. Halévy, p. 327.

53. See my '*Barnaby Rudge*: A Vade Mecum for the Theme of Domestic Government in Dickens', pp. 101–2. For additional comment on the political backgrounds to *Barnaby Rudge*, partially assimilated into this essay, see my '*Oliver Twist* and the Genesis of *Barnaby Rudge*', *Dickens Studies Newsletter*, 4 (March 1973), 10–15.

54. House, p. 182.

3

The Crowd in Dickens

by DAVID CRAIG

> . . . as Margaret reached the small side-entrance by the folding
> doors, in the great dead wall of Marlborough mill-yard, and
> waited the porter's answer to the bell, she looked round and
> heard the first long far-off roll of the tempest—saw the first
> slow-surging wave of the dark crowd come, with its threatening
> crest, tumble over, and retreat, at the far end of the street,
> which a moment ago seemed so full of repressed noise, but
> which now was ominously still. . . . There was no near sound—
> no steam-engine at work with beat and pant—no click of
> machinery, no mingling and clashing of many sharp voices; but
> far away, the ominous gathering roar, deep-clamouring.
> —Elizabeth Gaskell, *North and South* (1855), Ch. 21

Dickens's two main visions of the epoch just before his birth,
Barnaby Rudge (1841) and *A Tale of Two Cities* (1859), both
have at their centre an image of the mass of the people looting,
burning, injuring, killing, and destroying even themselves.
The Gordon Riot of 1780, in London, and the French Revolution of 1789–91, in Paris, are presented as unrelieved scenes of
demonic and bestial behaviour. A question this essay must
answer is whether Dickens saw such behaviour as typically
bygone, an aspect of backwardness, or whether it was present
to him as a tendency of 'the People governed'[1] which was as
liable to erupt as it had ever been.

Barnaby Rudge is much the simpler of the two novels in its
conception of how 'mobs' accumulate and behave, much the

more swingeing in its low view of militant crowds. The anti-Catholic rioters are stirred up by 'the worst passions of the worst men' (Ch. 45). For those few days in June 1780, Londoners were in a state of 'mania', which was all the more intense because the grounds for it were so flimsy; and once the rioting had started, a 'moral plague ran through the city' which made even 'sober workmen' drop their toolbags on their way home and join the crowds who were smashing house-fronts and burning roofs and furniture (Chs. 37, 53). (This mention of sober workmen is one of the rare hints that any of the rioters had regular jobs.) Dickens says that 'such of them as were really honest and sincere' never rejoined the rioters after the first few days. The crowd 'was composed for the most part of the very scum and refuse of London', of 'idle and profligate persons' whose behaviour was as 'terrible' and 'fickle'[2] as the ocean. In their siege of the Houses of Parliament (part demonstration, part attack), they are described in the classic language of abhorrence and condemnation: 'The mob raged and roared, like a mad monster, as it was.' They were 'like beasts at the sight of prey', and when they smashed up and looted a Catholic chapel, they were like 'hideous madmen', a 'dream of demon heads and savage eyes', 'so many phantoms' (Chs. 49–50, 52). Only three rioters are consistently given names and otherwise keyed into the story of fully-characterized people. They are: Dennis the public hangman, a cartoon monster of leering sadism; Hugh, an illiterate savage from Epping Forest, who is a kind of Caliban to Sir John Chester's malignant Prospero; and Barnaby himself, the innocent madman decked with feathers, a quasi-Shakespearean Fool or Wordsworthian Idiot Boy. The former two, who are the main whoopers-on of the pack, are described between bouts of riot as 'wallowing, like some obscene animals, in their squalor and wickedness', and the blatant villainy of this is matched by Gashford, secretary to the Protestant leader Lord Gordon, who is

> singularly repulsive and malicious. His beetling brow almost obscured his eyes; his lip was curled contemptuously; his very shoulders seemed to sneer in stealthy whisperings with his great flapped ears. (Chs. 52, 36)

Such are the passages which prompt us most tellingly to take a judging view of the riotous townsfolk. The sheer evocation of their behaviour is for the most part graphically detailed and convincing. It engages Dickens's powers as the most talented journalist of his time. In Chapters 49–70 the melodrama and whimsy which vitiate much of the novel are exchanged for a style which is masterly in its presenting of crowded occasions, incessant movement, physical details that bite into our minds unforgettably:

> On the skull of one drunken lad—not twenty, by his looks, who lay upon the ground with a bottle to his mouth, the lead from the roof came streaming down in a shower of liquid fire, white hot; melting his head like wax.

Passages like the description of the storming of Lord Mansfield's house in Bloomsbury Square take their place in the historical record; it would be hard to fault them as chronicles.[3]

From such writing we can see distinctly how the crowd behaved. Why they did so is another matter—they do not experience, they merely behave, and their motives are only thinly accounted for by Dickens's suggestion that the more groundless a hate-campaign is, the more inflammatory it is likely to be, or by his brief, liberal aside blaming the 'fostering' of the 'mob' on 'bad criminal laws, bad prison regulations, and the worst conceivable police' (Chs. 37, 49). For a convincingly inward account of what it is like to be collectively inflamed against a scapegoat and how this can issue out of, and then die back into, your ordinary experience as a person, we must go to a modern piece such as Steinbeck's wonderfully low-pitched story, 'The Vigilante', in which Mike the white lyncher's intimate emotions are precisely defined.[4]

A Tale of Two Cities offers a deeper account than *Barnaby Rudge* of how a rising gathers way. It is also more chastened and less righteous in its conception of destructive tendencies in social behaviour. A mature writer is at work now, and he has taken on a much more formidable subject—not a riot but a revolution. Again Dickens offers plenty of graphic descriptions of wrecking and killing, drawing heavily on Carlyle's *The French Revolution* (1837), which he had always greatly admired.[5] But the rioters here are not a motley mass, they are a class, with motives shown to be rooted in their poverty and the cruelty of the landowners, epitomized in the running-down and killing of a slum child by the carriage of Monsieur le Marquis (Bk. 2, Ch. 7). As such they are again evoked in imagery of the elemental, the bestial, the pathological. Again the crowd (the working men and women from the artisan district of Faubourg St.-Antoine, who storm the Bastille) are a 'sea of black and threatening waters', 'a vast dusky mass of scarecrows heaving to and fro', every person 'on high-fever strain and at high-fever heat', the women 'thirsting shrilly' for blood (Chs. 9, 21). When they dance the carmagnole, they are 'like five thousand demons', a 'mere storm of coarse red caps and coarse woollen rags', it is 'a fallen sport—a something, once innocent, delivered over to all devilry'—which recalls the passage in *Barnaby Rudge* in which the chapel-looters enact a kind of inverted parody of Christ's Passion, 'bleeding with the wounds of rusty nails . . . some with great wooden fragments'. And the French revolutionary crowd, specifically the members of a tribunal trying political suspects in the last phase of the novel, are once again 'The lowest, cruellest, and worst populace of a city, never without its quantity of low, cruel, and bad'.[6]

The marked difference from *Barnaby Rudge* is the stress on poverty and injustice as causes of the degenerated behaviour. This link is explicit in a short key passage from the Bastille chapter:

> The remorseless sea of turbulently swaying shapes, voices of vengeance, and faces hardened in the furnace of suffering until the touch of pity could make no mark on them.[7]

We have already been prepared for this by the child's death and it now issues in the extraordinary sequence in the chapter called 'Fire Rises' which gives the form of myth to the links between the ill-used townsfolk and the starving peasantry, between France under the *ancien régime* (the novel opens, and the child is killed, in 1775) and the events of 1789 and after. The bereaved father turns into a 'shaggy-haired man of almost barbarian aspect' who wanders the countryside like an avenging spirit. By an unobtrusive device—shifting the verbs into the conditional mood—he is presented as not one but many:

> in these times, as the mender of roads worked, solitary, in the dust . . . he would see some rough figure approaching on foot,

the like of which was once a rarity in those parts, but was now a frequent presence.

On this particular occasion road-mender and wanderer join hands and hint in monosyllables at an event set for the coming night. The road-mender exchanges his blue cap for a red one. And each calls the other 'Jacques'. Presently, from 'East, West, North, and South, through the woods, four heavy-treading, unkempt figures crushed the high grass and cracked the branches, striding on cautiously to come together in the court-yard' of the Marquis's château, and as it goes up in flames every villager sets a lighted candle in his window (Bk. 2, Ch. 23).

In sum the passage makes a powerful, stylized image of an oppressed class rising up. Together the men incarnate the traditional figure of Jacques Bonhomme, French for 'the common man', John Common in England, Iohne the Commonweill in Scotland, who from Renaissance times had stood for the mass of the people, peasantry and town workfolk. The burning is an archetypal jacquery—in Russian idiom, the setting of a 'red cock' on the lord's rooftree, which had been happening with mounting intensity throughout the revolutionary Hungry '40s of the nineteenth century: at least 800 peasant risings in Russia between 1845 and 1860, 230 serf-owners and bailiffs killed between 1835 and 1854, sixty or seventy a year by 1851.[8] To characterize an age (G. M. Young suggests in his essay 'Mid-Victorianism'), we should ask 'What were the people most afraid of?' And Charles Kingsley gave one contemporary answer: 'Look at France and see!'[9]

What the stylization of 'Fire Rises' precludes is any fine focusing of sympathetic understanding on the revolutionaries. We are rarely close to, let alone inside, any suffering workman or peasant. The principal named revolutionaries are the Defarges and they are not in poverty. Neediness, starvation, ill-use, powerlessness remain generalized bad things which the liberal novelist can invoke from time to time. A touchstone would be Silone's classic novel of peasant poverty, *Fontamara* (1934), where extremely broad stylization still leaves room for the personal experience of a lack of water and of land.[10] Consider how different *A Tale of Two Cities* would have been if we had been put amongst the families crying and dying for want of bread and flour at a price they could afford—if we had seen at close quarters the mother, say, who killed two of her three children for fear of famine, the people who killed themselves for the same reason, or dropped dead in the Paris streets, or the women who gathered in the Bonnet de la Liberté (Croix Rouge) and shouted 'Down with weapons! We want no more soldiers, because there is no more bread!'[11] This was still happening in 1795, after some years of Revolutionary government, but well before that time Dickens has lost all sight of the values professed ever more desperately by the people who had made the Revolution. The centre of his stage is occupied (against a background of gibbering sadists) by the lonely noble martyrdom of Darnay/Carton, doing his better thing and going to his better place—for reasons as purely (and coincidentally) personal as those for which Stephen Blackpool in *Hard Times* refuses to join the Lancashire cotton-spinners and weavers in their seven months' strike of 1853–54.[12]

In all these novels—and we may include *The Old Curiosity Shop* on the strength of the unemployed workers' march in a Midland city (Ch. 45)—Dickens is struggling to present, according to his lights, that most problematic social phenomenon, the militant crowd. Such crowds were present in the lives of British people in his day to an extent we may now have to recover by efforts of historical imagination. The eighteenth and early nineteenth century, says Edward Thompson, 'are punctuated by riot, occasioned by bread prices, turnpikes and tolls, excise, "rescue", strikes, new machinery, enclosures, press-gangs and a score of other grievances'. The commonest, he says, is 'the bread or food riot'. Dickens's second major case is from France in 1789, but 'Riots continued for many years after 1792: either upon specific issues . . . or . . . as insurrectionary climaxes to Radical agitation.'[13] In 1812, the year of Dickens's birth, Luddism—the rising of glovers, stockingers, and other textile craftsmen against the powered machines which were cheapening goods and undermining their livelihoods—reached a peak. In 1812–13 forty men were hanged for Luddite actions in the north of England alone. In the summer of 1812 more than 12,000 troops were stationed from York to Leicester:

It was a veritable army, larger than many actual armies with which British Generals had waged and won important foreign campaigns.

The social effects were permanent:

> Thereafter, and largely because of the lesson the authorities had learnt in 1812, the army in England was kept ready for internal and civil duty at a moment's notice.[14]

From these cases we can begin to see that to move back into history from Dickens's vision of it makes us take stock of class motives not only more imperative but also more humane and positive than either the fevered gullibility of the Gordon Rioters or the vengeful sadism of the revolutionaries in *A Tale of Two Cities*. It also makes us take stock of methods (forms of popular organization) and of results (advances in civilized social conscience) for which Dickens cannot find room in his vision of grassroots militancy as essentially chaotic.

So far as *Barnaby Rudge* is concerned, it is true that we have to look hard to find much sign of humane class motives, organization, or civilized conscience among the rioters who burned the libraries of peers favouring Catholic Emancipation or choked and poisoned themselves to death by lapping scalding gin from a Catholic-owned distillery. No doubt the brutality of this riot is a major reason why it fascinated Dickens and lent itself to one of his styles. Nor should we scout his insight into the tendency of people to become more excited and destructive the less valid the grounds they have for hating the particular scapegoat. When we read in Ch. 37,

> terrors and alarms which no man understood were perpetually broached, both in and out of Parliament, by one enthusiast who did not understand himself, and bygone bugbears which had lain quietly in their graves for centuries, were raised again to haunt the ignorant and credulous . . . so that stocks and stones appeared infected with the common fear, urging all men to join together blindfold in resistance of they knew not what, they knew not why,

we are horribly and specifically reminded of how Fascists fomented the hounding and destroying of Jews in Hitler's Germany, and of how they are doing so in Argentina at this moment.[15] Horrible though this is, it is not enough just to

81

abhor. The turbulent crowd itself becomes a bugbear haunting the ignorant unless we understand in what conditions
people run wild, and clear understanding is not much furthered
by imaging rioters as 'demons' or 'scum' or resorting to the
favourite blanket notion that 'it is the manner of a crowd' to
behave 'in a very disorderly and irregular way' (Ch. 43). The
most recent historian of the Gordon Riot—who is perfectly
unpartisan and who uses the familiar imagery of the crowd
'like a sea', impelled to violence by a 'sensual, reactive
impulse' and 'losing their identities in a fusing welter of
destruction'—also does careful justice to what causes such
behaviour:

> The poor were in revolt against authority. For as long as any
> of them could remember they had been insulted, frustrated and
> ignored; the victims of laws specifically directed against them;
> the lower orders in a society which shamefully abused them.
> They rose up incoherently in protest, unprepared and inarticu-
> late, unsure even themselves of what they wanted or hoped to
> attain. . . .[16]

The contemporary records from the London archives confirm
much of this. The rioters were not 'idle scum' but craftsmen,
shopkeepers, and wage-earners, as were most of the revolutionary Parisians whom Dickens smears as the 'lowest and
worst' and whom French officialdom smeared as 'brigands'.[17]
The London prisons were attacked and opened, as Dickens
describes, but the people set free were not mostly thieves,
pickpockets, desperadoes, and convicts, as contemporary
middle-class observers and police informers called them:
debtors outnumbered criminals by eight to one in a total of
about 2,000.[18] In spite of Gordon's sweeping anti-Catholic
propaganda, it was mainly the rich and powerful among the
Catholics who were attacked. They included employers who
sacked Protestant workers first when business fell away, or
brought in blackleg labour from among the needy London
Irish, and also a publican with a bad reputation as a thief-
taker—thief-takers used to magnify the offence of the accused
because the rewards they were after were graduated.[19] It
strikes me as a civilized conscience that shows through in the
remark of a barge builder from Bermondsey: 'Protestant or

not, no gentleman need be possessed of more than £1,000 a year; that is enough for any gentleman to live upon.' The same egalitarianism was at work among the crowd when they collected money 'for the poor Mob' and when they made their target the bastions of wealth and its expert servants: the Inns of Court, magistrates' houses, toll-houses, and the Bank of England.[20]

Toll-houses, and the excise mentioned by Thompson, were prime targets because they were among the most exorbitant means of wringing profit from thousands of people on or below the verge of destitution. The tolls or duties levied at city gates and bridges, or on country turnpikes, unbearably increased the cost of the means of life (herds and flocks driven along roads, produce brought in to town markets) and it is for this reason that in Paris in summer 1789 the first riots involved the systematic destruction of forty out of fifty-four customs posts. The documents, receipts, and registers were burnt along with the furnishings and the huts themselves. Looting was sternly discouraged.[21] In Britain the most famous action against tolls was the 'Rebecca' movement in Wales. The key moments in its history show how many essentials of class struggle joined their forces on this issue. For some years militancy had been gathering in the countryside. Houses of enclosing farmers were burned, as were houses of speculators who had bought up enclosed commons. In 1838 the effigy of a farmer was burned in his own yard. In January 1839 one of the new workhouses, which since the New Poor Law of 1834 had been dubbed 'Bastilles', and which housed 250,000 men and women by 1840, was burned down at Narberth. In February a Chartist 'missionary' was active near there. In May the first toll-gate was destroyed—it belonged to a trust notorious for neglecting its roads—and when it was put up again, it was wrecked again, by men disguised as women with blacked-up faces. By 1842 all this trust's gates in Carmarthenshire had been destroyed, the troops were powerless, within months few gates were left throughout Wales, threatening letters were being sent to clergymen notorious for exacting high tithes, ricks and plantations owned by unpopular magistrates were being burned, and 400 horsemen in disguise rode into Carmarthen under the slogan 'Justice' and ransacked the workhouse until dragoons drove them off.[22]

Such activity, which of course seemed lawless and disorderly to conservative people at the time, is remarkable for its own internal order, its own kind of method, and also for its stamina and its concentration on economic and presently on political goals. For several years the 'Rebecca' movement was masterly in its secrecy, even to the putting about of false news of its movements, and its petitions were drafted by a Chartist, i.e. by a member of the movement for most of the political rights we now enjoy. Such 'mobs', far from being 'fickle', were often remarkable for their concerted tactics and their sense of goal. Early in the Hungry '40s, when disturbances broke out all over the south of Scotland and the north of England against wage cuts and under the slogan 'A fair day's wages for a fair day's work', the plugs were driven out of the boilers to stop blacklegs doing the work. Machines were wrecked, and this can be seen as 'wanton' destruction. For the militants it was indispensable—a prototype of the picket; and when farms and bakeries were pillaged, which will have seemed barbarous to the law-abiding, it was to distribute flour and bread to the strikers—again a necessity in the days before union funds and strike pay.[23] In the climactic Chartist year of 1848, when a slump made thousands destitute, an armed 'mob' in Glasgow looted gunsmiths' and jewellers' shops. Chaos and disorder? or a bid for an alternative kind of order? In fact the leaders spent the night 'concerting a more methodical insurrection' for the following day: they would march on the factories, make them close, seize the gasometers and turn off the city lights, and in the darkness free the prisoners from the gaols.[24] This kind of planning and the self-control to carry it out is a notable feature of our social history, remarkably so when the experience and the tools of government belonged so exclusively to the ruling class.

Less than a week after the Plug Riots broke out in Lancashire, according to F. C. Mather,

> the mob found itself for a while virtually in command of large towns like Stockport and Bolton, and that violence and destruction of property did not take place on a large scale was solely due to the restraint of the working men.[25]

Only those possessed by the bugbear of the demonic mob should be surprised by this. The militant crowd was usually purposive and in its own way ordered because it was impelled by rational motives—the need for food, the ideal of equality. The Nottingham framework knitters in the Luddite movement wanted to raise wages and prevent frauds, and the Lancashire Luddites wanted to prevent speculation and profiteering in foodstuffs. In the opinion of their historian,

> But for the Luddites and the Blanketeers Manchester and Birmingham might have been unrepresented in Parliament, as well as without local systems of police, wage-earners might have been without the right to form trades unions, factory acts might have been delayed much later than they were.[26]

That is because so many of the rights and measures we believe to be civilized necessities were not offered us on a plate by our rulers but wrested from them by a show of force which they could smear as lawless or anti-social but which we may prefer to see as completely responsible.

This shows throughout the period that Dickens represents by demonic riot. In 1766 in Honiton the lace workers seized the farmers' corn, sold it at market themselves, and returned the money and the bags to the farmers. In 1783 in Halifax the weavers forced the corn merchants to sell wheat and oats at a reasonable price, and to make their action stick they had to control roads and market-places, monitor prices, and write and print handbills explaining what they were doing. (Their leader was hanged.) In the climactic year of 1795, with famine or extreme scarcity throughout Europe, the Privy Council had almost lost control of the food supply as fair sales of grain, flour, and loaves were enforced by the Nottingham house-wives, the colliers in the Forest of Dean, the Cornish tinners, the labourers in Norfolk, the townsfolk of Newcastle and Carlisle. In London a major flour mill, the Albion, was burned twice—when people suspected adulteration of the flour. This militant action as usual had its own lively style. At the mill-burning 'ballads of rejoicing' were sung from printed sheets, and in Nottingham the women made an emblem of a loaf, streaked with red ochre and tied up in black crêpe, to symbolize 'bleeding famine decked in Sackecloth'.[27]

In France similar traditions prevailed, from the time of *la guerre des farines* in the early 1770s, when loaves were seized or bakers forced to sell them cheap, to the late '80s and early '90s, when grain was seized from monasteries and sugar, bread, meat, and wine were taken from warehouses to be sold at low prices. (One 4lb. loaf was liable to cost an unskilled labourer's weekly wage, and prices were rising.) Was such commandeering chaotic and disordered? or a bid for a new kind of order? The orderly reaction of the law-keepers was to fire on crowds in narrow streets, to sabre a demonstration by youths 'armed' with torches and laurel branches, to shoot dead many dozens of demonstrators at the house of a manufacturer in the Faubourg St.-Antoine who had spoken against a rise in wages, hang three of them, and brand others before sending them to the galleys.[28] The terror which Dickens makes climactic in his novel was in fact the last stage of an escalation whose pace was forced relentlessly by successive governments and their troops, Town Guards, and so on. The stages in this blur beneath Dickens's lurid imagery of a blood-curse working itself out. They are further obscured by the plot with its jumps in time and from Paris to London and back again. Finally he distorts the record by the propaganda device of mentioning the atrocities done by one side only: e.g. during the siege of the Bastille at least 150 citizens were killed against seven of the garrison, but the only blood-letting Dickens brings fully onto camera is the beheading of the governor.[29]

That Dickens looked right past (or to one side of) the hundreds of Radical risings and chose episodes more than half a century old for his exhibition of mob violence may suggest that he saw it as typically bygone, and it is true that early in both novels he emphasizes the backwardness of the later eighteenth century: the illiteracy, the bad roads, the thieving in unlit streets (and in the drawing-rooms at Court), the heavy drinking, the public hangings.[30] But several points combine to make me feel that he senses mob violence to be present or immediate rather than distant. First, if the London crowd are fatally gullible in *Barnaby Rudge*, they are no less so at the Eatanswill by-election in *Pickwick Papers* (Ch. 13), where a crowd in the later 1820s do nothing but roar, fight, and get helplessly drunk, or at the strike meeting toyed with by the rabble-rouser Slackbridge in *Hard Times*, a novel for which Dickens went to Preston in January 1854 to get up-to-the-minute copy.[31] Similarly, the 'bands of unemployed labourers', in *The Old Curiosity Shop*—written at the start of the Hungry '40s—are seen as demonic emanations from a modern industrial city seen as Hell. Among the foundries, figures are 'calling to one another with hoarse cries', 'the people near them looked wilder and more savage', and 'maddened men', incited by leaders at a torchlight meeting, 'rushed forth on errands of terror and destruction, to work no ruin half so surely as their own'.[32] Here Dickens can get no further than the other outstanding socially-conscious novelists of his time—Disraeli describing the Sheffield cutlers as the 'subterraneous nation of the cellars', Elizabeth Gaskell describing the Manchester iron workers as 'demons'.[33] In their vision the crowd is a faceless mass—individuals are indistinguishable—the imagery which comes naturally to the writers is of swarming or herding animals. It was early in the nineteenth century that 'rookery' and 'warren' came commonly to be used to mean congested, poor accommodation; an earlier meaning for 'warren' had been 'brothel'. This works in with the novelists' image of the workers erupting from the other end of town. When they do acquire individual faces, they are deformed, by violent passions, bad breeding, or disease. Contemporary theorists likened convicts to animals (wolves, lions) and explained lawless behaviour as the fulfilling of a genetic warp or 'hereditary curse'.[34] This came out in the face. Near the start of *London Labour and the London Poor* Mayhew suggests that the people of the streets typically have features such as 'high cheekbones and protruding jaws'.[35] Just this face occurs again and again in the anti-Radical caricaturists from Gillray and Cruikshank to Hablot Browne, who as 'Phiz' was Dickens's most prolific illustrator. In their drawings (one of which is on the front-cover of the jacket of this book) the mouths of the 'mob' gape or turn sharply down at the corners, their lower jaws sag, their noses are beaky, their eyebrows dip sharply to meet just above the nose, their lips protrude, their nostrils flare or spread, their chins stick out. . . . The emotions we seem meant to read into these physical details include ferocity, sadistic glee, unseeing wild-eyed 'sent' states of various kinds, jeering, cackling, stupefaction. . . . 'Phiz' also sets his figures

into a characteristic reeling or spiralling motion, slanting them
heavily left or right in little clusters, sucking them towards a
vortex somewhere near the bottom of the picture. . . .[36] The
effect is of an uncontrollable giddiness, of helter-skelter figures
who must keep running or staggering or they will fall. Of
course people can be in such a state—on the football terraces?
in a lynch mob? My point is that Dickens and his illustrator
use this state of frightening collective fever to typify not only
wild gangs but also workers' groups (an unemployed 'demo', a
revolutionary tribunal) who more likely than not would have
been self-controlled.

Dickens, we know, worked very closely with Hablot Browne,
often instructing him in detail, so we may take it that the
graphic images corresponded fully with what he had in
mind.[37] Well before he wrote, such faces and such motions
were commonly attributed to townsfolk in the mass in the
cartoons that Hogarth and Rowlandson, Gillray and Cruikshank made to be sold as prints, and they presently appear in
the work of standard illustrators for the new picture magazines.[38] That is to say, long before the Gordon Riot (let alone
the Plug Plots or Chartism), the well-to-do already saw the
common people as a barbarous horde, since this view of them
was given, not so much from an actual history as from a long-
standing syndrome of fears, worries, insecurities, on the part of
the have's. It was replenished by each moment when the have-
not's challenged them again. Today the syndrome lives on in
the Dickens critic who abolishes the concrete reasons for
rebellion by saying (about *Barnaby Rudge* and *A Tale of Two
Cities*) that 'the same guards disperse the same riots ready to
erupt at any time and on any pretext'[39]; in the historian who
says of the Hungry '40s that 'the demon of destruction still
lurked beneath the surface of English social life, ready to break
loose in times of stress',[40] which is really a version of the belief
that as a species we have a quantity of aggression bred into us
which will out[41]; and in the Conservative Prime Minister who
said after the Toxteth riot in June 1981 that unemployment
was 'no justification' for the wrecking. The ethical term 'justification' evades the paramount social need, not to justify, but
to explain the behaviour of people who do something which
they would never do if they were in good heart and living well.

NOTES

1. The phrase is from a well-known address that Dickens gave to the Birmingham and Midland Institute in 1869: quoted from Arnold Kettle, 'Dickens and the Popular Tradition', in David Craig (ed.), *Marxists on Literature* (1975), p. 225.
2. 'Mob' is derived from *mobile vulgus*, the fickle or unstable mass (of the people) and according to the *O.E.D.* was first used about the London crowd, by aristocratic politicoes of the Restoration. Its use to mean the working people as a whole, as distinct from a politically-active minority of them, is a secondary meaning, for which the radical Swift criticized the conservative Addison.
3. Chs. 55, 66.
4. John Steinbeck, *The Long Valley* (1939; 1958 edn.), pp. 108–15.
5. *A Tale of Two Cities*, Preface; Edgar Johnson, *Charles Dickens, His Tragedy and Triumph* (1953), p. 947.
6. *A Tale of Two Cities*, Bk. 3, Ch. 5; *Barnaby Rudge*, Ch. 50; *A Tale of Two Cities*, Bk. 3, Ch. 6.
7. *A Tale of Two Cities*, Bk. 2, Ch. 21. The same image of the workman as hardened in bitterness, no doubt understandably, occurs in George Eliot's *Felix Holt the Radical* when she refers to the 'rather hard-lipped antagonism of the trades-union man' (Ch. 30: for a discussion of the social viewpoint behind such judgements, see my 'Fiction and the "Rising Industrial Classes"' in *The Real Foundations*, 1973, pp. 134–40).
8. B. H. Sumner, *Survey of Russian History* (1947; 1961 edn.), p. 124; Alexander Herzen, *Selected Philosophical Works* (Moscow, 1956), p. 491.
9. Quoted from Geoffrey Pearson, *The Deviant Imagination* (1975; 1980 edn.), p. 159.
10. Discussed in detail by myself and Michael Egan in *Extreme Situations* (1979), pp. 178–86.
11. George Rudé, *The Crowd in the French Revolution* (1959; 1967 edn.), pp. 148–51.
12. Discussed in detail in *The Real Foundations*, pp. 124–30.
13. E. P. Thompson, *The Making of the English Working Class* (1963), pp. 62–3, 74.
14. Frank Ongley Darvall, *Popular Disturbances and Public Order in Regency England* (Oxford, 1934; 1969 edn.), pp. 260–61.
15. Jacobo Timerman, *Prisoner Without a Name, Cell Without a Number* (1981; 1982 edn.), pp. 60–80.
16. Christopher Hibbert, *King Mob* (1958; 1959 edn.), pp. 92, 140.
17. George Rudé, *Paris and London in the Eighteenth Century* (1970), p. 283; Rudé, *Crowd in the French Revolution*, pp. 57–60, 67, 98, 101, etc.
18. Rudé, *Paris and London*, p. 280.
19. Hibbert, *King Mob*, p. 140; Rudé, *Paris and London*, pp. 286–87, 289; Thompson, *English Working Class*, p. 61.
20. Rudé, *Paris and London*, pp. 274, 289–90.
21. Rudé, *Crowd in the French Revolution*, p. 49.
22. David Williams, *A History of Modern Wales* (1950; 1951 edn.), pp. 198–211;

English Economic History: Select Documents, ed. A. E. Bland, P. A. Brown, and R. H. Tawney (1914), p. 663; Asa Briggs, 'The Local Background of Chartism' in Briggs (ed.), *Chartist Studies* (1960), p. 11.

23. Elie Halévy, *Victorian Years (1841–1895)* (1951; 1961 edn.), pp. 33–4; F. C. Mather, *Public Order in the Age of the Chartists* (Manchester, 1959), p. 16.

24. Halévy, *Victorian Years*, p. 238.

25. Mather, *Public Order*, p. 228.

26. Darvall, *Popular Disturbances*, pp. 172, 217. Similarly, in Wales, the 'Rebecca' movement gave rise to the setting up of county road boards, uniform tolls, and provision for a local enquiry before any private Enclosure Bill was promulgated (Williams, *Modern Wales*, pp. 208–11).

27. Thompson, *English Working Class*, pp. 64–7.

28. Rudé, *Crowd in the French Revolution*, pp. 23–5, 29–31, 35–43.

29. Rudé, *Crowd in the French Revolution*, p. 56; Dickens, *A Tale of Two Cities*; Bk. 2, Ch. 21.

30. *Barnaby Rudge*, Chs. 1–2, 16; *A Tale of Two Cities*, Bk. 1, Ch. 1.

31. John Forster, *The Life of Charles Dickens* ('Gadshill Edition', n.d.), II, pp. 147–48.

32. Ch. 45.

33. Benjamin Disraeli, *Sybil* (1845), Ch. 9; Elizabeth Gaskell, *Mary Barton* (1848), Ch. 19.

34. Pearson, *Deviant Imagination*, pp. 151, 155.

35. Henry Mayhew, *London Labour and the London Poor* (1849–62; 1967 edn.), I, p. 3.

36. Among the many examples, see esp. illustrations to Chs. 49, 52, and 66 of *Barnaby Rudge* and the cover of the Penguin English Library edition (1973); in *A Tale of Two Cities*, illustrations to Bk. 2, Ch. 22, and Bk. 3, Ch. 1; and in *The Old Curiosity Shop*, illustration to Ch. 45.

37. F. R. and Q. D. Leavis, *Dickens the Novelist* (1970; 1972 edn.), pp. 442–63.

38. Among the many examples, see esp. Hogarth's prints of the 1750s 'Gin Lane', 'Election Entertainment', and 'Chairing the Member' (Frederick Antal, *Hogarth and His Place in European Art*, 1962, plates 121a, 122a, 124a); and Gillray's cartoon of the London Corresponding Society (1795): see *Peterloo and Radical Reform*, ed. John Langdon-Davies (1965), item no. 1. An *Illustrated London News* cartoon of the 'Rebecca' rebels is reproduced in Williams's *History of Modern Wales*.

39. Joseph Gold, *Charles Dickens: Radical Moralist* (Minneapolis, 1972), p. 240.

40. Mather, *Public Order*, p. 14.

41. Popularized by Robert Ardrey in *The Territorial Imperative* (1966) and *African Genesis* (1972). A much more cogent explanation of aggression— that it is caused by shortage of food and space—is given by Claire and W. M. S. Russell in *Violence, Monkeys and Man* (1968).

4

Polyphony and Problematic in *Hard Times*

by ROGER FOWLER

The polarization of critical response to *Hard Times* is familiar enough to make detailed reporting unnecessary, but since this polarization is a fact relevant to my argument, I will recapitulate it briefly.

Popular reception of the novel has been largely antagonistic or uninterested. The character of the earlier novels has led to the formation of a cheerful and sentimental 'Dickensian' response which finds *Hard Times*, like the other later novels, cold and uncomfortable, lacking in the innocent jollity, sentimentality and grotesquery of the earlier writings. When Dickens's anniversary was mentioned in a T.V. spot on 7 February 1983, the novelist was identified through a list of his works which totally excluded the later 'social' novels.

In other circles, there has been a keenly appreciative response to *Hard Times*: in some quarters more academic, and in some quarters more socialist. Committedly positive evaluation is found as early as 1860 in Ruskin and then in this century in Shaw, whose appreciation of the book as 'serious social history' initiated a line of evaluation more recently reflected in, for example, Raymond Williams and in David Craig. Then there is a famous and extravagant essay by Leavis:

> Of all Dickens's works it is the one that has all the strength of his genius, together with a strength no other of them can show—that of a completely serious work of art.[1]

If Leavis was over-enthusiastic, others, some such as John Holloway and David M. Hirsch provoked by Leavis's surplus of commendation, have insisted on faults in the novel both as art and as social history. Even that majority of modern academic critics who accept and praise *Hard Times* concede some faults. Among the flaws cited by both camps are the following. A failure of a documentary kind is the presentation of the demagogue Slackbridge—'a mere figment of the middle-class imagination. No such man would be listened to by a meeting of English factory hands' (Shaw). Similarly, the use of a professional circus to represent Fancy as opposed to Fact has been faulted on the grounds that Dickens might have found Fancy in the native recreations of working people (Craig). A more 'ideological' criticism would allege that Dickens's *concept* of Fancy was, judging from the symbols by which he represented it, too trivial to weigh effectively against the Fact of Utilitarian economic theory and philosophy of education (Holloway, Lodge).[2] Other critics have admitted faults of characterization—the girl Sissy is sentimentally presented and emerges as inadequate: her childhood attributes do not ground her later strength on Louisa's behalf. Again, Stephen and Rachael are said to be too good to be true; Stephen's martyrdom to a drunken wife is a cliché; his refusal to join the union is not motivated and therefore puts him into a weak, contradictory position in relation to his fellow-workers. Now these allegations of faults of construction are not naïve 'Dickensian' complaints. There is real evidence that many things are not quite right with the book, for whatever reason: because of the unfamiliar constraints of small-scale writing for weekly parts, because of the secondhand nature of Dickens's experience?

Since *Hard Times* has gained a very positive reputation in this century, we should beware of condemning it by totting up 'faults'. Perhaps the yardstick which we unconsciously apply, the tradition of the humanistic novel already well established by 1850, is not entirely relevant. It might be preferable to revise our conception of what type of novel this is, or at least to suspend preconception. *Hard Times* is problematic for the critics, and that response itself is perhaps evidence of peculiarities of form. And what we know about the genesis of the novel suggests that it was problematic for Dickens too, involving him in compositional innovations. By this I do not refer merely to the structural consequences of weekly serialization (a discipline he had experienced only once before, in writing *Barnaby Rudge* (1841)), though this mode undoubtedly imposed constraints on episodic and thematic structure, and demanded compression. I mean by 'compositional innovations' new and defamiliarizing dispositions of language in response to new themes and unprecedented *and unresolved* ideological complexity.

A possible model for the structure of *Hard Times* is provided by Mikhail Bakhtin's theory of the 'polyphonic' novel; a theory which has the great benefit, for my purpose, of being interpretable in linguistic terms.[3] In a complex argument, partly theoretical and partly historical, Bakhtin proposes that there have existed two modes of representational fiction: monologic on the one hand and polyphonic or dialogic on the other. The monologic novel, which he claims has been the dominant traditional form, is authoritarian in essence: the author insists on the particular ideology which he voices, and the characters are 'objectified', dependent on the authorial position, and evaluated from the point of view of that position. In the polyphonic novel, on the other hand, the characters (or the 'hero', according to Bakhtin) are more liberated: they achieve voices, and points of view, which challenge the validity of the authorial position. The musical metaphor of polyphony refers to the co-presence of independent but interconnected voices. 'Dialogue' means implicit dialogue, not turn-by-turn speeches: it refers to the fact that one person's speech-forms reflect consciousness of the actual or potential response of an interlocutor, orientation towards a second act of speech. But there is a stronger meaning which Bakhtin seems to have in mind for 'dialogic', and that is 'dialectical'. The dialogic relationship confronts unresolved contrary ideologies, opposing voices in which conflicting world-views resist submersion or cancellation. The dialectical nature of Bakhtin's aesthetic can best be seen in his discussion of *carnival*, which was in his view the medieval forerunner of the polyphonic novel.[4] Carnival, with its boy kings and other multifarious travesties, mediates opposites, associates them while preserving their autonomous identities. It rejoices in extremes, negation, inversion, subversion, antithesis. The rhetorical figures generated by the logic of carnival are clear: they include prominently hyperbole, litotes, negation, syntactic inversions, paradox, contradiction. In social terms, the carnivalistic dialectic is the tension between mutually supportive but antithetical partners such as ruler and subject, employer and worker, teacher and pupil, husband and wife. And we would expect these differences of role, and antagonisms, to be articulated in the language of carnivalistic structures.

At a superficial level, the application of these ideas to *Hard Times* seems well justified. Three of the role-clashes just mentioned (employer/worker, teacher/pupil, husband/wife) figure directly and importantly in the plot. Then the novel contains a large number of diverse characters and groups of characters of very different social origins and affiliations, putting forward many and clashing points of view. The circus performers are an almost literal case of carnival: their diversity and deviance are strongly emphasized, as is their challenge to the authority of Gradgrind and Bounderby (Bk. I, Ch. 6). But polyphonic or dialogic structure is by no means limited to these circus artistes, but exists in the ensemble of numerous voices of opinion and conflict: Slackbridge, Bounderby, Stephen Blackpool, Harthouse, Louisa, Sissy, etc. The task for the analyst who wishes to make sense of this medley of voices is twofold. First, it is necessary to show in detail the linguistic and semiotic characteristics of the various voices (including the narrating voice) which participate in the dialogic structure. Second, the polyphonic structure, the multiplicity of voices, needs to be interpreted in terms of the author's ideology. A plurality of voices does not in itself mean a non-authoritarian narrative stance.

Turning to language itself, Bakhtin does not give a very clear guide as to how the structure of language contributes to the dialogic aesthetic. In fact, he appears to be quite negative on the dialogic value of stylistic variety. But this caution is strategic. He has to concede that Dostoyevsky, his main subject, is stylistically flat, but he must claim, of course, that his thesis works even in this linguistically undifferentiated case. He observes that marked linguistic individuation of fictional characters may lead to an impression of closure, a feeling that the author has definitively analysed a character and placed a boundary around its imaginative or moral potential: 'characters' linguistic differentiation and clear-cut "characteristics of speech" have the greatest significance precisely for the creation of objectivized, finalized images of people.' This seems to me not so much a limitation as an illumination, specifically an insight into our response to Dickens's grotesques: Peggotty, Micawber, Mrs. Gamp, and here, Slackbridge. All such characters seem to be clearly delineated, completely known, striking but uncomplicated. But we also need Bakhtin's more positive concession concerning the dialogic potential of speech styles; this potential is effective under certain conditions:

> the point is not the mere presence of specific styles, social dialects, etc., . . . the point is the dialogical *angle* at which they . . . are juxtaposed or counterposed in the work . . .

and

> dialogical relationships are possible among linguistic styles, social dialects, etc., if those phenomena are perceived as semantic positions, as a sort of linguistic *Weltanschauung*.

That is to say, speech styles need not be just caricaturing oddities, but to transcend caricature they must encode characters' world-views as dialectical alternatives to the world-view of the author and/or, I would suggest, other characters. Thus we might investigate whether, say, Stephen Blackpool's speech, or Bounderby's, encodes in its specific linguistic form a world-view, a set of attitudes; and how the two attitudes relate—in this case, antithetically. Similarly, and perhaps easier to demonstrate, we can look at the dialogic relationships between Gradgrind and Sleary on the one hand, and Gradgrind and the author on the other.

How to proceed in this project? The examples just mentioned are merely striking instances of many, perhaps dozens, of semiotically significant stylistic oppositions which permeate *Hard Times*. To provide a full account would require a book, not a chapter. As essential as space, however, is analytic methodology. Bakhtin provides no tools for analysing linguistic structure, but there is one linguistic theory which explicitly covers Bakhtin's condition that speech styles should be treated as embodying world-views: M. A. K. Halliday's 'functional' theory of language. I must send my readers elsewhere for details,[5] but Halliday's main premise is that linguistic varieties within a community, or 'registers', encode different kinds of meaning, different orientations on experience. Halliday offers a number of analytic systems such as 'transitivity', 'mood', 'cohesion', 'information structure' which I and others have found very valuable in analysing texts for the world-views which they embody.[6] I will use some of these categories below, but my analysis is constrained by space to be largely untechnical.

A list of distinct speech styles in the novel would show that there is an exceptional range of clearly differentiated voices: Sissy, Sleary, Slackbridge, Harthouse, Childers, Bounderby, Stephen, Gradgrind, etc. The length and diversity of the list are of less importance than the specific meanings of the voices and of their structural relationships, but sheer diversity is of some significance for the notion of polyphony. It could be argued merely on the basis of this multiplicity and variousness of voices and people that *Hard Times* makes a *prima facie* claim to be a polyphonic novel. The case would be putative as a global observation, more concrete and demonstrable in relation to specific sections which are explicitly carnivalistic in conduct. The best instance of the latter is the scene at the Pegasus's Arms in Book I, Chapter 6, when Gradgrind and Bounderby, in search of Sissy's father, are confronted by the members of the circus troupe, who speak 'in a variety of voices' (p. 82)[7] and who are combative and subversive in their address to these gentlemen. This scene, which is both challenging and farcical, threatens an anarchic overriding of utility and authority, and touches on antitheses which are more thoroughly debated elsewhere in the book.

I shall now look more closely at how the multiple languages of *Hard Times* signify and intersect by examining samples under three headings: *idiolect*, *sociolect*, and *dialogue*.

An idiolect is the characteristic speech style of an individual. Like dialect, it is a set of background features of language, supposedly constant and permanent characteristics which distinguish a person linguistically. In its most sophisticated realization it is the complex of features, mostly phonetic, by which we recognize our acquaintances' voices on the telephone. Now idiolects apply to literature in two ways. First, the elusive 'style of an author' might be thought of as an idiolect. I mention this only to observe that *Hard Times* had no consistent authorial idiolect (unlike, to cite a comparable example, Mrs. Gaskell's *North and South*). Second, in fiction foregrounding of idiolect produces caricature; and although caricature is a fixing, objectifying process as Bakhtin has indicated, it is a device for making statements, and that is something we are looking for in *Hard Times*. The two sharp instances in this novel are the union demagogue Slackbridge and the circus-master Sleary. Each has a mode of speech which is quite idiosyncratic (with a quali-fication in the case of Sleary, below) and absolutely self-consistent.

Slackbridge conducts himself with a violent, biblical rhetoric:

> Oh my friends, the down-trodden operatives of Coketown! Oh my friends and fellow countrymen, the slaves of an iron-handed and a grinding despotism! Oh my friends and fellow-sufferers, and fellow-workmen, and fellow-men! I tell you that the hour is come, when we must rally round one another as One united power, and crumble into dust the oppressors that too long have battened upon the plunder of our families, upon the sweat of our brows, upon the labour of our hands, upon the strength of our sinews, upon the God-created glorious rights of Humanity, and upon the holy and eternal privileges of Brotherhood!

It has been objected that no trades unionist of the time would have spoken like that (although, apparently, this is not beyond question). But fidelity to the language of the delegates' plat-form is only part of the issue. The point is that Dickens does not represent *any* social role in a focused way. He has created a symbolic language for his conception of 'Slackbridges', but this language signifies nothing precise: it is a generalized bombast which might inhabit the pulpit, the House of Lords, or any kind of political or public meeting. Conventionally, of course, this sort of language connotes vacuousness and insin-cerity, and presumably it does so here; but Slackbridge's appearance is an intervention in a complex moral dilemma (Stephen's refusal to 'combine', and his subsequent ostracism by the work-mates who know and respect him) and the sig-nification of his speech style is inadequate to the situation. So Dickens is forced to comment directly on what Slackbridge represents:

He was not so honest [as the assembled workmen], he was not so manly, he was not so good-humoured; he substituted cunning for their simplicity, and passion for their safe solid sense.

These judgements cannot be read off from the language in which Slackbridge is presented. His role remains puzzling, and since he is dramatically foregrounded as the main speaker against Stephen in this scene, the troubling nature of the scene (stemming largely from the unclarity of Stephen's motives and therefore of his relations with others at the meeting) remains provocatively unresolved.

Sleary is the second linguistic grotesque in the novel. Whereas Slackbridge's language is dominated by a bombastic rhetoric, Sleary's speech is submerged under brandy-and-water. Sibilants are drowned: [s, z, ʧ, ʃ, ʤ, ts] all reduce to a sound spelled *th*:

> Tho be it, my dear. (You thee how it ith, Thquire!) Farewell, Thethilia! My latht wordth to you ith thith, Thtick to the termth of your engagement, be obedient to the Thquire, and forget uth. But if, when you're grown up and married and well off, you come upon any horthe-riding ever, don't be hard upon it, don't be croth with it, give it a Bethspeak if you can, and think you might do wurth. People mutht be amuthed, Thquire, thomehow, . . . they can't be alwayth a working, nor yet they can't be alwayth a learning. Make the betht of uth; not the wortht.

But Sleary's function in the plot and in the thematic structure of the novel make him more than a comic drunk. In his first appearance (Bk. I, Ch. 6), he is a firm leader of the circus-people in their challenge to the bullying of Gradgrind and Bounderby, and effectively presides over the passage of Sissy into the care of Gradgrind. At the end of the novel, he has been harbouring Gradgrind's criminal son Tom, and (carnivalistically, through the good offices of a dancing horse) manages Tom's flight from apprehension. He is then given virtually the last word, an almost verbatim repetition of the sentiment just quoted. His interventions in the story are directly implicated in Gradgrind's fortunes, and he is the philosophical antithesis to Gradgrind's utilitarian educational thesis: Sleary's Horse-Riding stands for Fancy. This notion of Fancy may well be too trivial for Dickens's purpose, as has been conceded; but at least Sleary is so constituted as to demand attention. The idiolect is insistently defamiliarizing: it 'make[s] forms difficult . . . increase[s] the difficulty and length of perception' as Shklovsky puts it.[8] It takes effort to determine what Sleary is saying, because of the completeness and the whimsicality of the phonological transformation which has been applied to his speech. The reader is compelled to decipher a radical, and not entirely consistent, code which deforms everyday English words into momentarily unrecognizable spellings: *bitterth*, *prentitht*. These difficulties do not guarantee that what Sleary says is of any great interest; but the fact that Dickens has placed these difficulties in our way indicates that Sleary is *meant* to be listened to, that he is designed as a significant voice against Gradgrindism in the polyphonic structure of the book.

There is another interesting aspect of Sleary's speech, and one which further distinguishes his discourse from that of Slackbridge. Beneath the idiolect, there are markers which suggest a social dialect or sociolect. Dickens builds into Sleary's speech hints of working-class morphology and lexis: eathy (easily), ath (who), wouldn't . . . no more, took (taken), plain (plainly), winder, lyin', etc. (plus some odd spellings which suggest deviance from the middle-class code, but obscurely: natur, fortun, wurthst, conwenienth); and slang and oaths: morrithed (morrissed, 'fled'), cut it short, damned, mith'd your tip (missed your tip, 'jumped short'), cackler, pound ('wager'), etc. These characteristics link Sleary with the working class—in this novel, the interests of the 'hands'—and with the circus fraternity—the spokespeople for Fancy. These links not only 'naturalize' Sleary by providing him with social affiliations, but also broaden the basis of opposition to the Utilitarian philosophies embodied in Gradgrind (whom Sleary first meets in a confrontation).

The novel contains many other contrasts of speech style, and on the whole they can be explained sociolectally rather than idiolectally: Dickens seems to have accepted the principle that now provides the theoretical basis for Hallidayan linguistics, namely that registers of language characterize social groups and encode their values. Consider, for example, the contrasting speech of Harthouse and of Stephen Blackpool. The former is first introduced as an idle waster ('carelessly lounging') with a languid, verb-less, fragmented speech (Bk. II, Ch. 1). When he is established in Louisa's favours, however, this affectation is replaced by the syntax of 'elaborated code':

> Mrs. Bounderby, though a graceless person, of the world worldly, I feel the utmost interest, I assure you, in what you tell me. I cannot possibly be hard upon your brother. I understand and share the wise consideration with which you regard his errors. With all possible respect both for Mr. Gradgrind and for Mr. Bounderby, I think I perceive that he has not been fortunate in his training. Bred at a disadvantage towards the society in which he has to play, he rushes into these extremes for himself, from opposite extremes that have long been forced— with the very best intentions we have no doubt—upon him. Mr. Bounderby's fine bluff English independence, though a most charming characteristic, does not—as we have agreed—invite confidence. If I might venture to remark that it is the least in the world deficient in that delicacy to which a youth mistaken, a character misconceived, and abilities misdirected, would turn for relief and guidance, I should express what it presents to my own view.

Hypotaxis—the use of multiple subordinate clauses—dominates the syntax, which is further complicated by parenthetical clauses such as '—as we have agreed—'. Main clauses are delayed by preposed adjective clauses ('Bred at a disadvantage . . .') and by suspect protestations of diffidence or sincerity ('If I might venture . . .'). Nouns are liberally modified by adjectives, many of them evaluative and evocative of extremes (*graceless, worldly, utmost, wise, opposite, very best*, etc.). Modals are also prominent, emphasizing the speaker's claim to epistemic and deontic involvement in what he says: *cannot possibly, all possible, very best, no doubt, most, least*. Touches of rhetoric of more identifiable origin than Slackbridge's are present: 'a youth mistaken, a character misconceived, and abilities misdirected' is a literary, educated form associated with writing, not oratory—the key to this literariness being the inverted structure N + Adjective (there is only one inversion, Verb + Subject, in all of Slackbridge's speeches: p. 173).

Harthouse's speech in this episode is marked as middle-class, elaborated, evasive.[9]

At the other pole, socio-economically and linguistically, is Stephen Blackpool. There is a detailed effort to make Stephen's language indicate his representativeness of a class. A number of different features of his language combine to make his language suggest the regional, uneducated and oral properties of the language of the Hands. He is first shown in an intimate conversation with Rachael, an introduction which makes an immediate point that his speech style is shared, not idio-syncratic. I must quote a sizeable extract, including some commentary by the narrator which offers a clear contrast of style:

'Ah, lad! 'Tis thou?' When she had said this, with a smile which would have been quite expressed, though nothing of her had been seen but her pleasant eyes, she replaced her hood again, and they went on together.

'I thought thou wast ahind me, Rachael?'

'No.'

'Early t'night, lass?'

''Times I'm a little early, Stephen; 'times a little late. I'm never to be counted on, going home.'

'Nor going t'other way, neither, t'seems to me, Rachael?'

'No, Stephen.'

He looked at her with some disappointment in his face, but with a respectful and patient conviction that she must be right in whatever she did. The expression was not lost upon her; she laid her hand lightly on his arm a moment, as if to thank him for it.

'We are such true friends, lad, and such old friends, and getting to be such old folk, now.'

'No, Rachael, thou'rt as young as ever thou wast.'

'One of us would be puzzled how to get old, Stephen, without t'other getting so too, both being alive,' she answered, laughing; 'but, any ways, we're such old friends, that t'hide a word of honest truth fro' one another would be a sin and a pity. 'Tis better not to walk too much together. 'Times, yes! 'Twould be hard, indeed, if 'twas not to be at all,' she said, with a cheer-fulness she sought to communicate to him.

''Tis hard, anyways, Rachael.'

'Try to think not; and 'twill seem better.'

'I've tried a long time, and 'ta'nt got better. But thou'rt right;

101

'tmight mak fok talk, even of thee. Thou hast been that to me, through so many year: thou hast done me so much good, and heartened of me in that cheering way, that thy word is a law to me. Ah lass, and a bright good law! Better than some real ones.'

'Never fret about them, Stephen,' she answered quickly, and not without an anxious glance at his face. 'Let the laws be.'

'Yes,' he said, with a slow nod or two. 'Let 'em be. Let everything be. Let all sorts alone. 'Tis a muddle, and that's aw.'

A minimum of deviant spellings here serves to hint at the vowel sounds and the elisions of a northern accent. Elsewhere, Dickens indicates the accent by a more radical set of ortho-graphic, lexical and morphological peculiarities:

'My friends,' Stephen began, in the midst of a dead calm; 'I ha' hed what's been spok'n o' me, and 'tis lickly that I shan't mend it. But I'd liefer you'd hearn the truth concernin myseln, fro my lips than fro onny other man's, though I never cud'n speak afore so monny, wi'out bein moydert and muddled.'

Detailed analyses of these dialect notations are unnecessary. Different novelists (e.g. Mrs. Gaskell, Emily Brontë) use different notational devices: some use more archaisms, others more 'non-standard' morphology, and there is variation in the spelling conventions for vowels. There are two simple points to grasp in all such cases. First, these are not to be judged as realistic transcriptions where fidelity might be an issue—they are simply conventional signals of socio-linguistic difference. Second, only a very slight deviance, as in the conversation between Stephen and Rachael, is needed to persuade middle-class readers that they are in the presence of a social group below their own.

More significant is the syntax, which is in sharp contrast to Harthouse's elaborated forms. Halliday maintains that speech and writing have different information structures, and there-fore different modes of syntactic organization. Writing, which can be scanned and re-scanned for complexities and qualifica-tions of meaning, is a medium which can accommodate the kinds of indirections which we noted in Harthouse's language. Speech, according to Halliday, is more straightforwardly linear, and it releases its meanings in a sequence of short chunks or 'information units'; these units are segmented off by intonation patterns, rises and falls in the pitch of the voice. Syntactically, they need not be complete clauses, but are often phrases or single words, and often loosely linked by apposition or concatenation. The overall style is not strictly speaking paratactic, because the conjoined constituents are not clauses of equal weight; but in its avoidance of clause subordination it is much more like parataxis than hypotaxis.

Once the existence of this mode of speech has been pointed out, it takes no great analytic expertise to recognize that the description fits the conversation of Stephen and Rachael. The point is that Dickens has—in *writing*, of course—deliberately constructed a very *oral* model of language for these two humble characters, contrasting with the formal, written model used for some unsympathetic middle-class speakers such as Harthouse. I think there is a contrast of values intended here: solidarity and naturalness on the one hand, deviousness and insincerity on the other. I cannot prove this by reference to the language alone; I simply suggest that Dickens is using speech style stereotypes to which his readers, on the basis of their socio-linguistic competence and of their knowledge of the novel's plot, assign conventional significances.

So far I have offered examples of significant individual voices, and of speech styles which seem to take the imprint of social values ('social semiotic' in Halliday's term). Other examples could be discussed; together they would assemble a picture of a text articulated in a multitude of voices. These voices are, overall, discordant and fluctuating in the kaleidoscope of views they express. Furthermore, the opposing points of view do not neatly align. Though Sleary confronts Gradgrind directly, so that the symbol of Fancy and that of Fact are in direct opposition, Harthouse and Stephen are not immediately opposed, nor many other significant antitheses of voices. Dickens's intellectual scheme for the book does not seem to have been symmetrical: his socio-linguistic symbols embodied in characters do not relate diagrammatically, and so the relationships among theoretical issues such as factual education, exploitive capitalism, statistics, social reform, play, etc., are not dramatized neatly in the linguistic or narrative relationships between the characters. The story and the language figure the ideological debates in an unsettled, troubled way. I think this raggedness is a strength. But before commenting on it directly, I want to refer to other areas of linguistic instability, different from the 'unpatternedness' of the global canvas. These areas involve dialogue, explicit or implicit, and figure shifting organization in the style of the voice.

Stephen Blackpool visits Bounderby's house on two occasions, and each time finds himself in a stand-up argument. The debates start with each speaker using his characteristic speech style. Bounderby is blustery and bullying, his speech packed with commands and demands:

> Well Stephen, what's this I hear? What have these pests of the earth being doing to *you*? Come in, and speak up. . . . Now, speak up! . . . Speak up like a man. . . .

Bounderby continues in this register (which is his constant idiolect, or a major part of it), while Stephen's responses begin quiet and polite, in a language heavily marked for the dialectal phonology, and based on the short information units noticed earlier:

> 'What were it, sir, as yo' were pleased to want wi' me?' . . .
> 'Wi' yor pardon, sir, I ha' nowt to sen about it.' . . .
> 'I sed as I had nowt to sen, sir; not as I was fearfo' o' openin' my lips.'
> 'I'm as sooary as yo, sir, when the people's leaders is bad. They taks such as offers. Haply 'tis na' the sma'est o' their misfortuns when they can get no better.' . . .

Pressed to state how he would solve the troubles of the weaving industry, Stephen moves into a sequence of five long speeches; their sheer length is a sign of departure from character, against the norm of his conversation with Rachael. The spelling peculiarities are maintained to a large degree, as is the syntax of spoken information; this from the third long speech:

> Look round town—so rich as 'tis—and see the numbers of people as has been broughten into bein heer, fur to weave, an to card, an to piece out a livin', aw the same one way, somehows, twixt their cradles and their graves.

104

The fifth of these speeches has Stephen, under intense provo-cation, voicing sentiments of 'man' against 'master' which on independent evidence, as well as the evidence of the novel, can be associated with Dickens's own humanitarian point of view. Stephen cannot say what will right the world, but he can say what will not: the strong hand of the masters, *laissez-faire*, lack of regard for the humanity of the mill-workers, and so on. When Stephen gives voice to these sentiments, the overall structure of his language changes to the parallelistic rhetoric of a public speech: a succession of balanced sentences, steadily increasing in length, is used to enumerate his arguments; here are two of them:

> Not drawin' nigh to fok, wi' kindness and patience an cheery ways, that so draws nigh to one another in their monny troubles, and so cherishes one another in their distresses wi' what they need themseln—like, I humbly believe, as no people the genelman ha seen in aw his travels can beat—will never do't till th'Sun turns t'ice. Most of aw, ratin 'em as so much Power, and reg'latin 'em as if they was figures in a soom, or machines: wi'out loves and likeins, wi'out memories and inclinations, wi'out souls to weary and souls to hope—when aw goes quiet, draggin on wi' 'em as if they'd nowt o' th'kind, an when aw goes onquiet, reproachin 'e, for their want o' sitch humanly feelins in their dealins wi' you—this will never do't, sir, till God's work is onmade.

Some of the elaborated syntax noticed in Harthouse's language can be found here in the internal structure of clauses, in the qualifications and self-interruptions. And the overall format of repetitive structure recalls the insistent harangue of the book's opening scene, in the schoolroom.

When Stephen engages with the moral issues which concern Dickens centrally, then, his language deviates sharply from what had earlier been offered as his own characteristic socio-linguistic style. I do not point this out as an inconsistency of characterization, but as an application of the dialogic principle in the language through which Stephen is constituted. The stylistic shift shows strain in Dickens's use of a voice to express an ideological position that has become problematic through being assigned to that speaker. Stephen as originally set up by Dickens is inadequate to occupy the place in debate in which he has become situated: his language strains towards the rhetoric of a more public form of disputation than his social role warrants.

Surprising shifts of register occur in the speech of other characters, although none so remarkable as the transformation from tongue-tied weaver to articulate orator. I have no space to demonstrate any more of these changes; nor, most regrettably, can I show any selection of the range of styles of the narrative voice. Dickens ranges from subversive parody (Bk. I, Ch. 1, on Gradgrind on Fact), to complex animating and de-animating metaphors (Bk. I, Ch. 5, the superb evocation of Coketown) to pathos, and to simple direct judgement ('He was a good power-loom weaver, and a man of perfect integrity'). David Lodge has analysed some varieties of the narrative rhetoric of *Hard Times* in an excellent chapter of *Language of Fiction*: analysis which readers can consult to fill out this gap in my account. Lodge also relates these variations to uncertainties in Dickens's own position, as I do. But his judgement is essentially based on a monologic norm: '*Hard Times* succeeds where its rhetoric succeeds and fails where its rhetoric fails.' Generally, Lodge argues, this rhetoric is successful when Dickens is being antagonistic or ironic, but fails when he is trying to celebrate his fictional positives.

But it is more complex than that. The various styles are not just 'successful' or 'failed', but transcend a two-term set of values: it is the plurality of codes, their inconstancy, and their frequent stridency, which all together constitute a fruitful and discordant polyphony. Any account of Dickens's 'argument' in this novel is bound to come to the conclusion that he attacks an unmanageably large and miscellaneous range of evils (utilitarianism in education and economics, industrial capitalism, abuse of unions, statistics, bad marriage, selfishness, etc.); that he mostly over-simplifies them (e.g. fails to see the beneficial relationship between some fact-gathering activities and real social reforms); that he is unclear on what evil causes what other evil. On the other side, his proposed palliatives are feeble, misconceived in terms of purely individual initiatives and responsibilities, and sentimentally formulated. Most of this conceptual muddle stems from the crucial inadequacy of Dickens's idealized solution of tolerant rapprochement of the two parties to the industrial situation:

'I believe,' said I, 'that into the relations between employers and employed, as into all the relations of this life, there must enter something of feeling and sentiment; something of mutual explanation, forbearance, and consideration; something which is not to be found in Mr. McCulloch's dictionary, and is not exactly stateable in figures; otherwise those relations are wrong and rotten at the core and will never bear sound fruit.'[10]

Translation of all Dickens's insecurely based theses and antitheses into elements and structural relationships of this novel's form has produced the asymmetries and dissonances which my stylistic analysis has begun to display. But few people today would condemn *Hard Times* as a ragged failure. The inconsistencies and discords are an indication of the problematic status of the social and theoretical crises in question for a great imagination like Dickens who could not articulate unequivocally in fiction the (unknown to him) facile solutions which were consciously available to him as theory. The novel's lack of monologic authority fits Bakhtin's description, I believe; and the stylistic polyphony is provocative and creative, compelling the reader to grapple uneasily with the tangle of issues that Dickens problematizes.

NOTES

1. John Ruskin, 'A note on *Hard Times*', *Cornhill Magazine*, 2 (1860), reprinted in George Ford and Sylvère Monod (eds.), *Hard Times* (New York: W. W. Norton and Co., 1966), pp. 331–32; George Bernard Shaw, *Introduction to Hard Times* (London: Waverley, 1912), repr. Ford and Monod, ed. cit., pp. 332–39; Raymond Williams, *Culture and Society 1780–1950* (Harmondsworth: Penguin, 1968).
2. John Holloway, '*Hard Times*: a history and a criticism', in *Dickens and the Twentieth Century*, eds. John Gross and Gabriel Pearson (London: Routledge and Kegan Paul, 1962), repr. Ford and Monod, ed. cit., pp. 361–66; David Lodge, *Language of Fiction* (London: Routledge and Kegan Paul, 1966).
3. Mikhail Bakhtin, trans. R. W. Rotsel, *Problems of Dostoyevsky's Poetics* (Ann Arbor: Ardis, 1973).
4. Mikhail Bakhtin, trans. H. Iswolsky, *Rabelais and his World* (Cambridge, Mass.: M.I.T. Press, 1968).
5. M. A. K. Halliday, ed. G. R. Kress, *Halliday: System and Function in Language* (London: Oxford University Press, 1976); Halliday, *Language*

as Social Semiotic (London: Edward Arnold, 1978). Halliday has an *Introduction to Functional Linguistics* forthcoming. Most of the works cited in note 6 below give accounts of relevant aspects of Halliday's theory.

6. A seminal literary application by Halliday is his paper 'Linguistic function and literary style', in Seymour Chatman (ed.), *Literary Style, A Symposium* (New York and London: Oxford University Press, 1971). Relevant applications by others include R. Fowler, *Linguistics and the Novel* (London: Methuen, 1977); R. Fowler, 'Anti-language in fiction', *Style*, 13 (1979), 259–78; R. Fowler, R. Hodge, G. R. Kress and A. Trew, *Language and Control* (London: Routledge and Kegan Paul, 1979); R. Fowler, *Literature as Social Discourse* (London: Batsford, 1981); G. N. Leech and M. H. Short, *Style in Fiction* (London: Longman, 1981).

7. Quotations from *Hard Times* follow David Craig's edition (note 1), with a very few minor apparent printing errors corrected.

8. Viktor Shklovsky, 'Art as technique', in Lee T. Lemon and Marion J. Reis (ed. and trans.), *Russian Formalist Criticism* (Lincoln, Nebraska: University of Nebraska Press, 1965), p. 12.

9. On 'elaborated code' and its connotations see Basil Bernstein, *Class, Codes and Control*, Vol. I (London: Routledge and Kegan Paul, 1971); William Labov, 'The logic of non-standard English', in P. P. Giglioli (ed.), *Language and Social Context* (Harmondsworth: Penguin, 1972).

10. Reprinted in Ford and Monod, op. cit.

5

Charles Dickens: The Solo Performer

by DAVID PONTING

He had always been a gifted mimic. As a very young child, his proud parents had encouraged him to perform for the benefit of their house-guests. No doubt the visitors were amazed and amused by the mimicry of this precocious boy, and no doubt the more perspicacious among them would have worried about which particular foible or idiosyncrasy of theirs would shortly be paraded to entertain the next set of guests to Charles Dickens's parental home at Chatham. Forster wrote: 'He must have been a horrible little nuisance to many un-offending grownup people who were called upon to admire him.'

By the time he was 10, young Charles was also an avid reader and was adding dramatic recitations to his repertoire. Mary Weller (who was a servant to Dickens's parents in prosperous days) recalls that 'a rather favourite piece for recitation by Charles at this time was "The Voice of the Sluggard" from Dr. Watts, and the little boy used to give it with great effect, and with *such* action and *such* attitudes.' Not only did the 'little nuisance' recite, he also sang, in clear treble, comic duets with Lucy (the girl next door) or with Fanny, his sister.

A few years later, his keen observation and his ability to impersonate, made Charles popular at school (at least with his

109

classmates) and, later still, amused his associates and colleagues at the various jobs in which he was employed: from
Warren's Blacking-Warehouse (which Charles subsequently
rarely mentioned because it was a time when his father was in
the debtor's prison at Marshalsea), through his one year as a
solicitor's clerk (when he was 15), to his first 'real' job as a
shorthand reporter with various newspapers, ending up with
the *Morning Chronicle* when he was 22. During all this time, his
passion for reading continued and his ability to write more
than mere reportage, developed.

In his writing, he concentrated on documenting the real
people around him: as much about the poor, as the rich—and
about himself. His powers of observation of mankind, which
became no less acute as he grew older, were now utilized to
reconstruct, not in performance, but on paper the stories of
people and places and actions, and, although not yet published, he knew that he was good at it.

He had two other important gifts: boundless energy, and a
driving need to do everything with perfection; to be *among* the
best was not good enough, he had to be *the* best. This was
manifest in his writing but also in his desire to scoop the rival
newspapers, to get his story back to Head Office and on the
streets before the opposition. If that meant relentlessly driving
himself for more hours in the day than was good for him or
hard-riding through the night and getting drenched for his
pains, then so be it; he was young, and rest would soon put
him right.

With the same drive with which he seemed to do *everything*,
he threw himself into the theatrical life of his day. At the age of
15 he was a regular and avid theatre-goer but, more important
from the point of view of this study, he took up his interest in
performance again, and started acting lessons with the idea
that he would become a professional actor. Like all his
enthusiasms it became all-consuming, and every spare moment
was spent practising walking, sitting, standing, gesturing with
face and body, and declaiming. He wrote to Forster in 1845,
describing that time: 'I practised immensely (even such things
as walking in and out, and sitting down in a chair): often four,
five, six hours a day: shut up in my own room, or walking
about in the fields.'

His natural performance gifts allowed him to imitate all the famous actors of his day—to 'do' them better than they did themselves. One of them (who had a strong influence on the young Dickens) was Charles Mathews, a popular comic actor who was also very versatile: he sang, performed feats of magic, and, most important of all, he had amazing vocal and postural ranges which allowed him to play all the characters, in one-act plays specially written for him. These solo performances were ones that Dickens never forgot.

By 1832, Charles felt that he was now ready for the theatrical life and arranged for an audition at the Lyceum Theatre. He was told that if he wished, he could perform anything of Mathews, and that he would be auditioned before that actor himself and Charles Kemble. On the appointed day Dickens, with 'a terrible bad cold' (a disease to which I shall return), failed to keep his appointment and, although he says that he intended to, did not arrange another.

New horizons were opening up to him for, in December 1833, a short story that Charles had written was printed in the *Monthly Magazine*, and his professional career now began to move in a different direction. Some of his links with the theatre were no less strong for, from the age of 15 until his marriage in 1836, he attended the theatre pretty well every night, and it was about this time that he began to write plays and to perform in a whole series of amateur theatrical productions. On the evening of 27 April 1833, Charles and his family and friends took part in a theatrical 'experience' at his home in Bentinck Street. The playbill for that occasion shows that besides writing the introductory prologue, which preceded the opera *Clari* and *The Favourite Interlude of the Married Bachelor*, Mr. Charles Dickens also produced, directed and performed a major role in each section, as well as stage-managing, designing the sets, producing the sound effects and playing the accordion. He certainly would not have enjoyed the professional theatre had he moved in that direction for, even in Dickens's day, demarcation would have prevented his taking quite so many different roles!

In 1836 he married Catherine Hogarth. He was now a successful writer with a future which must have seemed assured. Private theatricals were still a passionate interest and a trip to the United States in 1842 was interrupted so that Charles could travel to Montreal and take part in an amateur performance with the officers of the Coldstream Guards. Further trips abroad included one to Italy in 1845, but within three weeks of his return from there he was treading the boards again. This time it was *Everyman in His Humour* by Ben Jonson, which was played before an invited audience of about 200 in a private theatre in London.

Of course, the theatre was not Dickens's only concern. By 1847 he had published thirteen major novels, received the freedom of the city of Edinburgh, visited the United States, Canada, Italy and France; and been six times a new father. He had also started a series of 'Splendid Strolls'—amateur theatrical tours of the provinces. These went on intermittently over the next six years and were interspersed with the writing of *David Copperfield* and *Bleak House*, editing and writing for the magazine *Household Words*, and producing the remainder of his ten children. Four children in six years could hardly be called unproductive, but with only two novels completed in that period, those years may have seemed to be so to Dickens. He was restless, and somehow ill at ease. He needed a new challenge and, almost apologetically, he suggested one to his friends: public readings of his work. For charity, of course.

In 1843, he had given a private reading of *The Christmas Carol* to John Forster and others in his circle. A year later there had been another private reading, this time of *The Chimes*. The small audience for *that* reading had included the actor Macready. Now, in order to raise money for the Birmingham and Midland Literary and Scientific Institution, Dickens suggested (in a letter addressed to Mr. Arthur Ryland and dated 7 January 1853), that he should give a *public* reading of *The Christmas Carol*. 'It would take about two hours', he wrote, 'with a pause of ten minutes half-way through. There would be some novelty in the thing as I have never done it in public, though I have in private and (if I may say so) with a great effect on the hearers.' When he had given the private reading of *The Chimes* he had subsequently told his wife, 'if you had seen Macready last night—undisguisedly sobbing and crying on the sofa, as I read—you would have felt (as I did) what a thing it is to have power.'

The first public reading was on 27 December 1853. The weather was awful but a crowd of 2,000 had gathered to see the great author. There was applause as he walked out to his table. Apparently calm, he opened his book and the hall fell silent. 'A Christmas Carol in Four Staves. Stave 1, Marley's Ghost. Marley was dead to begin with. . . .' As each character was introduced the audience saw and heard him or her, not Dickens. It did not last the two hours that Dickens had predicted; it was more than three, but nobody complained.

Two more readings completed the group that Dickens had promised he would give to benefit the same literary and scientific institution. On the second occasion he read another Christmas story *Cricket on the Hearth* and, in the third, he repeated *The Christmas Carol*. In both cases the audience's reaction was just as ecstatic as it had been to the first.

Now more charity readings were set up and given and Dickens began to feel himself inundated with requests, and under pressure. He wrote from Folkestone to Forster on 16 September 1855 (*Life*, II, 431); 'I am going to read for them here on the 5th of next month, and have answered in the last fortnight thirty applications to do the like all over England, Ireland and Scotland.' He could not possibly do them all and some institutions, recognizing this, tried to secure his acceptance by the offer of a fee.

Clearly when the success of the charity readings was so obvious, the temptation to make money from professional performances must have been very strong. He was not poor but, as he said, he had never been left anything but relations, and the financial demands his extended family were now making of him were considerable. So he needed money; but this in itself was not a sufficient reason for accepting reading fees. His publisher's advance on his next novel would be £6,000; a short story now commanded a fee of £1,000; a two-month professional reading tour across England *might* bring in a net profit of only £3,000. So money may have been a necessary, but was certainly not a sufficient reason for moving into the professional arena.

There were other pressures. His health was not good; he was restless, irritable, and cracks were now showing in his twenty-two year old marriage. He certainly felt he needed a

113

new challenge. He was 46, and had already been writing (it must have seemed almost non-stop) for twenty-five years. Outwardly to his friends, his prodigious gift of character and incident invention seemed unabated; inside, he worried because he felt that he might have written himself dry. In the period of twelve years following his first professional reading, he wrote four major novels. In the previous two years, he had written none, while in the nineteen years before *that*, he had completed seventeen major works.

One other factor was almost certainly more important; he had discovered the unequalled thrill, which started in terror and (for him) ended in total power over, and subjugation of, his audience. Playing with *other* actors on stage and receiving, with them, the rapture of an audience is one thing, but to have it all concentrated entirely upon oneself is another. With a single word, a simple gesture, he held them in his hand. It was a drug he had sipped and he could not put it down.

So far Dickens had only experienced audience *rapture*, but he could not be sure that the drug would always work. A rapturous audience in one performance unaccountably might be a contemptuous one on another occasion. Why does the chemistry sometimes fail? It could be that the hall was too cold, too hot; that sightlines were bad; that the audience could not hear. The performer almost certainly will blame the audience: 'Very unresponsive tonight!' It may be them, but it is more likely to be the performance itself.

There were other important thoughts which must have gone through Charles Dickens's mind. First, performing for an approving audience of friends and relations, or before those who are warmly aware that their entrance money and the performer's efforts are all directed towards raising funds for a charitable institution, is one thing; to do so before a coldly 'professional' audience, who will demand value for money and who will heckle and interrupt if that is not forthcoming, is another. Secondly, Dickens knew that, when he read, the words spoken would be almost as well known to his audience as to himself. Those who now *heard* him previously would have read and re-read them in the published versions of his novels. Then, out of the descriptive passages and the published illustrations, the private reader would have already conjured each character; and these mental images would be *perfect*, like the perfect 'sets' in radio plays. Now Dickens would have to provide a real, physical shape to each character, a distinctive body attitude, and, perhaps most difficult of all, he had to provide a *voice*, and convince them all that his was definitive.

Charles Dickens had before him the example of Charles Mathews as a one-man performer. The important difference between these two men was that Dickens was also the author of the work he read; Mathews was essentially a performer and interpreter of others' writings. One-man performances of today tend to fall into the same two camps, although Emlyn Williams has introduced a third when he started *his* Charles Dickens readings, being an actor playing an author reading the author's own work.

Of all the writers who also have performed publicly their own work (and this group includes Thackeray—a *gentleman* writer who did not feel at all degraded by indulging in public readings for money), with the exception of Dickens, none has been outstandingly successful as an *interpreter* of his creation. Instead, what success each may have enjoyed has arisen more out of a public voyeurism, a desire to *see* the great author rather than hear him read. This same impulse was true of the audience which first came to see Charles Dickens. His additional talent was there apparent for all to see: he *was* an outstanding performer and interpreter. The next question is whether he was a writer who could act or an actor who could write; or indeed whether his success lies elsewhere.

With hindsight, I believe that it is possible to see that, from a very early age, Dickens was moving towards a career as a professional reader. This may well have been clearer to Dickens himself than he was ever prepared to admit. His enthusiasm for the theatre, first as spectator and then as amateur actor, was life-long. As a solo performer, a period of ten years elapsed between the first tentative private readings and those given publicly later. This was, of course, less by design than by the pressure of his other work. However, it was an important period, allowing him to 'internalize' (to use an awful word for which, in this instance, I can find no substitute) and organize himself and his thoughts. Whether this was a considered process is doubtful; but it happened.

Dickens recognized, above all else, the need to be fully prepared and was astute enough to use out-of-town try-outs to give him the experience of reading to an audience and to experiment with the material of his books. He would have appreciated immediately the strength of the argument where someone trying to persuade him to give him a reading wrote:

> Here is an opportunity to test the matter without risk. An antidiluvian country town, an audience of farmers' sons and daughters, rural shop-keepers and a few country parsons;—if interest can be excited in the stolid minds of such a Boeotian assemblage, the success of the reader will be assured wherever the English language is spoken. On the other hand, if failure results none will be wiser outside this Sleepy Hollow circle. (*Pen Portraits*, 26)

Dickens used these opportunities well and by the time *The Christmas Carol* had reached the second of its 'final' reading lengths, it had been very heavily cut to a performance length of two hours.

Existing copies of Dickens's own reading scripts show just how he began to turn the book into the reading. Most of the descriptive material disappeared, particularly that describing people. There was little need for it.

> Marley was dead to begin with. There was no doubt whatever about that. The register of his burial was signed by the clergy-man, the clerk, the undertaker, and the chief mourner. *Scrooge* signed it. And Scrooge's name was good upon 'Change for anything he put his hand to . . .'

and at the mere mention of his name, *Scrooge* it was who stood before the audience; the body was right, the posture and movements were right; and the voice was right. The audience knew him for a 'tight-fisted hand at the grindstone'.

Dickens cut up the texts and rearranged them, added notes on characterization and on voice production, and indicated 'action' directions. If a piece could be acted out, it *was*; and the words were deleted from the reading. 'Fagin raised his right hand, and shook his trembling forefinger in the air' is masked in the manuscript, and the word 'action' written in the margin. Whole sections were coloured in washes of red and blue inks and marked with directions: 'snap your fingers', 'rising action', 'Scrooge melted' and 'soften very much'. All the action was tightened up and dialogue made much more specific to a particular character. Sometimes great comic strip balloons of extra dialogue were added, and surprised audiences heard:

> And Squeers out-Squeers himself when, turning to poor Nickleby, he asks 'Do you wash?'
> 'Occasionally.'
> 'Humph! I don't know what towel to put you on. I know there's a place on somebody's towel; but if you make shift with your pocket handkerchief tomorrow morning, Mrs. Squeers will arrange that, in the course of the day.'

His listeners would have known *Nicholas Nickleby* well but would have been amazed by that witty exchange since it was not in any of the published book versions of that time. He frequently ad-libbed as the mood took him during a performance, and some of these were incorporated permanently into later presentations by being added to the growing number of notes appearing in his reading scripts.

So a great deal of rearranging, adding and subtracting were done to the original material; but not perhaps as much as one might have suspected. Philip Collins (a Dickens authority and himself a reader of Dickens's work) wrote:

> As a performer, I certainly become aware of felicities of rhythm, accuracy of pointing, and control of the emotional curve of a scene, which are, for anyone with a modicom of platform skill much easier to demonstrate in performance, than to describe analytically. (*The Listener*, 25 December 1969)

It seems clear that Dickens, from very early times (and whether he knew it or not), was already writing to be read publicly by a solo performer.

However, for all his gifts, Dickens was an appalling writer of plays, the one area of his literary life in which he never succeeded. His strangely banal dialogue never seems to work, perhaps because the characters do not talk *to* each other, they 'announce' to the audience; already the narrator figure is present. This is one of the reasons why his novels adapt so

117

readily to one-man performance. There are other reasons. The novels are frequently written in the first person and the present tense, and are constructed so that the various characters express themselves more in monologue than dialogue.

As far back as 1832, Dickens had told the Stage Manager at Covent Garden Theatre, 'I believe I have a strong perception of character and oddity, and a natural power of producing in my own person, what I have observed in others' (quoted by Philip Collins in *Dickens Public Readings: The Performer and the Novelist*). This is graphically illustrated by Mamie (Mary), Dickens's oldest daughter, who in 1854 while convalescing was daily carried into the room where her father was writing. She recorded (quoted in *Interviews and Recollections*, 1, 121):

> On one of these mornings, I was lying on the sofa endeavouring to keep perfectly quiet while my father wrote busily and rapidly at his desk, when he suddenly jumped from his chair and rushed to a mirror which hung near, and in which I could see the reflection of some extraordinary facial contortions which he was making. He returned rapidly to his desk, wrote furiously for a few moments, and then went again to the mirror. The facial pantomime was resumed, and then turning toward, but evidently not seeing me, he began talking rapidly in a low voice. Ceasing this soon, however, he returned once more to his desk, where he remained silently writing until luncheon time. It was a most curious experience for me, and one of which I did not, until later years, fully appreciate the purport. Then I knew that, with his natural intensity, he had thrown himself completely into the character he was creating, and that for the time being, he had not only lost sight of the surroundings, but had actually become in action, as in imagination, the creature of his pen.

Mamie Dickens also recorded, in her book *My Father*, that Dickens had said to the philosopher and critic George Henry Lewes that 'every word said by my characters were distinctly *heard* by me.'

Almost certainly both of Mamie's stories relate to the period when Dickens was writing *Hard Times*. Many years later, when he was working on his *last* book *The Mystery of Edwin Drood*, George Woolley, gardener at Dickens's home at Gad's Hill, recalled, in an interview in 1838:

Opposite the house was a sort of wood the master called the Wilderness. He used to go over there to write. . . . I used to hear what sounded like someone making a speech. I wondered what it was at first, and then I found out it was Mr. Dickens composing his writing out loud.

In a very real sense, performance preceded the writing; or to put it in another way, although the performance was instinctive, the writing was calculated.

What kind of material, then, did Dickens choose to turn into the scripts for his one-man performances? Perhaps the time of year of the first readings dictated that he chose from the Christmas stories and subsequently, although the *Cricket on the Hearth* and *The Chimes* were rarely read, *The Christmas Carol* soon became a great favourite of his, and of his audiences. Success with one script creates its own problems. I know from my own experience that one doubts one's own ability to 'do it again' with new material and the greater the success with the old, the more difficult it becomes to move on.

Perhaps it is a rationalization to say that as long as audiences are able to offer the required concentration on the actor's well tried and 'comfortable' material (because it is a new and involving experience for them), the performer will not grow tired of it, nor does he feel that as yet he has extracted from the presentation the maximum amount of juice. Of course the actor/audience involvement is cyclic, hopefully a growing circle; but it is often difficult to say in performance which leads the other. Further, the actor's confidence, as the material becomes more and more familiar, allows him to take risks which can release unsuspected reserves. Dickens wrote to William Henry Wills (who was the Assistant Editor on Dickens's magazine *Household Words*) that he did 'exactly one million one hundred thousand and one new things with Marigold, while the audience seized each with exactly one million one hundred thousand and one rounds!'

Several factors now affected his choice of material: he selected stories or excerpts which were strong in broad comedy and/or pathos, and they had to have 'characters'. This last requirement is interesting because it is much more difficult for an actor to play a nondescript, Mr. Average, than it is to create a character with a twisted body, or a streak of violence,

119

or a speech impediment. Clearly Dickens's audiences often found his Sam Weller character something of a disappointment, although it must be said that the whole of 'The Trial' from *Pickwick* was a long way short of Dickens's better adaptations. Kate Field writes in *Pen Photographs of Charles Dickens's Readings* (p. 111): 'Is it strange that many are disappointed? Dickens's Sam Weller is a human being, very like other human beings belonging to the same profession . . . [and] nothing in the world can save Sam from being entirely eclipsed by Justice Stareleigh . . .'—for whom, of course, Dickens was able to create a stereotype.

Further, it is very difficult indeed in a one-man presentation to create the necessary differences between Mr. Average One and Mr. Average Two so that the audience is clearly able to identify them as individuals. So Dickens stuck to the comic, the tragic and the absurd, believed that his best material for reading was *David Copperfield* and ignored all the dramatic possibilities of some of his later writing.

Having completed the various adaptations, Dickens had to get *himself* ready. He certainly aimed at very high professional standards and set about achieving them. 'You have no idea how I have worked at [the Readings]', he wrote to Forster,

> finding it necessary, as their reputation widened, that they should be better than at first, I have learnt them all so as to have no mechanical drawback in looking after the words. I have tested all the serious passion in them by everything I know; made the humorous points much more humorous; corrected my utterance of certain words; cultivated a self-possession not to be disturbed and made myself master of the situation.

He learnt each adaptation by constant repetition, going over them 'often twice a day, with exactly the same pains as at night, over and over and over again'. One piece of evidence, albeit circumstantial, is that in private Dickens always wore spectacles and needed them to read; it never was reported that he appeared at any public reading wearing spectacles.

As he rehearsed each role within each reading, one sees the dedication and enthusiasm of the actor described by Mr. Crummles in *Nicholas Nickleby*: 'We had a first tragedy man in our company once, who, when he played Othello, used to black himself all over! but that's feeling a part and going into it as if you meant it.' Dickens meant it; and always blacked himself all over.

By 1858 he had five performances in his repertoire: *The Christmas Carol*, *The Cricket on the Hearth*, *The Chimes*, 'The Story of Little Dombey' and a triple bill consisting of two short stories, 'The Poor Traveller' and 'Boots at the Holly-tree Inn', and an excerpt, 'Mrs. Gamp', taken from *Martin Chuzzlewit*. *Cricket* and *The Chimes* were not very popular and the former was dropped completely and the latter rarely used. Later the same year, he added 'The Trial' from *The Pickwick Papers* and, shortening *The Christmas Carol* and 'Little Dombey' each to about one hour, he offered either of those with 'The Trial' as a single programme. In the summer of 1861, he prepared 'The Bastille Prisoner' from *Tale of Two Cities* and an abstract from *Great Expectations*; neither was ever performed. Excerpts from *David Copperfield*, *Nicholas Nickleby* and 'Mr. Bob Sawyer's Party' from *The Pickwick Papers* went straight into the repertoire and 'Mr. Chops, the Dwarf' was prepared at this time but it was considered too slight (it was the shortest of all the readings) and, after a few performances, was dropped.

No more readings were prepared until 1866 when 'Dr. Marigold' was distilled from the *Medical Man's Prescriptions*, a collection of short stories published the previous December. Even with all his (by now) considerable experience, Dickens wanted a private try-out of the 'Marigold' adaptation and it was given on 18 March 1865 before an invited audience (which included Robert Browning and Wilkie Collins). George Dolby, who was Dickens's manager for the readings, recorded some years later:

> It is hardly necessary to say that the verdict was unanimously favourable. . . . but too seldom . . . do we find a man gifted with such extraordinary powers, and, at the same time possessed of such a love of method, such will, such energy, and such a capacity for taking pains. . . . Although to many of his hearers at that eventful rehearsal of 'Dr. Marigold' it was the first time it had been read, Mr. Dickens had, since its appearance as a Christmas number only three months previously, adapted it as a Reading, and had rehearsed it to himself considerably over two hundred times—and this in addition to his ordinary work.

'Dr. Marigold' was the only real success out of the six prepared at that time. Of the others, 'Barbox Brothers' and 'The Boy at Mugby' had a few performances but 'The Haunted Man', 'Mrs. Lirriper's Lodgings' and 'The Signalman' were never read.

Only one more item was to be added: the notorious 'Sykes and Nancy'. Dickens wanted to include on his Farewell Tour an item which would live long in the imagination of those who witnessed it, and so he set about preparing as a Reading the murder of Nancy. Charlie (Dickens's son) described what happened:

> presently I heard a noise . . . as if two people were engaged in a violent altercation or quarrel which threatened serious results to somebody . . . I soon discovered the cause of the disturbance. There, at the end of the meadow, was my father, striding up and down, gesticulating wildly, and, in the character of Mr. Sykes, murdering Nancy with every circumstance of the most aggravated brutality.

Dickens's friends and family wondered whether such a violent presentation *could* be performed to a mixed audience, or indeed to *any* audience, so realistic and brutal was the performance. Dickens was determined it *should* be given, and arranged another private reading to test it upon friends, family and critics. Charlie Dickens continues:

> the trial performance was given before a very representative and critical audience, whose verdict, unfortunately, confirmed my father in his opinion of the effect the reading would produce upon the public, and the moment he spoke to me (afterwards)— eager, triumphant, excited— . . . I knew that no advice or expostulation of mine would avail. 'Well, Charlie, and what do you think of it now?', he said to me as I came up to where he was receiving the enthusiastic congratulations of such good judges of dramatic effect. . . . 'It is finer than even I expected', I answered, 'but I still say, don't do it.'

But he did.

On the evening of 29 April 1858, in St. Martin's Hall, London, Dickens gave his first professional reading. Very well aware that in accepting payment for his presentation he was risking public regard and respect (particularly in view of the scandal which now linked his name with that of the actress Ellen Ternan), he began his performance by addressing the audience directly:

> Ladies and Gentlemen. It may, perhaps, be known to you that, for a few years past, I have been accustomed occasionally to read some of my shorter books to various audiences, in aid of a variety of good objects, and at some charge to myself, both in time and money. It having at length become impossible in any reason to comply with these always accumulating demands, I have had definitely to choose between now and then reading on my own account as one of my recognised occupations, or not reading at all. I have had little or no difficulty in deciding on the former course.

> The reasons that have led me to it—besides the consideration that it necessitates no departure whatever from the chosen pursuits of my life—are three-fold. Firstly, I have satisfied myself that it can involve no possible compromise of the credit and independence of literature. Secondly, I have long held the opinion and have long acted on the opinion, that in these times whatever brings a public man and his public face to face, on terms of mutual confidence and respect, is a good thing. Thirdly, I have had a pretty large experience of the interest my hearers are so generous as to take in these occasions, and of the delight they give to me, as a tried means of strengthening those relationships, I may almost say of personal friendship, which it is my great privilege and pride, as it is my great responsibility, to hold with a multitude of persons who will never hear my voice, or see my face.

> Thus it is that I come quite naturally to be here among you at this time. And thus it is that I proceed to read this little book, quite as composedly as I might proceed to write it or to publish it in any other way . . .

and he opened the book (on this occasion *The Cricket on the Hearth*), and started to read.

In an age which takes *television* for granted, it is difficult, perhaps, to imagine the excitement of the living theatre in Dickens's day; not, of course, that Dickens often played in *theatres*. Many among his audience would not have entered such a place, perceived as they were as dens of sin. However the 'cultural experience' that Dickens offered was another thing; people of all classes flocked to hear him and the 444 professional performances that he gave during the period of twelve years until his death in 1870 were rightly regarded as one of the wonders of the age.

The halls where Dickens performed usually had some kind of raised stage and, while the audience was coming in, this would be lit by *low* gas jets. There was rarely a front curtain. Beyond the hissing of gas and the lack of seating comfort, what would have struck an audience of today would have been the simplicity of the stage setting. At the back of the platform was a large screen of maroon cloth. Below the screen and centre stage a desk was placed, but there was no stool. The desk top had three levels: on the right, when one stood upstage of it, was a shelf which carried a carafe of water and a glass. On the desk top proper rested the book which was to be read at that performance, and at the left-hand side was fixed a cube of wood on which the reader's elbow rested and which also supported the open book and hand during the reading. The upright wood of the desk legs was thin and the top was not covered by a cloth, all of which was intended to ensure that as much as possible of the reader's body upstage of the table was visible to his audience. The desk had been designed by Dickens specifically for the readings. In an earlier amateur production, he had found himself inside a kind of Punch and Judy booth, which allowed his head to be seen while totally obscuring the second most articulate part of the actor—his body. *That* would not happen again!

Besides the desk and his other props, Dickens toured with his own lighting man. It was *his* responsibility to see that gas was available, and to set up the jets, with their tin reflectors, twelve feet or so above the platform and downstage of the desk. They were fed gas from vertical pipes each side of the platform and from the middle of each of these was another powerful jet with a glass chimney. So all the lighting was in front of the performer; behind, the stage area went off into shadow.

Right on the appointed hour, the stage gas jets would be turned up and Charles Dickens would walk out to centre stage to take the applause. Many in his audience would have been as familiar with his writing as was Dickens himself, but, in an age without television, or photographs in newspapers or on the dust jackets of his books, few would have known his face.

Knowing what a great novelist *should* look like, many in the audience appeared to have been disappointed; what they saw was a man of medium height, iron grey hair with full beard and moustache, and a red face, which was rather empty, with his features in repose. He would remove his gloves and put them on the shelf to the right, pick up the book, open it and begin to read. Quite soon his eyes would be raised from the book to catch the audience's; rarely did he look down again. Slowly at first he would begin to draw the crowd into himself . . . starting loudly to gain their attention and make them listen. (A critic in one of the audiences whispered to his companion early in a reading: 'Dickens's voice is limited in power, husky and naturally monotonous. If he succeeds in overcoming these defects it will be by dramatic genius.') Soon he would begin to project less; lower and lower; the audience would have to be quiet to hear him; their silence built his, and their, concentration; a whisper now would fill the room. He had them: in his hand. This was the reason he drove himself on relentlessly across the country, across Europe and across America—for the heady high of this kind of power, to carry his listeners with him; to make them laugh or cry or both; at will . . . *his* will. And he could do it; it was a new magic and he could not produce enough of it. The audience no longer saw *him* and heard *him*. Instead, it was the voice he had had in his head when he had written the story; the novelist of average height with iron grey hair and full beard was gone. In his place stood variously a portly and laughing gentleman, a grasping scrawny miser, a maimed child, a cheapjack hustler. The audience wept for Little Nell and roared for Mrs. Gamp . . . and it was Oh! so sweet! Dickens wrote to his sister-in-law:

> I have never seen *men* go into cry so undisguisedly . . . they made no attempt whatever to hide it, and certainly cried more than the women. As to the Boots at Night, and Mrs. Gamp too, it was just one big roar with me and them, for they made me laugh so that sometimes I *could not* compose my face to go on.

And again:

> there was one gentleman . . . who exhibited the profoundest grief. After crying a good deal without hiding it, he covered his face with both his hands and laid it down on the back of the seat

before him, and really shook with emotion. He was not in
mourning, but I supposed him to have lost some child. . . .
There was a remarkably good fellow too, of thirty or so, who
found something so very ludicrous in Toots, that he *could not*
compose himself at all, but laughed until he sat wiping his eyes
with his handkerchief; and whenever he felt Toots coming
again, he began to laugh and wipe his eyes afresh; and when
Toots came once more he gave a kind of cry, as if it were too
much for him. It was uncommonly droll, and made me laugh
heartily.

By the end of the first section of the Reading, the same critic
who had earlier doubted the quality of Dickens's voice is
obviously now won over and is reported as saying: '*Dickens is
an actor!*' (*Pen Portraits*). There can be no possible doubt that
he *was*; *sensational*, with all the overtones that that word
possesses. Ladies fainted for him and strong men fought for the
petals which had fallen from his carnation.

There were no doubts about the way Dickens reconstructed
the two characters in 'Sykes and Nancy'. The audience
watched in petrified horror as Sykes rained down the appalling blows on Nancy's upturned face. She can only murmur
'Bill, dear Bill', as blinded by blood, she dies. 'And there was
the body—mere flesh and blood, no more—but such flesh and
so much blood! the very feet of his dog were bloody!' Dickens
forced this reading into as many performances on his 'Final
Tour' as he could. Against advice based first on his standing as
an author and performer, and then on medical criteria, he
pursued this short reading relentlessly and presented it with a
morbid passion which moved into mania. As if foreseeing his
end to be near, he wanted to leave behind a performance of
greatness by which to be remembered. He must also have been
well aware that violence and lust are the things that sell tickets
and I do not believe that Dickens ever did anything without
considering the consequent effects. He was the kind of man
who, having done something well, needed now to do it better.
Where before an audience had numbered 1,000, now it numbered 2,000; and, although he would have denied it with his
dying breath, the financial return was important, at least as a
measure (as *he* saw it) of his success.

Dickens was a man of extraordinary talents. There are few

who are great writers; there are few who are great actors, there are, therefore, very few indeed who have a combination of both these talents. He had one other important characteristic: he was an enthusiast, who did not start something he could not finish; and having started, involved himself with that activity in a way which represented one hundred per cent of himself. It was Charles Dickens speaking when he wrote for David Copperfield:

> Whatever I have tried to do in life, I have tried with all my heart to do well; whatever I have devoted myself to, I have devoted myself to completely. . . . there is no substitute for thorough-going, ardent, and sincere earnestness. Never to put one hand to anything on which I could throw my whole self, and never to affect depreciation of my work, whatever it was, I find now to have been my golden rules.

At the end of each reading, he would close his book and place it upon the desk. He would accept the applause of the audience as part of his due reward, and walk slowly from the platform. He was always thoroughly exhausted. The audiences, often still sobbing, would make their way home. Another day, another town, another show.

Having written the last six words, I shall now try to guess something of the personal reality behind Dickens's day-by-day living on those reading tours. What I have written before has been based largely on the factual reports of the day. One must assume that they were carefully observed and honest, but they are often the writings of Dickens's friends and do not tell the whole truth, although the sub-text can sometimes be seen, glinting between the lines. Part of what is missing lies in the unrevealed personal feelings of Dickens the actor, some of which, I suspect, are common to *all* performers. From this point on, I unashamedly admit to some speculation and conjecture and put off one hat to put on another; for I too have toured a one-man show and given hundreds of performances in one-night stands.

Almost every day, Dickens would have travelled on, as I have done, to a new place, a new performance. Travelling is exhausting, particularly when it is followed immediately by the setting up of a new show with different theatre personnel.

If yesterday had been a reading day as well, then last night would have meant a performance, followed almost invariably by a party of some kind. These are welcome periods of relaxation given by kind strangers who provide a comfortable environment in which to relax and unwind—essential after a performance. For your hosts, it is one late night in a week; for you it is a late night *every* night; inevitably fatigue and exhaustion follow. They do for all touring actors, and Dickens was no exception. However, travelling also has a positive aspect. If Dickens, *Mouse Trap*-like, had had to give 444 performances in *one* theatre, he would have become bored and jaded long before he reached the end of the first hundred. Different locations, therefore, help you to keep an edge on your performance.

So, yet another hall. The setting-up begins. The lighting man fits the gas pipes, jets and chimneys. You meet and begin to get to know the new front-of-house and stage managements. If they have not seen your presentation, they will have no scale against which to evaluate your performance. However, you *will*; and almost all actors in that situation would tend to move behind a defensive line. For Dylan Thomas, it was drink: 'I shan't be able to do it if I'm not drunk enough', his argument would go,

> And if I *am* drunk enough, they (my friends who, because they've seen it all before, will now fail to be impressed by what I do, together with those for whom the performance is new), *they* will all perhaps understand and excuse, make allowances if the performance is down, a bit flat, or not very good, or a total bloody disaster. Because after all, I am bloody drunk, aren't I? and you can't keep on doing it bloody brilliantly, can you?

Dickens did not use 'drink', but he did exploit his illnesses in this way. Many years before, he had failed to turn up for his audition at the Lyceum Theatre, because he had a heavy cold. That, and the fact that he never arranged an alternative date, probably meant (for a character of Dickens's resolve) that he had real doubts about *that* course of action anyway. Now, later in his life, when he reads, he frequently complains of being ill; but with maladies which will affect his performance: a cold, a sore throat, exhaustion.

128

Washington, February 7th, 1868: 'My birthday and my cold worse than ever'. A friend called to see him that afternoon and found him covered with mustard poultices, *apparently voiceless*. 'Surely you will not let him read tonight?', he asked Dolby, to which Dickens's manager replied, 'I have told Mr. Dickens at least a dozen times today that it will be impossible for him to read; and, but for my knowledge of him and his wonderful power of changing when he gets to the little table, I should be even more anxious about him than I am'. Dickens wrote to his sister-in-law describing that same occasion: 'After five minutes of the little table, I was not (for the time) even hoarse'.

I am not saying that Dickens did *not* have a cold, but what I am saying is that there was an element of psycho-soma about the way he uses these illnesses which shows a behaviour pattern that most actors will recognize immediately.

Another pattern that is instantly recognizable (and not just by actors) is what I shall call the 'good luck ritual'. Many actors (and solo performers in particular), who come into a new performance space, are trained to go through a kind of checklist as a way of making certain that everything will be ready, in its right place, and will work when that moment in the presentation comes. Many (if not all) will do as Dickens did: check the acoustics of the hall by trying out voice projection whilst somebody stands at the back to test audibility. Is there a gallery? Can I 'hit the back wall'? Today, actors will also check the position of the exits and their signs to see if the faint light from them can be used as a guide for getting off stage when they have been left on at a blackout.

Very quickly the checklist becomes a ritual to which are added many activities having nothing to do *directly* with the success or otherwise of the performance: the meal eaten before the show, drinks during it, the routine between the Acts and so on. Thus, like the cricketer who always puts on his right pad before his left and looks around the field one particular way before the other, the actor soon develops a ritual of idiosyncratic behaviour which *must* be carried through completely and in order, so that the performance will succeed. If something in the ritual is left out for whatever reasons, the performance really may not be so successful, because the performer will worry; something in the back of his mind will give him uneasy feelings of sins of omission or commission. Was this true of Dickens? On days when he was due to perform, he was fastidious in his preparations and demanded an unchanging ceremony before and during the presentation. At seven in the morning, in bed, he had a tumbler of fresh cream and two tablespoonfuls of rum. At noon, he had a sherry cobbler and a biscuit. At three o'clock, he had a pint of champagne and at five minutes to eight, before going onto the platform, an egg beaten up in a glass of sherry. In the intervals between the Readings he had a cup of strong beef tea and at a quarter past ten, a bowl of soup. 'After dinner, reading days, he would take a cup of strong coffee, a tiny glass of brandy, and a cigar, and . . . lie down for a short time to get his voice in order' (Annie Field's *Diaries*, quoted in *Interviews and Recollections*). '. . . he would go down to the empty hall long before the hour appointed for the Reading, to take the bearings, as he would say, or, in other words, to familiarize himself with the place beforehand.' I wonder a bit about his eating and drinking patterns, but while most of the activities are all perfectly normal and even functional, the regularity of them, and Dickens's insistence upon them, place this behaviour as part of a 'good luck ritual'. Further, these lists must show only the iceberg's tip of the nightly routine of which only Dickens himself in the deep recesses of his mind was aware, or perhaps unaware.

Now, the gods appeased, he stands ready in the wings; the voice of the audience rises and falls; he waits. The stage gas hiss increases and he steps out into the garish light and feels . . . fear? 'Not in the least,' he is reported as saying, 'I felt as much confidence as though I had already done the like a hundred times.' He goes on to say that he only felt fear once and that was when he overheard in a shop a lady asking for a copy of his magazine. When she was shown the current issue, she said, 'that, I have read. I want the next one!' 'Listening to this unrecognised', reported Dickens, 'and remembering that not one word of the number she was asking for was yet written, for the first and only time in my life, I felt frightened.' All *I* can say is 'Nonsense!' I am convinced that Dickens was far too good an actor not to have been scared at the start of each performance, from the first to the 444th! As all actors know, to be frightened, to go through a low period before, when one says to oneself 'I don't want to do this', is not only to be accepted, it is to be welcomed. For it is through the re-channelling of this energy that the actor comes to terms again with his role and re-creates it anew for each fresh audience; in this respect, I do not believe that Dickens was any different from the performers of today. Kate Field reports that a 'supernumerary' declared at one of Dickens's early performances that the great author's legs shook from the beginning to the end of the reading. So Dickens was being less than candid when he protested that he was not frightened as he stood in the wings waiting.

Looking back a hundred years, it is difficult to know whether a late twentieth-century audience would have recognized the greatness in Dickens's performances. To modern eyes, used to the close media of film and television, he would have appeared grotesquely melodramatic. However, his circumstances nearly always dictated that his performances *had* to be large. Some of the halls in which he played sat (in some discomfort) 2,000 spectators or more. That such a large audience would have had difficulty in seeing him, and what he was doing for each character, was obvious. What he did do had to be big. Yet, in spite of the ad-libbing (which, having no director and being the author, he could self-indulgently allow himself and which in any case can only be done safely and under control in a one-man show), each was a disciplined performance and one can see from the contemporaneous criticism that he maintained a very high professional standard indeed.

Dickens would soon have found that, after a certain point, the more he performed the same material, the more difficult it became. An increasing level of concentration has to be created and then maintained, and he might very well have allowed himself some sort of organic development within each reading text so that he was continually presented with new challenges. The more the same material is performed, the wider becomes the actor's personal scale which he uses to chart (in *his* terms) failure and success. Inevitably, some performances are good, and some are not so good. When a performance was down, Dickens rationalized, as we all do, and blamed the audience without perhaps recognizing that the further along the success curve one moves, the greater the effort required to go higher.

Yet the people who came to hear Dickens usually were warmly supportive of him, while coming quickly and easily under the power of his suggestion through the images he created. Indeed, if we are to believe the contemporaneous descriptions of Dickens's performances, we are forced to the conclusion that all his audiences seemed to do was to howl, either in mirth or in anguish. Now, I think that my Dylan Thomas one-man presentation has its moments of humour and pathos, but only rarely can I reduce my audience to tears of either kind. Setting aside the obvious facts that he was clearly a more skilful performer and manipulator than I, and that modern audiences have long lost their innocence and been desensitized by a continuous media stream of death and destruction, I felt there might be other reasons to explain why late eighteenth- and nineteenth-century audiences appeared to be so much more emotional than those of today. First, of course, such behaviour was an affectation; people went to the theatre to cleanse themselves of their tensions by a semi-contrived, public display. However, work I have been doing on a recent film suggested to me another possibility of which, the more I explore, the more certain I become. By modern standards, halls and theatres in Dickens's day were over-crowded. In 1941, when the Theatre Royal, Bristol, was up for sale it was stated that it seated 1,800 people. Even allowing for the hyperbole of an over-enthusiastic estate agent, 1,800 is nearly three times the seating capacity of that theatre today. All reports are that Dickens played to packed houses. So his audiences were always desperately tightly packed together. Then, halls and theatres were lit by fire of some kind (in Dickens's day by *gas* jets) and naked flames consume oxygen; natural ventilation was inadequate and forced ventilation was non-existent. Thus, the burning of gas, together with the overcrowding, might have resulted in the audiences and the performers becoming mildly hypoxic, and the first sympton of hypoxia is a kind of drunkenness where emotions are brought easily to the surface. I am confident that this is at least one factor in explaining the gross emotional responses of nineteenth-century audiences, and it is something that I am currently pursuing.

By the end of each performance, Dickens was exhausted.

This is in no way surprising. He was 46 when he gave his first professional reading and he lived in a time when life expectancy in his social group was about 10! Throughout the twelve years that Dickens was a professional reader, he did not enjoy the best of health. Of course he was exhausted by his efforts; he was working under strain, a great deal of which he created for himself by the passion and aggression within his performances. They might have been better had they been less intense; but there was no one near him courageous enough to tell him that; and so the strain continued. However, to imagine (as all his many biographers have done) that this kind of tension in itself would be enough to kill him is clearly wrong. Daily exertion to a point where the pulse rate is significantly raised is the current recommendation by the medical profession to those who want to get or stay fit. It is even advised for some who have diagnosed heart disease. Regularly created and subsequently *relieved* emotional stress is strongly approved of for good mental and physical health; and this is the kind of tension/relief cycle through which a working actor daily passes. I cannot accept that the strain of performances (divorced from his life style) killed Charles Dickens.

One must ask the question why Dickens, generally in poor health as he was, continued to perform. As I have said before, money was certainly a factor but not the most important. I think the need to go on proving himself (to himself and to others: you are only as good as your last performance) is best summed up in an article by Philip Collins published in *The Listener* on 25 December 1969. He quotes John Butt as saying that his (Dickens) life-long love-affair with his reading public was by far the most interesting love-affair of his life. Something very similar might be said about *my* other passion, Dylan Thomas. Would it be going too far to suggest that both these men spent their later years searching for their ideal love and in the end had to settle for second best: adulation of a rapturous audience? Both Charles Dickens and Dylan Thomas exposed something of their individual needs in, respectively, *Great Expectations* and *Adventures in the Skin Trade*. In the former, Pip finds his ideal love; but she is cold, distant and unobtainable, *never* to be possessed (had Dickens had the emotional courage to stick with the ending he intended originally for *Great*

Expectations). On the other hand, when Dylan Thomas seeks his ideal in *Adventures*, she is evanescent as steam and he spends his time in a nightmare of searching, searching and never finding. For both men, the drug that healed the symptom was an audience's adoration and Thomas became hooked on it as had Dickens a hundred years before. As one observer who had attended a reading in Glasgow during Dickens's first tour in 1858 recorded: 'when he sat down (after the performance), it was not mere applause that followed but a passionate outburst of love for the man.' Dickens had found a mistress and she was devoted to him.

6

Adapting *Nickleby*

by DAVID EDGAR*

I had already made several discoveries about the adaptation of books for the stage, before embarking on the task of adapting *Nicholas Nickleby* for the Royal Shakespeare Company. Through the adaptation of two autobiographical works (*Mary Barnes* and *The Jail Diary of Albie Sachs*) I'd found out that, in many ways, the business of adaptation was very similar to the business of 'normal' playwrighting (and no less hard work). I had realized the paradoxical truth that the mediation between my own craft and another writer's required even more concentration than usual on the playwright's perpetual catechism: '*Why* am I dealing with this material?'; '*Why* have I chosen this incident as against another?'; '*What* am I wanting to say through this material?' And I'd discovered that the world did not take a similar view of the adaptor's craft: my work, I was told, had ceased to be 'original'; I was probably only doing it for the money; or maybe I'd 'dried up', but sooner or later would doubtless return to the fold and start writing 'real plays' again.

But most importantly of all, I'd understood that the only way to adapt books seriously is to view the final product as a play, in large part, about *the author of the original work*. Easy with auto-biography, of course (though sometimes politically tricky if the authors are still alive). But in fact I think our adaptation of *Nicholas Nickleby* was also a play about Charles Dickens in

* 'Adapting *Nickleby*' is a talk, first given at a Conference of the Society for Teachers of English, at Oxford, in April 1982, and subsequently at the Chicago Arts Club, in January 1983.

his late twenties, about the world in which he lived, how he viewed it, and how we viewed both the man and his perspective. And I say 'we' because, although my name is on the poster as the adaptor and I physically wrote almost every word, how this adaptation came to be like it was can only be understood in terms of an essentially collaborative creative process; and to describe that process is the best, indeed the only way to explain the play.

First of all, however, I ought to come clean about how I came to be involved. During, roughly, the academic year 1978–79, I was in the United States on a fellowship, and I had been in correspondence with Trevor Nunn, artistic director of the R.S.C., about the possibility of writing a film adaptation of George Eliot's *Felix Holt*. In late October 1979—I was due to return in November—I received a dramatic transatlantic 'phone call, from Trevor Nunn, telling me that the R.S.C. had decided to make a version of a Dickens novel, and the choice was already down to two: *Our Mutual Friend* and *Nickleby*. I was asked to think about being the writer, and immediately I 'phoned my wife, who was in England (it was proving an expensive afternoon), to ask what I should do. The extent of my Dickensian scholarship can be judged from the fact that my first question was 'Is *Nicholas Nickleby* the one with Mrs. Gamp in it', and when we'd established that no, it was the one with Dotheboys Hall, her advice was to say yes if it was *Mutual Friend* and no if it was *Nickleby*. Happily, as things fell out, I departed from the habits of a lifetime and did not follow my wife's advice. I read the novel on the plane on the way home on the Friday, and started work with the company on the Monday, more unprepared for a project than I had ever been before, or ever intend to be again.

The process of work was one with which the company was familiar from its work on the classics and I was familiar from my work with small-scale touring companies. Basically, the company as a whole would research, discuss, experiment, undertake exercises and consider the results. Some kind of collective view of the work and its subject-matter would then emerge, at which point more conventional theatre processes would take over: the writer, in the case of a new play, would write; and the director or directors would direct the actors.

But the collective voice would not be silenced even now: the rewriting and rehearsal processes would be influenced by the fact that the company as a whole was pursuing a collective purpose. This, as I say, was a familiar process to most of us; but none of us had ever attempted it on anything like this scale. We began by sitting round in a large, forty-five-person circle, to talk about the novel, our reaction to it, our memory of other Dickens adaptations—we saw one or two of the movies—and so on. Then we began the exercise work, which was to last four or five weeks before a single part was cast or a single word written.

While preparing this, I was very struck by how many of the ideas that came up in those first weeks ended up as key elements of the adaptation. Indeed, the story of the adaptation *as a text* (as a theatrical production, things are rather different) can be largely told through the exploratory period, and three exercises in particular.

The first was the research project. Pairs of actors were assigned a subject to research and prepare a short submission on; the subjects covered Dickens himself, his life and his times, and various aspects, in particular, of the world of the 1830s. They were all good, but the most useful to me were the projects on social etiquette and manners, which significantly effected the eventual creation of Fanny Squeers, Mrs. Nickleby, the Wititterlies and the Kenwigs, of whom more later; an extraordinarily comprehensive report on sports and pastimes—which was immensely helpful for Hawk and his entourage; and a *son et lumière* presentation on the early Victorian theatre, which had not a little influence on the way we portrayed the engagement of a certain young actor with a provincial company of no mean repute. But I think most important of all were the projects on science, technology, the Empire and medicine, because they gave flesh and substance to our growing view that the 1830s was in many ways a mirror of our own times; it was the decade when the great technological revolution that had been brewing for fifty years suddenly flapped its great iron wings and flew. Two years before *Nickleby* was begun, Samuel Morse had built his first telegraph; four years before that, Michael Faraday discovered electro-magnetism, in the same year as Charles Darwin set off on his voyage of exploration with the *Beagle*. And *Nickleby*

137

was finished only ten years after the first steam locomotive line opened in the United States, between, if this matter is of interest, Baltimore and Ohio. Industrialism, it must have seemed, had taken nature by the throat and commanded it to bend to its will; as, meanwhile, imperialism was opening up the great uncharted continents to exploration and discovery.

But behind the unparalleled sense of excitement and opportunity lay a sense, too, of great if undefined loss. The old certainties—particularly those of the rural English village—were dissolving. Hundreds of thousands were crowding into the cities, where the old rules appeared no longer to apply. True, the out-moded hierarchies and snobberies were swept away by the winds of change; but something else had gone too: the idea of a social hierarchy which not only granted immeasurable rights to the powerful, but imposed obligations on them too. Less than ten years after *Nickleby* was written, two other great nineteenth-century literary figures were to describe what was happening in the following terms:

> The bourgeoisie, wherever it has got the upper hand, has put an end to all feudal, patriarchal, idyllic relations. It has pitilessly torn asunder the motley feudal ties that bound man to his 'natural superiors' and has left remaining no other nexus between man and man than naked self-interest, than callous 'cash payment'. . . . The bourgeoisie has torn away from the family its sentimental veil, and has reduced the family relation to a mere money relation. . . . All fixed, fast-frozen relations, with their train of ancient and venerable prejudices and opinions are swept away, all new formed ones become antiquated before they can ossify. All that is solid melts into air, all that is holy is profaned, and man is at last compelled to face, with sober senses, his real conditions of life and his relations with his kind.

When we began, we had only one rule: we were going to adapt the whole of *Nicholas Nickleby*, or, at the very least, we were going to tell the whole story. Anyone who knows the novel will understand that this principle forms itself quickly into a society for the protection of the Kenwigs plot, virtually the only section of the story that could be snipped out in its entirety. But we realized quickly that this plot encapsulated, in comic form, the obsessions of the whole. Mrs. Kenwigs, who has married beneath her, is desperately concerned to keep on the right side of her tax-collector uncle, whose promised covenant to her large and growing family is her only guarantee that her children will be kept in the manner—and manners— to which she is determined they will grow accustomed. The point, of course, is that fifty years earlier Mrs. Kenwigs would not have married beneath her, and the rules and regulations of family life would see to it that her inheritance would either be on the way or conversely not: but *there would be no doubt in the matter.* As there would be no doubt that Ralph Nickleby would look after his brother's widow and her children, or that Madeline Bray's predicament would be solved, one way or another, in a manner befitting her station. What the research we did on the 1830s demonstrated was that the technological revolution, and the social upheavals that followed from it, had created a world of unfathomable economic opportunity but also one assailed by bottomless social doubt.

The projects revealed something else too. Human beings were making the most incredible discoveries about how to adapt and control their external environment; but their knowledge of their own bodies had hardly progressed beyond the middle ages. Death—nasty, brutish and sudden—lurked behind the spinning jenny and waited in the next carriage of the railway locomotive, mocking humankind's Promethean pretensions. And that reality brings me to the second major exercise we undertook, and to the whole question of Smike.

The second exercise was a simple one. Each actor was sent away to prepare a two-minute presentation, from the book, of an aspect of a character in the novel. Performers were not restricted to age or sex or the part they wanted to play; some viewed it as an unofficial audition, but many others did not (Roger Rees, who ended up playing Nicholas, did his two minutes on Mr. Brooker; the actors who were to end up as Ralph and indeed Smike himself presented variations on the Gentleman in Small Clothes). There were eight Smikes, including two actresses, and all of them were full of perception. One actor, for example, spotted the tiny passage in which Smike, who has borrowed a book from Nicholas, attempts to do with it what he has seen Nicholas doing. His failure to make the thing work—Smike was not only illiterate but, one assumed, ignorant even of the principle of what reading was—

took the whole of the actor's two minutes, and was breath-taking. Even more significant was another performer who brought his own experience to bear on the almost equally tiny incident in the novel when Smike, having been extensively tutored by Nicholas, performs the part of the apothecary in *Romeo and Juliet*, to Nicholas's Romeo. The actor's two minutes showed Smike in the wings, waiting for his cue, and desperately going through the lines that Nicholas has drummed into him. So obsessed was he, indeed, that he missed the actual cue. It was moving and very funny, and it turned out to be the tip of an inverted pyramid in terms of the construction of the play.

A little later, when we had decided on a two-evening structure for the final work (how we ever thought we could do it in one go is a mystery), Trevor Nunn said that he thought the first part should end with a huge triumphant Crummlesian moment: Nicholas and Smike at a high point, surrounded by their strange new friends, with only the knowledge of Kate's persecution by Sir Mulberry Hawk to undermine the sense of happiness and achievement. I had read that, in the eighteenth century, *Romeo and Juliet* was frequently performed with a happy ending, and I thought that ending a well-known tragedy in uncontrolled mirth would be a cheerful metaphor for Nicholas and Smike's unawareness of the storm clouds that were lowering. Then, when writing the scene in which Nicholas rehearses Smike as the apothecary, I realized that many lines applied to other characters and other situations (Newman Noggs, 'so poor and full of wretchedness', Ralph's gold, 'worst poison to men's souls', and Kate's poverty, but not her will, consenting), and I constructed a double scene in which the London and Portsmouth events weaved in and out of each other. It was then pointed out—I think by Trevor Nunn—that the second half of *Romeo* had other resonances too: particularly, the Capulets' project of marrying Juliet to Paris had distinct echoes in Ralph's use of Kate as a bait for Lord Frederick Verisopht. And so that scene was inter-cut with Ralph's dinner party as well.

But matters did not stop there. I had already decided that one way to make Smike—a character who could easily slide into easy sentiment—work as a part was to develop those aspects of his dialogue which were at least equivalent to the medically observable behaviour of retarded or schizophrenic people. (At the same time, and marvellously, the actor David Threlfall developed the physical characteristics of a twenty-year-old who had suffered profound environmental and nutritional deprivation.) One frequent habit of schizophrenics is to invest particular words and phrases with an immense metaphorical and often punning significance; there is a wonderful passage in R. D. Laing's *The Divided Self* where he makes intelligible a young schizophrenic's obsession with the idea that she is called Miss Taylor on the basis of a series of interlocking puns which culminate in her self-definition as a 'tailored maid'. I initially took Smike's obsession with the words 'home' and 'away' (for him, reversed: 'home' was dangerous and nasty, and 'away' was potentially cosy and comfortable), invested them with meaning, reversed them and turned them back again; and the same things happened with Squeers's imposed definition of Smike as an 'outcast, noun substantive'. But then I realized that if echoes of Smike's misery would be of immense significance to him, then memories of his period of greatest contentment would be so too. So the words of the apothecary scene—Smike's greatest triumph—kept reappearing on his lips in part two of the play, and formed the basis of his dying speech, which concluded with the apothecary's opening words 'Who calls? Who calls so loud?'

Genuinely, then, a whole track of the play was based on one actor's perception in a two-minute improvisation. Similarly, the third initial project, which dealt with narrative techniques, was an open sesame for the solution of a number of pressing dramatic problems. The exercises on how the company could collectively represent key passages of the book were most obviously useful in two great descriptive passages in Part Two of the play, which were assembled largely by the directors, with very little textual interference by me. But the revelation that it was possible to use Dickens's narrative in a vast number of ways, and, particularly, that characters could step out from themselves and narrate their own feelings about themselves or other people, in the third person, was a mighty discovery. Specifically, it opened the door to the solution of a problem that was obsessing me, which was how to make the young women in the novel active participants, rather than insipid victims, in the story. At a simple level, we found that by transferring certain key passages about Kate Nickleby from reported speech ('Kate thought', 'Kate felt') to direct speech, we were creating a much gutsier character, and one, further-more, who was clearly capable of surviving the privations and sufferings to which she is subjected in the story. (Incidentally, this trick of looking at what the women actually do, rather than what they say, helped with Madeline Bray as well. In the novel, she spends the scene of her greatest crisis, when she is about to be married off to the ghastly Arthur Gride, in a dead faint; we woke her up, and she is an active, indeed the most active, participant in the scene where Nicholas and Kate interrupt Arthur Gride's gruesome wedding morning.)

The use of narrative was also important, in a more complex way, in our treatment of Fanny Squeers. All Dickens's petty snobbery, London contempt for the provinces, and, dare I say it, sexism, come out in his own comments on Fanny; but his portrayal of her is imbued with much greater understanding of the desperately limited options open to a plain and not very bright little girl, stuck in the middle of an appalling family on the edge of a bleak Northern moor, and blessed, if that is the word, with an extremely pretty and only friend. No surprise, then, that she resorts to a pathetic and grandiose gentility; and it is evidence of Nicholas Nickleby's lack of sensitivity in the early part of the novel that he treats her with such undisguised contempt. Theatrically we represented this reality by using Dickens's own words about Nicholas's feelings, initially, and then by using Dickens's own long paragraph of attack on Fanny, but put into Nicholas's own mouth, to turn the audience's own attitude from one of contemptuous mirth against Fanny to a kind of sympathy with, or at the very least understanding of, her situation. And by establishing the principle that Nicholas's attitudes to the women who fall for him are revealed by his own third person narrative, we were able to make clear the progression from his boorish dismissal of Fanny, through his ironically detached flirting with Miss Snevellicci, to his passionate declaration that he would know his beloved Madeline Bray 'in ten thousand'.

Much of the ultimate shape of the plays, therefore, was

defined during these first three exercises. I should add a fourth, which was a series of long discussions between me, the two directors, and the assistant director, in which we hammered out, in thematic form, the story we wanted to tell, which revolved, in a way we did not quite expect, around the figure of Nicholas Nickleby himself. It is possible to view the character, in the original novel, as a kind of courier, the chap at the front of the bus, who, though of little interest himself, introduces you to the wonderful sights you are passing. Increasingly, we discovered that the novel's title is no accident. Nicholas comes to London an innocent and is rudely thrown up against cynicism, brutality and sham. He discovers that goodness is not a function of status, indeed that more often than not human decency is to be found among the low-castes or outcasts, rather than in the halls of the great; and he and we discover this truth in the most theatrical manner, through the relationships that Nicholas forges, of antagonism or friendship, with moneylenders, rakes, schoolmasters, members of parliament and misers (on the one hand), and bluff and simple corn-dealers, alcoholic clerks, and mentally-retarded simpletons (on the other). For Nicholas, all that is solid has indeed melted into air, all that he thought of as holy has been profaned, and, as Marx and Engels predicted, he is at last compelled to face, with sober senses, his real conditions of life and his relations with his kind.

As I've said, I firmly believe—although somewhat to my retrospective surprise—that the main thematic structure of our *Nickleby* was built in those early sessions, and as someone who is committed to collaborative play-making techniques, it's a pleasant discovery. Even when we moved into the more conventional business of writing the text, designing the set, and rehearsing the shows, however, our initial ideas had to be developed and deepened, and indeed thrust along through the great length of the novel (predictably, much of the exercise work had concentrated on the early part of the book). Most importantly, we had to sort out the great struggle between two radically different types of capitalist—Ralph Nickleby on the one hand, and the benevolent Cheerybles on the other—which forms the arch of the last third of the story.

In a review of the New York production, in the conservative

journal *Commentary*, I was berated for missing the point of *Nicholas Nickleby* (I think the implication was, deliberately) by choosing to emphasize the social criticism which I believe lies at the heart of the novel. 'Far from being the result of unjust social arrangements,' the reviewer stated, 'violence in *Nickleby* is a consequence of the original, inborn nature of man, in which aggression forms a constituent instinct.' Indeed, the whole novel 'subverts the notion that nature endows all creatures with innocent and praiseworthy impulses', and, 'for Dickens, the state of nature is not holy but Hobbesian, the war of all against all.' And indeed, citing Burke as well as Hobbes (he might have added Hume), the reviewer goes on to argue that the point of the philanthropic Cheerybles is that, being without a wicked instinct, they are fairy-tale figures, too good to be true; and further that *Nickleby* as a whole was a staging-post en route to the wholesale attack on the original barbarism of man that lies at the centre of *Barnaby Rudge*.

Well, yes, you can see it like that, but I—and we—became much more convinced by the thesis put forward by George Orwell in his incomparable essay on Dickens (a constant script-side companion). As Orwell pointed out, Dickens has been seized upon as a champion by supporters of all ideologies and religions. He has been claimed as a fellow-traveller by Catholics and humanists, by Communists and capitalists, by the most ardent revolutionaries, and—like the *Commentary* reviewer—the most avid supporters of reaction. But, for Orwell, Dickens fits neatly into none of these categories. 'In every page of his work', he writes 'one can see a consciousness that society is wrong somewhere at the root', but Dickens provides no specific solutions to the social ills he describes. Indeed, it's possible to extract from his work a message that, at first glance, looks like an enormous platitude: 'if men would behave decently the world would be decent.' Orwell was by no means convinced, however, that this perception is as shallow as it sounds. 'Most revolutionaries', he goes on,

> are potential Tories, because they imagine that everything can be put right by altering the *shape* of society; once that change is effected, as it sometimes is, they see no need for any other. Dickens has not this kind of mental coarseness. The vagueness of his discontent is a mark of its permanence. What he is out

against is not this or that institution, but, as Chesterton put it, 'an expression on the human face'.

For me, what is wrong with the conservative view of Dickens is contained in Orwell's simple sentence, 'if men *would* behave decently the world *would* be decent.' Dickens's vision is *conditional*. Of course he was horrified by the brute instincts of the mob, see *Barnaby Rudge*, see *A Tale of Two Cities*, and see the forces unleashed at the break-up of Dotheboys Hall, which I hope we represented honestly. But Dickens is not just positing his horror at and pessimism about what *is*, he is also expressing not just a hope but a conviction that things *could be* different. Of course the Cheerybles are impossible—they dole out largesse to the needy with a gay abandon which in the real world would drive their business into bankruptcy in an afternoon. But surely Dickens is asking, wouldn't it be good if the Cheerybles could exist, or, to return to the Communist Manifesto, wouldn't it be wonderful if one could retain all the obligations and kindnesses and generosities of rural relationships, and somehow impose them on the exciting, challenging and democratic age that technology was ushering forth? Or, put even more simply, wouldn't it be great if iron capitalism could have a smiling feudal face? The Cheerybles are not there to be scoffed at as fairies, beside the cold reality of Ralph Nickleby. They are—they must be—at least a possibility.

And Dickens provides ample proof that they are. Ralph Nickleby is a classic Hobbesian figure; he knows the world, he knows himself, and at base both of them are about naked self-interest. But, as it turns out, Ralph's judgements about other people and indeed about himself are consistently and grossly wrong. The gull Lord Verisopht, the unctuous Mr. Snawley, the besotted Madame Mantalini, the drudge Newman Noggs, and the supposedly self-seeking Nicholas himself, all *in fact* turn out to be considerably nobler, finer and more selfless creatures than Ralph believes them to be. And at the very end, he suffers the frightful realization that *he himself*, through his love for his niece and his desperate grief at the death of his son, is not the man he thought himself to be, is *better* than he thought himself to be, and the discovery kills him.

I don't think any of us realized fully the importance, for

representing the conditional essence of the novel, of a development in the narrative principle which occurred quite early, but didn't reach fullness until we began work on the second play. The directors were strongly of the view that the whole company should be regarded as the story-teller of the whole tale: that they had possession of it, collectively, they all knew how it began, continued and ended, and their joint ownership of it was more important than any individual's part. And the theatrical effect of that, particularly towards the end, was that our forty actors—who knew how it was to end—were expressing a huge, collective 'wouldn't it be good if' aspiration, as they watched and told the unfolding events. This distancing device, which in Brecht is supposed to clear the mind of emotion, had in our case the effect of directing and deepening the audience's own visceral longing for Ralph's vision of the world to be disproved.

I think it will be clear what I'm saying. I began talking about our *Nicholas Nickleby* as a play about Charles Dickens. Often, in radio adaptations, there is actually a character called Charles Dickens, who reads selected pieces of narrative. We decided really rather early that no one was going to don a frock coat, beard and moustache, and stand at the side of the stage with a big book. Nor was our collective story-teller to be viewed as a forty-strong embodiment of the Great Man. Because what they were was a group of late twentieth-century actors, who sympathized profoundly with what Dickens wrote and his aspirations for society and the human beings within it, but who were telling his story six generations later, and who knew 150 years' worth of things about men and women and their affairs that Charles Dickens did not know.

There has been a lot of comment, in the press and elsewhere, about the way we chose to end *Nicholas Nickleby*. What happens is that the concluding chapter—in which we hear how our heroes and heroines enjoyed an absurdly happy ever-after—was represented as a narration by a kind of Christmas family photograph of the central protagonists, surrounded by the rest of the company singing that most Dickensian of carols, 'God rest you merry, gentlemen'. As the carol reached its climax, however, Nicholas, alone, notices that, outside in the snow, a Dotheboys Hall boy, the boy in fact who took over

146

from Smike as the Squeers' general factotum, is sitting in the bleak darkness. Nicholas leaves the party, goes to the boy, picks him up in his arms, and, watched by his wife and his sister, holds the child out to us, as a reminder that for every Smike you save there are still thousands out there, in the cold. I have on previous occasions justified this departure from the text by pointing to the fact that the novel does indeed end with Nicholas and Kate's children playing round the grave of Smike, and their eyes filling with tears, as 'they spoke low and softly of their poor dead cousin.' But I think that I was probably being dishonest. Orwell points to the unsatisfactory ending of the novels, where all conflicts apppear to be resolved by the acquisition of 'a hundred thousand pounds, a quaint old house with plenty of ivy on it, a sweetly womanly wife, a horde of children, and no work', a world where 'everything is safe, soft, peaceful, and, above all, domestic.' Clearly, the conditional operates here *par excellence*: 'wouldn't it be just marvellous', Dickens is saying, 'if it could be Christmas every day.' But I think we, with our 150 years of experience of things turning into air, are more certain than he was that it can't be Christmas all year round, and more doubtful that decency alone can warm what Marx and Engels call 'the icy water of egotistical calculation'. And, while I believe that Dickens was aware, if only subconsciously, of the impossibility, or at the very least the conditionality, of his ending, of his freezing of his characters' lives into an unending and unchanging state of pure contentment, I think that our ending was not just the conclusion of an adaptation of a Charles Dickens novel, but of a play of which Dickens himself was the subject-matter.

I began by attempting to justify the business of adaptation as a legitimate artistic process. Whatever may be thought of what we did to *Nicholas Nickleby*, I hope I have justified that position at least. I know that the directors of *Nicholas Nickleby* gave real directions, the designers produced real designs, and the actors delivered real performances. I like to think—well, no, actually, I *do* think—that I wrote a real play.

7

Dickens and Film:
101 Uses of a Dead Author

by MIKE POOLE

From the early days of original serial publication, through to
his exploitation by the Victorian stage and the more recent
attentions of film, radio and television, Dickens has always
been a mass media phenomenon. As a result, he has assumed
a massive cultural profile that is in many ways quite distinct
from his strictly *literary* identity. What many people understand by the term 'Dickens' may, in other words, have very
little to do with the Victorian novelist of literary history. This
has yet to be at all adequately reflected in critical writing
about his work, even though any estimate of Dickens's significance clearly cannot afford to exclude that other 'Dickens',
as it were, who circulates in *extra*-literary forms. The present
essay is a modest attempt to fill that gap by offering a short
history of how film and television have treated Dickens. First,
however, I would briefly like to try and characterize why
conventional literary criticism has largely eschewed this kind
of analysis.

Traditionally, literary criticism has tended to have a dual
focus: on texts and on authors. Occasionally, the two are
articulated with history to produce, say, Eliot's notion of
a Tradition. Mostly, though, and particularly within the
academy, criticism has evolved almost exclusively as the practice of author-centred textual analysis. And, historically at

least, there are good reasons why this should have been so. Yet beyond a certain point—arguably reached as long ago as the mid-nineteenth century, with the advent of mass communications—it rapidly becomes inadequate, outmoded by the changes in its own object of analysis. In the new mass cultures produced by urban society, the literary object was radically reconstituted. Developments, first in education, printing and newspapers, then in music-hall, cinema and radio gave literary culture an extra-textual dimension of a previously unprecedented kind. These changes involved a degree of cultural democratization that can in some ways be described as a re-opening of Literature to popular memory. By which I do not mean that as an institution Literature became any the less élitist, merely that it circulated more widely—in the classroom, the cheap abridged edition, the newspaper serialization, the stage or the film adaptation. And, inevitably, this kind of cultural exchange—in which texts were re-used, re-cycled and, to some extent, *re-made*—produced a whole range of new meanings, readings and understandings in a meeting, of sorts, between popular and literary traditions. Few authors illustrate the process more vividly than Dickens, a writer whose career coincides with the beginnings of mass culture and whose hold on popular memory is as firm as his place in the literary canon. Yet, as has already been noted, the Dickens of popular memory does not always overlap with the Dickens of literary history. In the difference between the two lies not just the cultural history of Dickens's novels—the manner in which they have circulated at various times in the culture—but the history of that culture itself: the dynamic of its evolving response to new media like film and television.

The history of Dickens and film is the history of a curious symbiosis. It's not just that Dickens adaptations were among the first films ever made; or that television returns to the novels again and again. Rather, and rather surprisingly, it's a question of aesthetics. For, through the figure of D. W. Griffith, Dickens would seem to have exercised a decisive influence on the whole development of narrative cinema. The pioneer film-maker and director of *The Birth of a Nation* acknowledged a huge debt to the novelist in the matter of close-ups, dissolves and parallel storylines. Once, for instance, when berated by his cameraman, Arthur Marvin, who was appalled by the use of such devices, Griffith is said to have simply replied: 'Well, doesn't Dickens write that way?'[1] In a famous essay written in 1944, the Soviet director Sergei Eisenstein, who was a great admirer of Griffith's work, enumerated this Dickensian influence with a number of close textual readings from the novels, including the opening sentence of *The Cricket on the Hearth*—'The kettle began it'—which he described as a 'typical close-up'.[2] Eisenstein was at pains to point out that there was nothing piecemeal about the way Griffith drew on Dickens. There was, he argued, a clear 'genetic . . . line of descent':

> From here, from Dickens, from the Victorian novel stem the first shoots of American film aesthetic. . . .[3]

The essay also noted the way Griffith's fondness for 'rounded but slightly exaggerated characters'[4] echoed Dickens's own preference for a peculiarly heightened form of characterization. The connecting link was, of course, via Victorian melodrama, which helped shape the moral and aesthetic climate of both the nineteenth-century novel and the early silent cinema. And, immediately, this common legacy in a popular form, developed specifically for an urban audience, tells us something quite crucial about Dickens's enduring appeal for filmmakers and, more latterly, television producers. To paraphrase the typically perceptive Eisenstein, the novels bore the same relation to their contemporary audience as 'film bears to the same strata in our time'.[5]

Dickens, that is to say, was addressing a mass audience long before film ever arrived. Serial publication, with per-instalment print-runs of up to 100,000 in the case of *The Old Curiosity Shop*, ensured his work a cultural currency greatly in excess of its merely literary reputation. Even as early as 1836 and the publication of *Sketches by Boz*, Mary Russell Mitford could write:

> I did not think there had been a place where English was spoken to which 'Boz' had not penetrated. All the boys and girls talk his fun—the boys in the street; and yet they who are of the highest taste like it the most.[6]

This wide-ranging appeal was intimately bound up with the fact that Dickens's novels worked and re-worked the popular traditions of the new urban culture, drawing on a rich variety of non-literary sources in the process—from newspapers and the theatre, through to songs and spoken stories. As Raymond Williams has observed, his is 'a crowded, many-voiced, anonymous world of jokes, stories, rumours, songs, shouts, banners, greetings, idioms, addresses'.[7] This in turn produced Dickens's characteristically *direct* mode of address, that highly self-conscious narrative style described so accurately by Robert Garis as 'theatrical'.[8] And these two elements—the popular and the theatrical—are perhaps the key to understanding the various ways in which Dickens's novels have been appropriated and re-cycled by film and television.

It is worth remembering that the exploitation of Dickens's texts by other media began in his own lifetime with the stage. Pirated versions of the novels, scripted by hack dramatists and funded by theatrical impresarios, regularly appeared on the West End stage before Dickens had even written the final instalments. *The Cricket on the Hearth* held the record in this respect, turning up in no fewer than *eleven* stage versions in London alone within months of being published at Christmas 1845. According to F. Dubrez Fawcett, the Adelphi theatre virtually became 'a Dickensian repertory company'[9] so frequently did it adapt his work. Dickens had railed against this state of affairs in *Nicholas Nickleby*, when he had Nicholas meet a pirate adaptor responsible for having dramatized some 'two hundred and forty-seven novels':

> . . . you take the uncompleted books of living authors, fresh from their hands, wet from the press, cut, hack, and carve them to the powers and capacities of your actors and the capability of your theatres, finish unfinished works, hastily and crudely vamp up ideas not yet worked out by their original projector, but which have doubtless cost him many thoughtful days and sleepless nights. . . . Now, show me the distinction between such pilfering as this, and picking a man's pocket in the street. . . .[10]

The cap fitted one W. T. Moncrieff well enough for him to have replied with a manifesto-style declaration defending his work as an adaptor against what he described as Dickens's 'intemperate and vulgar caricature'.[11] Moncrieff was, of course, perfectly within his rights; *legally* there was nothing Dickens could do to protect his copyright. Eventually, he decided to make the best he could of the situation by giving his blessing to selected adaptations in return for a cut of the profits. Indeed, by Christmas 1846 there was even a suggestion that he might have been tailoring his novels for the stage in advance. Certainly *The Battle of Life*, Dickens's fourth 'Christmas Book', fell rather too neatly into three acts, and when it did reach the West End stage, Dickens himself significantly supervised the final rehearsals.

What is perhaps most instructive about this phase of theatrical adaptation is the brash, totally unself-conscious verve with which Dickens's texts were bowdlerized. There was no question of audiences in any sense paying to see dramatizations of the originals. West End managements were simply in the business of exploiting Dickens's peculiar hold on popular consciousness for a quick return. It was really a primitive kind of franchise system. As long as a production had 'Dickens' stamped on it, it was likely to make money and so the same novels could be endlessly re-adapted and re-cycled, now as comedy, now as melodrama, now as musical. This entrepreneurial opportunism was, of course, a perfect mirror-image of Victorian capitalism at its most self-confident. And this perhaps explains why there seems to have been an absence of any real critical debate about precisely *what* audiences were getting. It wouldn't have occurred to anyone to have worried over the kind of questions about 'authenticity' and 'faithfulness' to the originals that have come to dominate both academic and journalistic discussion of adaptation today.

Thus, when the fledgling cinema industry superseded theatre and music-hall as the single most important source of mass entertainment, it inherited a thoroughly liberal tradition of adaptation. Which was just as well since, as George Bluestone has argued:

An art whose limits depend on a moving image, mass audience, and industrial production, is bound to differ from an art whose limits depend on language, a limited audience and individual creation. In short, the filmed novel, in spite of certain resemblances, will inevitably become a different artistic entity from the novel on which it is based.[12]

Before 1914, however, Hollywood was largely prepared to follow the melodramatic penchant of the stage in its treatment of Dickens. D. W. Griffith's experiments with close-up in *The Cricket on the Hearth* in 1909 aside, the most important development was probably Vitagraph's 1911 'serial' version of *A Tale of Two Cities*. In 1918, however, an Englishman named Maurice Elvey began recruiting some of the West End stage's best-known serious actors for a silent based on *Dombey and Son*, to be directed by himself for Ideal Films. The resulting film stood out so much—making earlier Dickens adaptations seem primitive in comparison—that it established a *theatrical* preference among producers of Dickens, which would persist through into the television era and which is still discernible even today. This approach, linked as it was to more 'respectable' stage traditions, was reinforced in the 1920s as the cinema began to cater for a new kind of middle-class audience. It came into its own with the advent of sound. Yet the results were often stodgy, as in American Pathé's over-solemn version of *Oliver Twist* in 1933. What sound did prompt was greater realism, and the 1930s see a determined effort to develop an adequate Dickens *décor*. The sort of period rhetoric that now dominates all forms of costume drama made its first appearance in productions like George Cukor's *David Copperfield*, made in 1935 with minute attention to details of furniture, dress and design. Just how *ersatz* and wide of the mark such period 'authenticity' could be is well demonstrated by the fact that all the costumes for Cukor's film were modelled *exclusively* on the 'Phiz' illustrations that accompanied the original text. Inevitably, the whiff of caricature spilled over into the acting itself, producing precisely the reverse of what was intended: a stress on individual eccentricity at the expense of historical typicality. Similar problems continue to dog most television adaptations of Dickens.

A certain *style* of adaptation is, then, emerging: strongly theatrical, lingeringly melodramatic and much concerned with period detail. But it is important not to lose sight of the fact that all these films also radically *re-write* Dickens in their own terms. Jack Conway's 1935 version of *A Tale of Two Cities*, for instance, patently discovers its own imperatives in Dickens's text, re-encoding it in ways that work to limit its possible meanings in line with what made good inter-war box-office. Thus Dickens's French Revolutionary novel is broken down into three distinct codes, each of which roughly corresponds to a Hollywood genre—love story, adventure epic, historical romance. In the first, Ronald Colman's Carton anticipates nothing so much as Humphrey Bogart's performance seven years later in *Casablanca* as the man discovering salvation of a kind in his first purely selfless act; while in the second, Conway's direction revels in de Mille style crowd scenes backed by a grossly portentous score. The third, more difficult to pinpoint, mobilizes a period iconography to conjure with a certain nostalgic image of Victorian London, particularly in the picture-postcard Christmas scenes. All three are, of course, cleverly inscribed back into the framework of the original narrative, but the film's (considerable) pleasures remain largely generic. So much so that one almost suspects a hint of irony in the celebrated opening sequences when 'authenticity' is signalled by the first page of the novel being framed, turned by an invisible hand and then dissolved into the action.

After the war, the focus shifted from Hollywood to Britain, where the film industry was enjoying a brief international boom based on successful adaptations of quintessentially English works, such as Laurence Olivier's *Henry V* and the most influential Dickens adaptation ever made, David Lean's *Great Expectations*. Lean abandoned the long tradition of theatricalizing Dickens in favour of strong narrative line, controlled character acting and atmospheric period feel. In particular, though, the film was a triumph of framing, with Lean using the full scope of the screen to suggest an allusive, haunting power in the original way beyond the range of any merely 'theatrical' dramatization. The marsh scenes, which pick out, track and dwarf the frightened Pip against an immense and darkening sky are still among some of the most memorable in all cinema. Yet despite forging a filmic language which offered *equivalence* rather than replication, Lean's film is informed throughout by a quite precise reading and understanding of Dickens's text. Pip's story is not presented as the passage of an *ingénue*—as it had been in a Universal production in 1934—but as the history of a painful class translation. The film's famous 'unhappy' ending—suggesting that Pip's 'expectations' are illusory—reinforced this class reading[13] of the novel in a courageous and, as it turned out, enormously prescient way: the enthusiasm for post-war reconstruction, in which the film clearly shares, was already souring along traditional class lines even as it was being distributed in 1946. Lean's *Oliver Twist*, two years later, was similarly incisive when it came to the class structure of Victorian Britain, but less impressive visually and heavily dependent on forceful characterization for its effect. The previous year, Ealing had produced a far more lightweight version of Dickens in Alberto Cavalcanti's *Nicholas Nickleby*. Sadly, though, this post-war trio of adaptations marked the end of an era. From the 1950s onwards, television would increasingly come to dominate the adaptation industry. The cinema had come of age and no longer needed to lean on a literary tradition, if indeed it ever had.

In 1947, John Ford directed a version of Graham Greene's *The Power and the Glory* and felt no qualms at all about turning Greene's whisky-priest into a martyr-hero and the communist lieutenant who pursues him across Mexico—in the novel a model of celibacy in contrast to the priest—into a degenerate sadist. Television, on the other hand, was still in its infancy and radically uncertain of its own cultural status. It needed the 'respectability' and sense of tradition that classic literature could provide. But the B.B.C.'s Reithian brief also included a commitment to 'entertain' as well as 'educate' and 'inform'. Dickens, whose critical stock had never been higher, was an obvious candidate to do all three and has been ever since, with on average at least one new B.B.C. adaptation being produced every year for the past thirty years. Television also had every reason to believe that as a naturalistic medium it was better suited to adapting Dickens than film. With its emphasis on studio production, it could pay careful attention to that minute re-creation of period detail that was now felt to be essential to any successful adaptation. (In the event, this is precisely what happened. Deprived of the scope, range and scale of cinema, television fell back on a meticulous attention

to detail that issued in a dogged kind of historical literalism
from which, arguably, it has yet to recover.) Moreover, as a
domestic medium, television could *serialize* Dickens, thus
retaining an approximation to the novels' real-time in a way
that had never been possible in the cinema.[14] A further
advantage being that transmission on a week-to-week basis
would neatly re-create the conditions of serial publication
under which Dickens's novels were originally both produced
and consumed. As it turned out, this proved more difficult
than anticipated. True, Dickens's own 'cliffhangers' could be
used, but that still left the problem of pacing, of finding room
for each strand of a multi-plotted narrative in *every* episode.
However, after some unwieldy experiments in the early years,
adaptors quickly learnt how to, as it were, encode the novel's
whole structure in each episode, and the style that emerged
from what we might call this Reithian phase survived through
well into the 1970s.

Typified by its concern with history as decor and its
dependence on character acting, it is a style that has changed
hardly at all in twenty-five years, apart from obviously reflecting the various technical improvements in the quality of
videotape, lighting and design, from which all forms of television drama benefited during the same period. The way
adaptations were scheduled also greatly contributed to the
overall impression of stagnation. The early evening slot on a
Sunday on B.B.C. became something of a ghetto and the
'family serial' tag that went with it had important effects on
what *kind* of Dickens dramatists felt able to offer. Invariably,
and to some extent inevitably, the bias was heavily weighted
towards the novelist at his most optimistic—his darker side
rarely broke through—and the results were often mawkishly
sentimental. One became aware of just how neutered some of
these productions were when, in 1976, the more prestigious
'Classic Serial' slot on B.B.C.2 adapted the disturbing *Our
Mutual Friend* almost as a gothic-expressionist piece. This
B.B.C.2 programming strand had largely been developed in
response to the new impetus given to costume drama by the
advent of colour television in the late 1960s.[15] Using its bigger
budgets to produce ever more sumptuous period patinas, the
slot began to discover overseas markets for its serializations,

spectacularly so in the case of Galsworthy's *The Forsyte Saga*, which even sold in the Soviet Union. But as costs soared and the sums required to put costume drama into production became more and more prohibitive, both the B.B.C. and the I.T.V. companies began to look for co-producers and the 'up-front' money they could provide. They found both, by and large, among giant American corporations like Exxon and Mobil, who were willing to defray a proportion of the production costs either as a straightforward investment or simply as part of a public relations image-building exercise—hence the term 'prestige' drama.

This co-production phase,[16] which really dates from the mid-1970s, has on the whole had a damaging effect on the development of indigenous British television drama,[17] but in the case of the literary adaptation it genuinely does seem to have temporarily reinvigorated what had by common consent become a thoroughly moribund area of programme-making. As the present writer has commented elsewhere:

> What [had] developed out of it was the cultured soap opera, that episode by episode unfolding of a reassuring pattern of identification and resolution which hooks mass audiences while respectfully paying its dues to Literature.[18]

Like Hollywood in its heyday, television was content to find only what it was looking for in literary texts. And, to paraphrase John Ellis's highly suggestive argument,[19] what television specifically looks for is stories that can become series, narratives that lend themselves to segmentation. The result was a deadening homogeneity in which one Dickens adaptation tended to resemble nothing so much as another Dickens adaptation. What was missing was any sense of a work of *interpretation*. To adapt had come to mean nothing more than its most literal dictionary definition: 'to make to correspond' . . . to, of course, television's own imperatives. However, with more money available from co-production deals, writers and directors—working to less restrictive deadlines and budgets—began to become more adventurous. We've already noted how *Our Mutual Friend* boldly discovered a gothic strain in Dickens. Two years later, Granada Television's *Hard Times*, scripted by Arthur Hopcraft and co-produced with Exxon, intelligently cut through the naturalist rhetoric traditionally associated with tele-Dickens to offer its own highly specific *reading* of the novel:

> [A] lavish concern with detail—aided by large amounts of co-production capital and Granada's biggest-ever location set—pays homage to realism only to break with it in a number of significant ways. For if at one level a landscape of urban squalor is given all the presence and weight of an active force shaping the destiny of those who inhabit it, at another it is simultaneously made to display what this sheer presence necessarily *excludes*. We are, that is to say, asked to go beyond what we can actually 'see'.
>
> The non-naturalistic gestures of the circus performers, as they troop through the streets in the opening sequences, call into question the kind of society those streets represent long before their realistic presence has had time to establish itself. This mixing of narrative styles disrupts our passivity as viewers, forcing us into an active relation to what we see—we are immediately more prepared to *construct* the historical implications of Dickens's baldly stated attack on Victorian attitudes to industrialization.
>
> This consciously interpretive approach to adaptation extends to other areas of the production. There is, for instance, no attempt to make the weak sub-plot concerning Stephen Blackpool's refusal to join a trade union any more convincing than it is in the novel. Dickens's diatribe against organized labour so obviously contradicts the rest of his depiction of working-class life that its inconsistencies are rightly retained.[20]

Hard Times probably represents a highwater mark in television's treatment of Dickens. Most co-produced literary adaptations in the 1980s have been high-gloss affairs, less concerned with interpretive strategies than with 're-packaging' the original texts attractively enough for the global television market. Thus, Jonathan Powell no longer produces *Hard Times* but *The Woman in White*, a meticulously confected mid-Atlantic 'entertainment', slickly scripted by Ray Jenkins, a writer specially drafted in from work on more down-market drama series like *The Sweeney* and *Airline*, and positively luxuriating in lushly visual countryscapes that have traditional 'Englishness' stamped all over them. Granada themselves move on to *Brideshead Revisited* and—again with the aid of

Exxon, the world's biggest multinational—spend a reputed £9 million on recreating Waugh's nostalgic elegy for a lost England. In this kind of climate, where an economic drive towards globalizing the television product meets a socially-led boom in nostalgia generated by recession, it seems safe to predict that in future Dickens adaptations, too, will be heavily weighted towards the picturesque, the reassuring and the traditional.

Unless, that is, the televising of the Royal Shakespeare Company's stage production of David Edgar's remarkable version of *Nicholas Nickleby* by Channel 4 in late 1982 produces a radical re-think. (Unlikely, given appalling viewing figures in Britain, even though it did considerably better in the U.S. ratings.) Using a single multi-purpose set, very few props and the cast as a kind of narrative chorus, the R.S.C.'s *Nickleby* broke with naturalism in ways unfamiliar to audiences reared on the 'classic serial' approach to dramatizing Dickens. The chorus, in particular, manufactured an entirely novel effect by foregrounding Dickens's narrative voice in the manner of the book itself and allowing its storytelling energy, its sheer *fictiveness* to come through. This, coupled with the absence of a realistic set, helped to set up a critical distance between novel and adaptation, encouraging a more objective understanding of the original, especially in terms of the kind of contemporary resonances that so often become muffled by the aspic-like effects of television's characteristically over-literal attention to period detail. A more radical attempt to open up Dickens to contemporary realities was made in another 1982 project—a video version of *Hard Times* produced at London's Royal College of Art[21] with the aim of offering both a formal and political gloss on the novel's sub-title: *For These Times*. Opening with shots of British Rail's latest generation of passenger trains, which are to recur throughout, the film intercuts dramatized sequences from the novel with historical documentation and further images of contemporary Britain to produce a whole range of understandings and meaning *for* the text. Dissolves, for instance, show maps being cut into the narrative in a way that places Coketown within the global economy of Victorian capitalism as a whole; voice-over readings from the reports of nineteenth-century Royal Commissions on factory conditions link Dickens's characters to a real and tangible history; while the slightly heightened, stylized acting and unexpected camera angles work against the kind of reading that would want to see the novel merely as an inter-personal drama played out between characters we, as viewers, can identify with. The R.C.A.'s *Hard Times* is an uneven and at times confusing piece of work, but it is ambitious and it does show that there are other ways of adapting Dickens than simply *dramatizing* the novels. Yet as the product of a beleaguered independent sector—at the time of writing it had still to find a transmission slot—it is sadly likely to have minimal effect on how mainstream television tackles adaptation.

What this history illustrates perhaps most, I think, is the ability of film and television to assimilate, re-make and re-cycle any literary entity in their own image. Yet while this may alarm purists, concerned about a 'debasing' of Dickens's currency, it also has its positive side. Novels are not just inert texts with fixed meanings, but imaginative structures open all the time to new readings, new uses—and television, especially, clearly does make Dickens *usable* again to audiences who would not otherwise encounter him. That said, there remain genuine worries about what kind of 'Dickens' results. Not, it should be stressed, because what is on offer fails to measure up to some quintessentially 'real' Dickens—who, of course, does not exist—but because it opens out on to wider questions of history and its representation. For, by a curious kind of slippage, Dickens has come to stand for the whole Victorian era in popular memory, and this means that adaptations of his work are often perceived as offering unmediated access to Britain's past. In this context, the standard visual rhetoric of adaptation—the ahistorical use of period detail merely as an aesthetically-pleasing backdrop—begins to look distinctly irresponsible. Certainly, it does nothing to place Dickens in the kind of continuing historical development that would connect him up with the contemporary world in important and increasingly pressing ways. This anaesthetized version of the past is the historical equivalent of the predominantly sentimentalized readings that adaptations tend to mobilize at the aesthetic level, and the result of both is the same cosy, nostalgic frame of reference: safe, undisturbing, unchallenging. Moreover, in the case of British television, this displacement— away from the more unpalatable, political side of Dickens— has itself had the effect of displacing other kinds of pro- gramming. Adaptations, like all forms of costume drama, tend as we have seen to attract large amounts of co-production capital and have therefore begun to oust other forms of drama from our screens, particularly the single play. Co-produced Dickens fits into the global television market in a way that the more indigenous single play, with its traditionally incisive concern with reflecting contemporary Britain, clearly does not. It is often said that were Dickens alive today his interest in contemporaneity, in providing society with a kind of instant image of itself, would have led him to work in television. But given that his concern with the present was also intimately bound up with understanding its past, I'm not so sure. More likely he would have been appalled to discover that television was using his work to deflect attention away from both history *and* contemporaneity. Which, in a sense, returns us to where we began, because if literary criticism refuses to get involved in this kind of debate, this contention over contemporary mean- ing, over what Dickens represents and how he in turn is represented, then it tacitly acknowledges that he has no importance outside the academy. And in the light of the crowded history outlined above, of perhaps no other writer could that be less true.

NOTES

1. Cited in Martin Williams, *Griffith: First Artist of the Movies* (Oxford, 1980), p. 35.
2. Sergei Eisenstein, 'Dickens, Griffith and Film Today', in *Film Form*, ed. and trans. by Jay Leyda (London, 1959), p. 198.
3. Op. cit., p. 195.
4. Ibid., p. 207.
5. Ibid., p. 206.
6. Cited in Edgar Johnson, *Charles Dickens, His Tragedy and His Triumph* (Penguin edn.), p. 109.

7. Raymond Williams, 'Introduction' to *Dombey and Son* (Penguin edn.), p. 15.
8. Robert Garis, *The Dickens Theatre* (Oxford, 1965), p. 24.
9. F. Dubrez Fawcett, *Dickens the Dramatist* (London, 1952), p. 74.
10. Charles Dickens, *Nicholas Nickleby* (Dent, Everyman edn.), p. 644.
11. Fawcett, op. cit., p. 50.
12. George Bluestone, *Novels into Film* (Baltimore, 1957), pp. 63–4.
13. Ray Durgnat went so far as to describe *Great Expectations* as 'a classic marxist fable about bourgeois confusion', *A Mirror for England* (London, 1970), p. 22.
14. After, that is, Erich Von Stroheim's disastrous *Greed* in 1923, a version of Frank Norris's naturalist novel *McTeague*, which at some twenty hours ran considerably longer than a reading of the text itself would have taken.
15. '. . . dresses that had formerly been mere shades of grey burst into elegant hues, backgrounds took on a new brilliance'—Shaun Sutton, *The Largest Theatre in the World: Thirty Years of Television Drama* (London, 1982), p. 35.
16. The best analysis of television co-production is still Michael Pilsworth's 'Buddy Can You Spare A Dime', *Sight & Sound*, Winter 1979–80, 51–3.
17. See Carl Gardner and John Wyver, 'The Single Play: From Reithian Reverence to Cost-accounting and Censorship', *Edinburgh International Television Festival 1980—Official Programme*, pp. 47–52.
18. Mike Poole, 'Englishness for Export', *Time Out*, 7–13 March 1980, p. 13.
19. John Ellis, *Visible Fictions* (London, 1982), p. 116.
20. Mike Poole, 'The Floss on the Mill', *Time Out*, 16–22 March 1979, pp. 16–17.
21. Produced and directed by Iain Bruce, Nick Dubrule and Ross Keith.

8

Circulation, Interchange, Stoppage: Dickens and Social Progress

by DAVID TROTTER

Collecting your thoughts about Dickens can be a tricky business. Characters you had supposed for years to belong to one novel turn up in another. Or, what is even worse, turn up in several—there is a youth with one fixed eye and one revolving eye who must have half-a-dozen incarnations. Themes, incidents and mannerisms not only recur, but become more memorable for their similarities than for their differences. The best studies of Dickens, like John Carey's *Violent Effigy*, acknowledge this by treating the entire sequence of novels as a single, diffuse text.

To put it another way, Dickens's strengths as a writer are incidental to the literary strategies which confer unity and singularity on a novel: plot, the representation of inner life, symbolism. He deployed these strategies ostentatiously enough, but often wrote best when ignoring them. Something else shapes and fires his work, and we read him because of the something else.

'It has occurred to me that I am rather strong on Voyages and Cannibalism', Dickens once told W. H. Wills (letter of 20 November 1854). He was also rather strong on corpses and molten lava and ship-shape cubicles, among other things, as

Carey has shown; and it was these vivid obsessions which—independently of plot or inner life or symbolism—provoked his best writing.

Carey concludes from the intensity of such obsessions that Dickens's creative impulse was essentially anarchic, and that we should therefore value him as an 'imaginative writer' rather than as a 'critic of society'. The distinction seems to me far too neat. What counts in the novels is usually the vivid obsession; but Dickens was vividly obsessed by banks and lawyers as well as by cannibals and conflagrations.

One proof of that enthralment by the social is his journalism and his magisterial editing of *Household Words* and *All the Year Round*. An important element in both journals was what he called the 'process' article: vivid, detailed accounts of manufacturing process. He relished the sheer activity of an industrial nation. He also wrote and commissioned many articles on what one might call 'social process', on the systems which sustain and regulate the activity of an industrial nation: banks, post offices, police forces, libraries and so on. These, too, caught his imagination.

For Dickens social process was, like Mr. Veneering, a 'veiled prophet, not prophesying'. Banks and post offices function; they do not declare a meaning. Yet we are tempted by the possibility that they might make a sign, that a pattern or principle might stir behind the veil. What Dickens saw moving behind the veil of social process was not a theory but a metaphor, an intimation of meaning which never became explicit, and thus never stopped drawing him back to interpret afresh.

My limited aim in this essay is to show how a particular metaphor informed Dickens's imagining of social process, and how that imagining itself informed the portrayal of character in novels he wrote immediately prior to or during his editorship of *Household Words* (1850–59): *Dombey and Son, David Copperfield, Bleak House, Hard Times, Little Dorrit*. Earlier or later novels and essays are by no means irrelevant to my theme, but I have preferred to concentrate on those in which the veiled prophet came closest to prophesying.

During the Great Exhibition of 1851, Dickens and Richard Horne wrote a piece for *Household Words* contrasting the wonders of the Crystal Palace with the quaintness of an accompanying display of artefacts from China. 'It is very curious to have the Exhibition of a people who came to a dead stop, Heaven knows how many hundreds of years ago, side by side with the Exhibition of the moving world' (5 July 1851). In their eyes, England and China represented the extremes of progress and reaction, movement and stagnancy: 'England, maintaining commercial intercourse with the whole world; China, shutting itself up, as far as possible, within itself.'

What interests me is the criterion of progress put forward by Dickens and Horne. England communicates with the world, and prospers. Its prosperity depends on a flow of goods and information within and beyond its borders; in short, on what they call 'interchange'. China shuts itself up within itself, refusing interchange, blocking the flow of goods and information. To compare China with England is to compare 'Stoppage' with 'Progress'.

No one, apparently, had told the Chinese about Free Trade, a doctrine triumphant in England since the Repeal of the Corn Laws in 1846. Dickens and Horne insisted that the Tories, who in 1851 had not yet shaken off the label of Protectionism, were trying to turn the country into another China. *Household Words* advocated the extension of free-trading as widely as possible throughout the world. One article attacked the Hudson Bay Company for preventing exploitation of the land under its control, and thus 'stopping the way for labour and capital'. In the writer's view, the Company might just as well have placed a huge 'NO THOROUGHFARE' sign across rivers and highways (7 January 1854). When Dickens and his colleagues talked of stoppage, they had something pretty concrete in mind. They meant that the channels through which goods and information should flow had been blocked.

It was the flow of money, one contributor said, which ensured that commercial interchange would proceed 'without unwieldy jerks or blank full-stops' (17 May 1856). When Dickens and Wills visited the Bank of England, they marvelled at 'the mighty heart of active capital, through whose arteries and veins flows the entire circulating medium of this great country' (6 July 1850). It was this metaphor of the circulation of blood which Dickens saw behind the veil of social process, this metaphor which articulated his enthralment with the 'great country' he lived in. He took the pulse of the great country. Instances of circulation and of stoppage excited him deeply.

However, it was the flow of information rather than the flow of commerce which came to obsess him during the 1850s. The British economy was expanding. But ignorance and mal-administration appeared continually to block the interchange of ideas, subjecting the most prosperous nation in the world to many an unwieldy jerk, and to the blank full-stop of the Crimean War. Dickens's views on the remedy, on the need for general education and administrative reform, are well known. Here I shall simply emphasize the insistence of the metaphor of circulation.

'Knowledge is the life-blood of Genius', declared an article in *Household Words*, 'and must, where it can, be spread and circulated' (28 September 1850). Knowledge was to be spread by education and by freedom of speech. Without these benefits, nations would either stagnate (as China had) or suffer revolution (as France had in 1789 and most of Europe had in 1848). Henry Morley thought 'political restrictions' rather than 'social evil' the cause of revolution; ideas and resentments damned-up when they should flow freely will eventually burst their bounds (16 November 1850). *A Tale of Two Cities* clearly subscribes to this anxiety, which Dickens felt throughout the 1850s. *Household Words* frequently attacked the political restrictions imposed by continental states—Dickens himself made a point of cursing the Austrian Police with 'extraordinary heartiness' (letter of 25 January 1854 to Shirley Brooks)—while advocating the general education and freedom of speech which would ensure progress at home and abroad. 'Free to think, and free to trade, Spain may become some of these days; she may have railways in abundance, then, and circulate rich blood through all her arteries' (13 September 1851).

Britain enjoyed a little freedom of thought and a lot of railways. Even so, bureaucratic stoppage brought misery to whole classes and ruin to individuals like William Barber, a solicitor who had been wrongly convicted of fraud, transported

166

for life and after much delay pardoned. Barber's assertion of his innocence had been ignored by two Home Secretaries, and Dickens considered this a 'tremendous illustration' of the inefficiency of aristocratic politicians who 'receive Memorials from innocent men in the agony of supposed guilt . . . put them away in drawers, and never so much as read them' (letter of 2 February 1849 to Macready). Barber had a lot to say about his innocence, and about the time he had spent as a convict. But Dickens fastened on an issue of little interest to Barber himself, and found for it a concrete image: the letter put away in a drawer.

When outrage at the incompetent handling of the Crimean War led to the founding of an Administrative Reform Association, Dickens was quick to subscribe; he spoke at a meeting in the Drury Lane Theatre on 27 June 1855. The Association aimed to expose the absues which had 'locked' the machinery of government and 'clogged the public departments with incapacity' (*First Report of the General Committee*, 8 August 1855). By way of illustration Dickens invented the Circumlocution Office, a department which always has it in hand

> to send a mail or two which was in danger of going straight to its destination, beating about the seas like the Flying Dutchman, and to arrange with complexity for the stoppage of a good deal of important business otherwise in peril of being done. (*Little Dorrit*, Bk. 1, Ch. 34)

The Circumlocution Office over-produces information, but this flow of memos and statements is so narrowly circular that it blocks the administrative system as effectively as the Home Secretary's drawer. (The Court of Chancery works in the same way, over-producing documents and circulating them among a closed group of lawyers.)

But Dickens was also excited by the *successful* interchange of ideas, and thus by two recent innovations, the Penny Post and the Electric Telegraph. In these systems the metaphor of circulation came alive. When the Penny Post was introduced in December 1839, it led to a huge increase in the number of letters mailed. *Household Words* celebrated the achievement handsomely, covering every aspect of the postal service right down to the kind of gum used on stamps. In the first issue

Dickens and Wills set the tone by absorbing the spectacle of the General Post-Office at St. Martin's-le-Grand:

> those enormous chambers, each with its hundreds of sorters busy over their hundreds of thousands of letters . . . those silent receptacles of countless millions of passionate words, for ever pouring through them like a Niagara of language, and leaving not a drop behind. (30 March 1850)

The post was exciting not only because of its scope and efficiency, but also because of its content: the mixture of ideas and emotions, commercial data and private confidences, which passed through it. For the health of the nation depended on the flow of information *and* the flow of feeling. One sign of an unhealthy nation would be the primitive nature of its postal service, with China once more the example: 'The letter bearers perform their journey at a gentle trot; being lightly clad and burdened only with a small umbrella, and a wallet thrown across the shoulders' (14 April 1855).

Perhaps the most excited article of all was written by Dickens himself, about a plan to close provincial post offices on Sundays. This, he said, would be like closing the London post offices on a working day, and

> the stoppage of Monday's Post Delivery in London would stop, for many precious hours, the natural flow of the blood from every vein and artery in the world, and its return from the heart through all those tributary channels. (22 June 1850)

It would have as terrible an effect as the Sabbatarian proposal to make Sundays 'a day of mortification and gloom' by banning all activity except worship. Working people would become bitterly resentful about such restrictions. 'Too tight a hand in these respects, is certain to engender a disposition to break loose, and to run riot.' That Dickens should sweep passionately from one minor example of stoppage to another, and then to the prospect of revolution, shows how much weight he attached to the metaphor of circulation. It also shows that a detail like the gloom of the Sunday on which Arthur Clennam returns to London must be regarded not as literary atmosphere or as irrelevant didacticism, but as an imagining of social process.

The Electric Telegraph proved almost as compelling an

embodiment of circulation and progress (it figured prominently on the British stands at the Great Exhibition). An article described how the 'electro-galvanic fluid' generated by batteries was sent on its 'eternal round through wire and earth', 'the interruption of which is to set the needle in motion, that messages may be read' (7 December 1850). Writing to Mrs. Richard Watson on 13 January 1854 about his recent continental tour, Dickens remarked that few things he saw had taken his fancy so much as 'the Electric Telegraph, piercing like a sunbeam, right through the cruel old heart of the Coliseum of Rome'. Instances of circulation, as well as instances of stoppage, found a vivid and concrete image.

It would not reduce Dickens's politics too absurdly to say that he was for circulation and against stoppage, and not at all afraid of the literal application of the metaphor to everyday life. He thought that the lives of the poor could only be made tolerable by the proper circulation of air and water. He was sickened by physical blockage, by enclosed congested spaces in the centre of the city, like Smithfield Cattle Market or urban graveyards (1,117 corpses per acres, according to *Household Words*, giving off 55.261 cubic feet of noxious gases per acre per year). He wrote an article fiercely criticizing Smithfield as a cause of massive inconvenience, danger and brutality to animals (4 May 1850). In *Great Expectations*, Pip wanders through it, 'and the shameful place, being all asmear with filth and fat and blood and foam, seemed to stick to me'.

But such physical applications of the metaphor, however important to Dickens's politics, do not really tell in the novels. In *Bleak House*, the subject of urban burial provokes him to anger rather than to memorable expression. The metaphor articulates the novels at a slightly abstract level, at the level of social rather than physical process. Thus the 'perpetual stoppage' of the fashionable Dedlock world connects more readily with the perpetual stoppage of Chancery than with the perpetual stoppage of the graveyard near Tom-All-Alone's. Character is often and strikingly defined by an intervention in the flow of ideas and data which constitutes social process. The Circumlocution Office, Gowan and the Merdles are all part of the same evil, Dickens said of *Little Dorrit*.

*   *   *

At a table in the post office visited by Dickens and Wills sat a 'hawk-eyed gentleman' whose job was to apply his 'hieroglyphic powers' to the decipherment of unintelligible addresses. Many letters would go astray were it not for his ability to discern the writer's intention, and thus the correct identity of the addressee. Unintelligibility could be seen as a kind of stoppage, since it blocked the passage of information from sender to receiver. That passage, so crucial to the health of the nation, could only be ensured by a considerable hermeneutic activity. Clerks operating the Electric Telegraph, for example, had to be skilled interpreters of the 'mystic alphabet' of the signals, the 'electric A,B,C' (7 December 1850).

Semantic stoppage engrossed Dickens. The metaphor of circulation which had catalysed his imagining of social process made unintelligibility (or mystery) an object of compelling horror. The worst and most exciting evil was that which kept people apart by obscuring what they said to one another. For Dickensian mystery is not just a literary device, an ignorance dispelled by the unfolding of the plot. He knew all about that, of course, and once advised the great virtuoso of literary mystery, Wilkie Collins, to strengthen the interest of a story by making its development 'a little more obscure' (letter of 19 March 1855). But the mystery in his own books derives its power less from a play on the credulity of the reader than from an imagining of social process.

Dickensian mystery takes root in people and institutions and landscapes. Think of the lawyer Tulkinghorn, in *Bleak House*. 'His calling', says Lady Dedlock, 'is the acquisition of secrets, and the holding possession of such powers as they give him, with no sharer or opponent in it' (Ch. 36). Tulkinghorn's vocation, his very being, is secrecy. He neither explains anything, nor is explained. He represents a NO THOROUGHFARE sign, a block to the hermeneutic activity on which the moving world depends for its movement.

In Dickens's books the secretive secrete. Like a gland, they extract matter from the bloodstream of society, remove ideas and feelings from circulation. And the matter they have extracted stagnates and festers in its hiding-places. It becomes a growth, a mould, a bad smell. On his way to visit his mother,

Arthur Clennam passes through dim streets which seem like 'depositories of oppressive secrets':

> The deserted counting-houses, with their secrets of books and papers locked up in chests and safes; the banking-houses, with their secrets of strong rooms and wells, the keys of which were in a very few secret pockets and a very few secret breasts; . . . the secrets of the lonely church-vaults, where the people who had hoarded and secreted in iron coffers were in their turn similarly hoarded, not yet at rest from doing harm. . . . (Bk. 2, Ch. 10)

We feel that it will take bulldozers and gallons of disinfectant, rather than a mere twist of the plot, to clear these secrets.

Dickens thrilled in particular to the idea of a gland secreting from the nation's commercial bloodstream. His banks and offices usually contain a functionary or an inner recess of spectacular mouldiness: the 'musty chambers' in the Bank of England where records of the National Debt are stored; the strong room in Dombey's office which looks like the cavern of an ocean monster; the mildewed clerks in Tellson's Bank.

In vivid contrast to these depositories of secrecy stands the bank above which the Gowans live in Venice. It contains two clerks ('like dried dragoons, in green velvet caps adorned with golden tassels'), an empty safe and a jug of water. Not a secret in sight, not a whiff of mildew. The clerks produce 'exhaustless mounds of five-franc pieces' merely by 'dipping their hands out of sight' (Bk. 2, Ch. 6). In the context of the novel, this Venetian bank becomes an image of natural interchange, almost of fertility.

But secretive Britain demanded stronger remedies. From *Bleak House* onwards, Dickens began to introduce characters whose function was not simply to resolve mysteries, but to enact the resolution of mystery; not simply to interpret, but to embody the hermeneutic activity on which social process depends. We can define their function against that of an unofficial resolver of mysteries, Mr. Nadgett in *Martin Chuzzlewit*. Nagdett is employed by the Anglo-Bengalee Disinterested Loan and Life Assurance Company to make enquiries. His hieroglyphic powers are formidable, and he tracks Jonas Chuzzlewit to and from the murder of Montague Tigg, thus bringing the story to a resolution.

171

Yet Nadgett's role in society is as ambiguous as that of the company which employs him. Secrecy is his 'ruling passion', and he deeply regrets having to make public what he has discovered about Jonas. Furthermore, he is strangely dried up, as though he has 'secreted his very blood'; and he short-circuits the postal system by writing letters, putting them into a 'secret place' in his coat, and delivering them to himself several weeks later, 'very much to his own surprise, quite yellow' (Ch. 27). Such an ardent secreter may dispel an occasional mystery when it suits him, but can hardly be trusted to do so in a regular and purposeful manner. Nadgett is no more an agent of circulation and interchange than Tulkinghorn.

What was needed to turn an unofficial 'informer' like Nadgett into an official hermeneut like the hawk-eyed gentleman at the post office was the establishment in 1842 of the Detective Police. Dickens seized on (or perhaps invented) the hermeneutic prowess of the Detective Department of the Metropolitan Police, and made it a major theme of *Household Words*. The Department's brief, according to Wills, was to combat crime and clear up 'family mysteries' (13 July 1850).

Further articles such as Dickens's 'A Detective Police Party' (27 July and 10 August 1850) built up an image of bluff, shrewd, respectable, middle-aged men with phenomenal powers of observation and interpretation. Dickens was convinced that each detective arriving for the party immediately took a silent inventory of the furniture and 'an accurate sketch of the editorial presence'. To him and Wills thief-taking looked like a science, and detectives were chiefly notable for the impersonal way in which they compressed 'marvellous' and 'romantic' adventures into 'the set phrase, "in consequence of information I received, I did so and so"'. Unlike the informer Nadgett, these men were integrated into society; their ruling passion was to make public what they had discovered, and so ensure the free flow of information.

In this respect, their role found analogies. George Sala wrote a piece about the canvassers or 'finders-out' who compiled names and addresses for that majestic aid to circulation, the *Post-Office London Directory*. The finder-out described by Sala bears a striking resemblance to the detectives described by his colleagues. He is bluff, shrewd, respectable, middle-aged, 'taciturn in responsion, but voluble in interrogation'. Like the detective sketching the editorial presence, he becomes 'a silent daguerreotypist, for ever taking your portrait in his printed camera' (9 December 1854). What emerges from these articles is a type which includes policemen and canvassers, and which is defined by its hermeneutic function. The magazine had found an answer to institutionalized mystery.

One of the most notable contributors to *Household Words*, Elizabeth Gaskell, was quick to spot the implications for the novelist of this newly created type. In a piece about mysterious disappearances, she described how a relative of hers who kept changing his address had eventually been tracked down with the help of a bluff, shrewd, respectable, middle-aged detective. She suggested that the imperturbable omniscience of such men had in effect removed 'the materials of pursuit and evasion' from 'the store-house of the romancer'. In Godwin's *Caleb Williams* the man whose privacy is invaded by Caleb sets off after the culprit himself.

> Now, in 1851, the offended master would set the Detective Police to work; there would be no doubt as to their success . . . It is no longer a struggle between man and man, but between a vast organised machinery, and a weak, solitary, individual; we have no hopes, no fears—only certainty. (7 June 1851).

Detectives were, of course, soon to be individualized, and the materials of pursuit returned to the store-house of the romancer. But we should not underestimate the appeal of hermeneutic certainty for a writer as alert to social process, and as disheartened by the stoppage of the 1850s, as Dickens was. Mr. Bucket, in *Bleak House*, does credit to the image of the Detective Police promoted by *Household Words*. He clearly belongs to a 'vast organised machinery', and his hieroglyphic powers are trained on the secrecy which threatens to bring the moving world to a halt. Nothing can resist them, not even Sir Leicester Dedlock's half-paralysed mumble, which he deciphers with astonishing 'velocity and certainty'.

Taciturn in responsion, voluble in interrogation, Bucket has a habit of putting words into other people's mouths. 'You're a man of the world, you know,' he tells Snagsby, 'and a man of

business, and a man of sense. That's what *you* are' (Ch. 22).
He displays a great 'fondness for society' and 'adaptability to
all grades'. He is a kindly man, treating Sir Leicester and
Esther Summerson with compassion, and adjusting the hand-
cuffs on George Rouncewell 'like a most respectable trades-
man, anxious to execute an order neatly, and to the perfect
satisfaction of his customer' (Ch. 49). Bucket's calling involves
the decipherment both of clues and of states of mind. He
ensures the flow of information by his hieroglyphic powers,
and the flow of compassion by his attentiveness to feeling
under inauspicious circumstances.

In *Little Dorrit*, Bucket's role is taken by Pancks, Mr.
Casby's rent-collector. Pancks tracks down Mr. Dorrit's
inheritance, showing 'a sagacity that nothing could baffle, and
a patience and secrecy that nothing could tire' (Bk. 1, Ch. 35).
He, too, secretes in order to make public. He shares Bucket's
kindliness, sociability and speech-habits (for example, when
talking to Casby in Book 1, Chapter 13). He is more fallible
than Bucket, persuading Clennam to invest in Merdle's ill-
fated bubble company. But since he is always compared to a
tug propelling larger and clumsier vessels, we can assume that
he is on the side of the moving world.

Pancks was followed by Wemmick in *Great Expectations*,
although here the role is vestigial, having perhaps lost some of
its urgency for Dickens. Wemmick does not dispel any
mysteries, but there is one episode in the novel whose main
effect is to link him with Bucket and Wemmick: the visit to
Newgate in Chapter 32. In Newgate, Wemmick acquires for
the first and only time Bucket's attentiveness, adaptability to
all grades and speech-habits (' "No, no," said Wemmick coolly,
"*you* don't care" '). Another detail which connects him with
the detectives at the Police party is his belief that last-minute
confessions by criminals are 'every one of 'em Lies, Sir'
(Ch. 25).

Wemmick is more like Pancks than Bucket. For the type did
evolve, as Dickens lost interest (or faith) in the scientific
expertise of a vast organized machinery. But its ascendancy
during much of the 1850s shows how seriously he took the
social problem of unintelligibility.

*　　　*　　　*

In Dickens's story 'Hunted Down', published in *All the Year Round* (4 and 11 August 1860), a villainous conman is brought to justice by the combined efforts of Meltham, the lover of one of his victims, and Sampson, Chief Manager of a Life Assurance Office. The romance-hero owes the success of his individual struggle to the hermeneutic prowess of a hawk-eyed gentleman. For a glass partition separates Sampson's office from the reception-area, 'in order that I might derive my first impression of strangers who came to us on business, from their faces alone, without being influenced by anything they said'. Through this instrument Sampson trains his hieroglyphic powers on the villain's face, and immediately becomes suspicious. (Although he might just as profitably have trained them on the villain's name, Julius Slinkton.)

The episode reminds us that physiognomy—the art of distinguishing character in facial and bodily features—was crucial both to Dickens's imagining of social process and to his portrayal of character. Nature's writing, he claimed in *Household Words*, 'as it may be read in the human countenance, is invariably legible, if we come at all trained to the reading of it' (14 June 1856). Detective and finder-out sought evidence of personality in the likenesses they took; and there are dozens of characters in Dickens's novels on whom they might have practised their art.

However, even the most skilful interpreter would have made hard work of those characters whose ruling passion is secrecy, and who consequently achieve a degree zero of expression. Tulkinghorn stalks through aristocratic mansions 'making no sign' (Ch. 48). He is as unlikely to reveal the secrets of his soul as he is those of his clients and victims.

Mrs. Clennam's 'immovable face' keeps *her* secret, and indicates that she is 'beyond the reach of changing emotions' (Bk. 1, Ch. 4). It has 'no thread of relaxation in it, by which any explorer could have been guided to the gloomy labyrinth of her thoughts'. She sits gazing at the fire with 'the impenetrability of an old Egyptian sculpture' (Bk. 1, Ch. 5). The dead cultures of the orient provided the Victorian mind with emblems of enigma, while the European explorers who penetrated them became equally powerful emblems of hermeneutic prowess. One of the churches in the secretive area around

Mrs. Clennam's house is said to be awaiting discovery by Giovanni Belzoni, an explorer whose achievements had already been described in *Household Words* (1 March 1851). Dickens referred to his friend Austen Layard, a noted orientalist, as the man who 'brought to light the hidden memorials of a long extinct people' (speech to the Commercial Travellers' Schools, 22 December 1859). Not even Belzoni or Layard, we infer, could have penetrated to the gloomy labyrinth of Mrs. Clennam's thoughts. Layard, incidentally, was one of the chief Parliamentary critics of the Government's handling of the Crimean War and a moving spirit in the Administrative Reform Association. We can glimpse here connections between the different kinds of impenetrability—physiognomic, cultural, bureaucratic—which preoccupy the novel.

But physiognomy also connects with another of Dickens's themes: the circulation of feeling through love and compassion. Arthur Clennam's upbringing had forced him to secrete and deny feeling (the 'locked-up wealth of his affection and imagination'). Then he met Flora Casby: 'That wealth had been, in his desert home, like Robinson Crusoe's money; exchangeable with no one, lying idle in the dark to rust, until he poured it out for her' (Bk. 1, Ch. 13). Dickens's heroes and heroines are usually obliged to hoard their love until the very last moment, when a ceremony of mutual recognition enables them to pour it out for the right person, to put it into circulation.

The basic medium of exchange of feeling is expression. As Sir Charles Bell remarked in his *Anatomy and Philosophy of Expression*, which Dickens certainly knew, 'expression is to passion what language is to thought'; it speaks our feelings, and thus determines how other people will respond to us. 'It is expression which raises affection, which dwells pleasantly or painfully in the memory.' Dickens's characters are so regularly and so inflexibly attracted or repelled by expression that they might almost be following the code outlined by Edmund Ollier in an article on 'Faces'. Ollier maintained that whenever one's attention is drawn to the lower parts of a face, the face is 'bad'; when the reverse happens, the face is 'good' (16 September 1854). A comparison between the effect of Carker's teeth or Rigaud's moustache, and that of Little Dorrit's eyes or Lucie Manette's forehead, might have proved his point.

Villains can at least be distinguished by the repulsive lower halves of their faces, and avoided. The most disquieting presences are not the villains, but the people who cannot be interpreted at all, who confound the physiognomic code. Tulkinghorn and Mrs. Clennam, making no sign, fall into this category. So do those few women in the later novels who are fully conscious of their sexuality.

Dickens tended to allow a consciousness of sexuality only to women in their prime (Edith Dombey, Rosa Dartle, Lady Dedlock, Miss Wade), or to women who mature too rapidly (Louisa Gradgrind, Fanny Dorrit, Estella). The ripeness of these women's bodies distinguishes them from the incorporeal child-brides, and from the refrigerated or sandpapered flesh of the harridans and bustling matrons. However, their embodied and recognized sexuality prevents them from entering into any 'proper' exchange of feeling. They either secrete the memory of some earlier, abortive exchange (Rosa, Miss Wade), or undertake a loveless marriage (Edith, Louisa, Fanny, Estella), or do both (Lady Dedlock). The consciousness of a sexuality they can neither enjoy nor escape remains to torment and divide them. They do not know whether they want to be ignored or desired.

That divided consciousness interferes with the physiognomic code on which the circulation of feeling depends. The women's faces speak in two languages: a decorous public language, which indicates that they don't care what people feel about them, and an enigmatic private language, which indicates that they strongly object to what people feel about them. The observer is confronted by a baffling alternation between languages.

Dickens once accused Emily Jolly of making the heroine of a story 'too convulsive' (letter of 30 May 1857), but no heroine ever convulsed to greater effect than Edith Dombey. Sometimes she maintains an impassive hauteur, sometimes she rages (her bosom heaves, her nostrils quiver, her head trembles). Dombey, who first sees her in impassive mood, thinks that her hauteur will complement his own nicely; Carker, who first sees her in convulsive mood, thinks that her enigmatic passion will answer his. Both men are baffled by her switching from a language they can recognize to one they can't.

177

But it was the enigmatic private languages of these women which really caught Dickens's imagination. In her convulsive moods, Edith seems to want to score her body, to damage it as an index of feeling and a screen for the signs which attract men like Dombey. Red stigmata appear on her white skin where she has clawed her breast or dragged a bracelet around her arm 'until the white limb showed a bar of red' (Ch. 40). These gestures are meant to stamp the body with enigma, and so disrupt the physiognomic code which would draw her into an exchange of feeling.

No body in Dickens's novels is marked more indelibly than Rosa Dartle's. A scar inflicted by Steerforth, whom she had once loved, cuts down through her lips. When she turns pale with anger, the scar becomes 'a dull, lead-coloured streak, lengthening out to its full extent, like a mark in invisible ink brought to the fire'. It starts forth 'like the old writing on the wall' (Ch. 20). The scar speaks through a medium designed to conceal or to amaze rather than to communicate. It stamps her face with enigma, breaks up the site of expression.

The spasms which punctuate Lady Dedlock's customary hauteur are quite as enigmatic. They pass away 'like the features of those long-preserved dead bodies sometimes opened up in tombs, which, struck by the air like lightning, vanish in a breath' (Ch. 29). Again the orient proposes an emblem of enigma. Layard's *Discoveries in the Ruins of Nineveh and Babylon* (1853), which Dickens owned, included several examples of this phenomenon, as no doubt did his conversation. But even the great orientalist could not have done much with evidence which decomposed at the moment of its appearance. Of such duration and intelligibility was the evidence of sexual consciousness.

In this essay I have tried to look at what Dickens did without the strategies of plot and inner life and symbolism, rather than at what he did with them. One of the things he did without them was to enable a metaphoric apprehension of social process to shape and animate character. In his novels stoppage took the form of unintelligibility, and circulation came to depend on the exercise of hieroglyphic powers. The strength of this transference can be seen both in the vivid detail it provoked and in the scope of the connections established between different kinds of behaviour. A culture such as our own, which is not generous in its provision for the imagining of social process, would be foolish to lose sight of this astonishing achievement, either among Dickens's other qualities or among the qualities of other novelists.

9

The Other Portion of *Bleak House*

by BERT G. HORNBACK

In his recent book on *Dickens and the Science of Criticism*, Bill
Stumps demonstrates brilliantly that *Oliver Twist* is an ana-
gram for *Sir Love Twit*, that *The Old Curiosity Shop* was Dickens's
loving, laughing recollection of his days at Oxford with all the
other fellows, that *Bleak House* is but an ironic title for an
essentially comic novel, and that *The Mystery of Edwin Drood* is
a mystery *by* Edwin Drood, and thus either not by Dickens at
all, or if it is by Dickens, then written in the persona of Edwin
Drood who disappears half-way through the novel in order to
foreshadow the modern fictional technique of obscured narration.

Bill Stumps has made his mark by speculating always from
the outside, and I must admit—grudgingly—that he has done
significant work. I have always written about books I have
read, and have tried to be faithful to the spirit of what their
authors wrote, and to elucidate their meanings when I could.
But Stumps has convinced me otherwise. And as Stumps cites
Mr. Pickwick as his model practitioner of the Science of
Criticism, so I cite Bill Stumps as mine, and propose to discuss
in this essay the other portion of *Bleak House*, or the part that
Esther never wrote.

You will recall that Esther Summerson begins her narrative,
in the third chapter of *Bleak House*, with reference to writing

her 'portion of these pages' (62). It would be easy enough, if one had read the novel—or even if one had read the two chapters preceding this third—to presume that 'these pages' is a curious reference to the novel itself, and that the other portion of *Bleak House* must be the portion written by the omniscient narrator. But surely there is another possibility: surely Esther could be referring to what she has herself not written, and suggesting that there is yet another portion of the novel which nobody has written at all.

Dickens never writes 'whodunnit' types of mysteries, and in *Bleak House* we know who murders Tulkinghorn as well as we know who marries Esther near the end. But this is not to say that Dickens doesn't tease us with mystery, or mysteries, or that what we don't know isn't just as important as what we do know. If Mr. Snagsby is the hero of *Bleak House*, it is precisely because he is keeping his secret so well. And he can keep that secret because he doesn't know what it is. Similarly, what is most significant about little Jo is that he 'don't know nothink'; otherwise, he is—as the omniscient narrator tells us—not worth our attention. What is important about Mr. Krook is that, like Jo, he is illiterate, and thus can't read all of those papers and documents he has collected. Tulkinghorn, 'an Oyster of the old school, whom nobody can open' (182), locks up everything he knows in his file boxes, thus keeping what he knows safely out of circulation. Bucket, wisely, is a fool, and can be counted on to chase the wrong man, or to drive off in the wrong direction. When Bucket is right about something, it is accidental: explaining how he discovered that it was Hortense who shot Tulkinghorn, he says, 'it flashed upon me, as I sat opposite to her at table, and saw her with a knife in her hand' (795). Mr. Bayham Badger, clever man that he is, doesn't think at all: he lets his wife do that for him, and thus never has to know anything himself. Harold Skimpole, an elder child, insists that he doesn't know anything about anything, and thus is responsible for nothing. The Lord Chancellor knows as close to nothing as is professionally possible, and the learned gentlemen who conduct the Inkwhich succeed in learning nothing about Nemo, or Nobody. Even the constable on the beat is significantly ignorant: he has insufficient instructions for dealing with the likes of Jo. When asked—by that puzzler, Snagsby—where

181

Jo is to 'move on' to, the constable replies, 'My instructions don't go to that' (320).

Phil Squod can't think, because of all the banging in his ears. Guster has fits every time knowledge—of anything—gets near her. Mrs. Jellyby is so intellectually nearsighted that she can't see anything closer to her than Africa. Caddy's baby is a deaf mute. Sir Leicester has a stroke when Lady Deadlock runs away, and never speaks again. Mrs. Barbary keeps her secret until she dies—and she dies of keeping it. Mrs. Rachel and her husband, that servant of 'Terewth' Mr. Chadband, stumble onto a secret, and honourably try to sell it to Sir Leicester so it won't get out into the light. Esther herself is temporarily blind. Tom Jarndyce—braver than his cousin John, who only hides from the world, and tries not to know it: Tom Jarndyce blows his brains out even before the novel opens.

Surely the theme of the novel is clear: knowledge is fool's gold, and to be wise is to be ignorant. Better not to know the world—so shut the book!

But there are some people in *Bleak House* who want to know things. Little Charley Neckitt wants to learn to read and write. Mrs. Snagsby follows poor, terrified Snagsby about, trying to discover his secret. Tulkinghorn, whose 'calling is the acquisition of secrets' (567), is killed by his curiosity, and 'the last great secret [added] to the many secrets of the Tulkinghorn existence' (633). Guppy, who thinks that lawyers should serve truth, wants to discover Esther's identity—for Esther's sake: 'What might I not get to know ... concerning you? I know nothing now, certainly, but what *might* I not' (177). Guppy again, with Tony Jobling, tries to discover Krook's secret—only to discover Krook himself, combusted (511–12). Caddy Jellyby wishes that Esther could 'have taught her', and is certain that she 'could have learnt much from' Esther (194). And Mrs. Pardiggle, though she is in need of no knowledge herself, and wouldn't accept any from anybody, desires most earnestly to instruct the rest of the world.

How are we to respond to these people? Dickens is loading the novel with knowings and not knowings, pushing us to make a decision about what it means to know—to know anything—in this world, and the value of such knowledge.

The character who most desires 'to know' is Esther. Bill

Stumps argues that since she wants to know, she must need to know; and if she needs to know, then clearly she doesn't yet know. And if she doesn't yet know, we had better not read what she has to say—or if we do, at least we must be careful not to place any value on her utterance.

I don't care to follow Stumps's lead, because I like *Bleak House*, and I value what Dickens is doing in the novel. But Esther does present a serious problem. Not only doesn't she know anything yet about the world; worse, she doesn't know why she is writing, or what she is supposed to be writing about. If ever in the history of fiction we have seen an incompetent narrator, Esther is it.

'I don't know how it is,' she says, 'I seem always to be writing about myself. I mean all this time to write about other people, and I try to talk about myself as little as possible . . . but it's all of no use' (162–63). Early on she tells us, 'It seems so curious to me to be obliged to write all this about myself! As if this narrative were the narrative of *my* life!' (71). Later she says:

> I hope any one who may read what I write, will understand that if these pages contain a great deal about me, I can only suppose it must be because I have really something to do with them, and can't be kept out. (163)

Given what Esther knows and doesn't know, we can determine several things, the most important of which would seem to be that the novel isn't about her. David Copperfield begins his novel wondering 'Whether [he] shall turn out to be the hero of [his] own life'; Esther, self-effacing always, suspects that she may have some role to play in her life, but would never dare to hope for anything more. And she is wise so to limit her expectations: the omniscient narrator, though he knows everything and insists on knowing everything, never even mentions Esther.

But if *Bleak House* is not about Esther, why is she the keeper of its keys? Anybody else in the novel would know—immediately—what to do with a bundle of keys. Even Jo would know what keys are for: he knows 'a broom's a broom, and knows it's wicked to tell a lie' (199), and could surely comprehend keys, and understand their use. But all Esther does is jingle them in her basket.

183

But Esther is important, and she grows more so as the novel progresses. What is most important about Esther—besides her being invited to write a 'portion of these pages'—is that she is very much concerned with knowing things, and not knowing them. The verbal gesture which characterizes her narrative is that of knowing. Sometimes she can say 'I know'; more often she must say 'I am sure I don't know.' No one would question the authority of the omniscient narrator, but Esther, in her insecurity, invites us to doubt her knowledge, her understanding, her authority. Even Caddy Jellyby challenges her:

> 'It's disgraceful,' she said. 'You know it is. The whole house is disgraceful. . . . Priscilla drinks—she's always drinking. It's a great shame and a great story of you, if you say you didn't smell her today. It was as bad as a public-house, waiting at dinner; you know it was!'
> 'My dear, I don't know it,' said I.
> 'You do,' she said, very shortly. 'You shan't say you don't. You do!' (93)

It is typical of the way Dickens works—I would call the method one of 'obsessive sympathy'—that because Esther needs to know, he makes knowing the central focus of the novel. Because there is something that Esther doesn't know, something that has been hidden from her, he teases all the characters with secrets. Because Esther feels herself to be ignorant of the world, he insists on showing us just how much or how little all the other characters know about the world. And because Esther always wants to learn, the rest of the characters must want to learn—Caddy, Charley, Guppy, Tulkinghorn, Mrs. Snagsby, Krook—or be exposed in their self-satisfaction—Sir Leicester, the Lord Chancellor, Mrs. Jellyby, Bucket. Snagsby doesn't know much, and is terrified of learning more. Jo would learn, if anybody wanted to teach him. Skimpole has learned a great deal, but it is all useless learning. John Jarndyce knows more than he can manage. Allan Woodcourt knows medicine, and uses it for good. Miss Flite sits—with her 'documents'—waiting for 'the Day of Judgement', when everything will out.

Esther begins her narrative telling us what she knows: 'I

know that I am not clever. I always knew that' (62). And she recalls, then, that when she was a child she would tell her Dolly this—'Dolly, I am not clever, and you know it very well'—and then would tell Dolly 'every one of [her] secrets' (62). Esther does, however, have 'rather a noticing way—not a quick way, O no!—a silent way of noticing' which makes her want always 'to understand . . . better' (62–3). Her 'understanding', she says, is 'not by any means a quick understanding'; but 'When I love a person very tenderly indeed, it seems to brighten' (63). Her 'comprehension is quickened when [her] affection is' (64).

Because her 'disposition is very affectionate' Esther is able to read in her godmother's face—to understand, without Mrs. Barbary's saying it—the horrible thought that 'It would have been far better, little Esther, that you had had no birthday; that you had never been born' (64). What is most remarkable about Esther, perhaps, is that, given this result of product of her intelligence, quickened by affection, she ever wants to know anything again, or dares to be affectionate.

Mrs. Barbary tells Esther that she is 'set apart', and she goes to bed with such an 'understanding of [her] sorrow' that she 'knew that I had brought no joy, at any time, to anybody's heart, and that I was to no one upon earth what Dolly was to me' (65). Still, she determines to 'strive as I grew', and 'to do some good to someone, and win some love to myself if I could' (65). Her godmother tells her that, being 'different from other children', she must live by the rubric of 'submission, self-denial, and diligent work'; but Esther translates these into a determination to be 'industrious, contented, and kind-hearted' (65).

Ignorance always separates us; affection draws us together. When the omniscient narrator shows us the world—or the universe—in the opening chapter, the only thing that holds us together is an ironic 'infection of ill-temper' (49). Jarndyce and Jarndyce—an example of that infection—is 'so complicated that no man alive knows what it means' (52). The Lord Chancellor, naturally and professionally ignorant, can't even get straight the relationship between John Jarndyce and the wards he is about to assign to Jarndyce:

'I will . . . [provide] for their residing with their uncle.'

. . .

'Begludship's pardon—dead.'

185

'With their . . . grandfather.'

'Begludship's pardon—victim of rash action—brains.'

Suddenly a very little counsel with a terrific bass voice arises . . . and says, 'Will your lordship allow me? . . . He is a cousin, several times removed. I am not at the moment prepared to inform the Court in what exact remove he *is* a cousin, but he is a cousin.' (54)

It is Conversation Kenge who knows that John Jarndyce is a cousin to Ada and Rick. But when asked if Esther is 'related to any party in the cause', Kenge answers—wrongly—'No, my lord' (79). Kenge, who prides himself on his knowledge as much as on his voice, doesn't know Esther's connection to Chancery—and doesn't know that this novel is about her.

Ignorance is everywhere. Mrs. Jellyby, 'with her fine eyes on Africa' (87), is ignorant of the world around her; Mrs. Pardiggle doesn't understand a thing about what people feel. Mr. Chadband perverts 'Terewth' (414) every time he opens his mouth. Detective Bucket, who pretends always to some kind of metaphysical understanding—'That's what *you* are, you know' (362); 'I know you' (404)—depends upon his ability to 'understand' things, and is regularly mistaken. Sir Leicester 'knows' how things should be, but finds that they are 'incomprehensible' (455)—but then Sir Leicester is, as Boythorne calls him, 'Sir Arrogant Numbskull' (299). The 'fashionable intelligence' presumes to know its world, but 'hardly knows' where Lady Dedlock is (270); and Lady Dedlock, caught in her own secrets—or even in her own ignorance—wonders, fearfully, 'how much [Tulkinghorn] knows' (217). Guppy admits, 'I know nothing now' (177)—but he expects to learn, and he does; his learning, however, accomplishes nothing. Tony Jobling can't get straight the name of Chesney Wold—he calls it 'Castle Wold' (332)—yet claims to 'know' both Miss Flite and Krook (335). But when Tony and Guppy set out on their 'mysterious and secret' venture to Krook's, what they discover is not what they planned on at all. Tony 'knows', he says, 'three things' (507)—but he doesn't know what he is going to find out and be so frightened by (512).

Snagsby is pathetic—and pathetically interesting—in his ignorance. Asked by Tulkinghorn where Nemo comes from, he

replies, 'I no more know where he came from than I know—'
(192) and he can't finish the sentence. And 'as to [Nemo's]
connections,' he says, 'if a person was to say to me, "Snagsby,
here's twenty thousand pounds down, ready for you in the
Bank of England, if you'll only name one of 'em," I couldn't do
it, sir!' (192). Bullied by Tulkinghorn and Bucket, Snagsby
'goes homeward so confused . . . that he is doubtful of the
reality of the streets through which he goes—doubtful of the
reality of the moon that shines above him' (371). 'Something is
wrong,' he knows, 'somewhere; but what something, what
may come of it, to whom, when, and from which unthought of
and unheard of quarter, is the puzzle of his life' (409). Bucket
and his 'confidential manner . . . persuade [Snagsby] that he is
a party to some dangerous secret without knowing what it is';
and he lives 'under the oppressive influence of [that] secret . . .
impelled by the mystery of which he is a partaker, and yet in
which he is not a sharer' (499–500), afraid always that 'the
secret may take air and fire, explode, blow up' (409).

Jo is the most pathetic character in the novel, and his
ignorance the most significant for Dickens. Jo is the central
symbolic character, and he symbolizes ignorance, in part. Jo
'don't know nothink', and his evidence, thus, is unacceptable:

> It must be a strange state to be like Jo! To shuffle through the
> streets, unfamiliar with the shapes and in utter darkness as to
> the meaning, of those mysterious symbols, so abundant over the
> shops, and the corner of streets, and on the doors, and in the
> windows! To see people read, and to see people write, and to see
> the postman deliver letters, and not to have the least idea of all
> that language—to be, every scrap of it, stone blind and dumb!
> It must be very puzzling to see the good company going to the
> churches on Sundays, with their books in their hands and to
> think (for perhaps Jo *does* think, at odd times) what does it all
> mean, and if it means anything to anybody, how comes it that it
> means nothing to me? (274)

In Jo's world, 'the great Cross on the summit of St. Paul's
Cathedral, glittering above a red and violet-tinted cloud of
smoke' is, as a 'sacred emblem', but 'the crown confusion of
the great, confused city' (326).

It is our lack of knowledge, however, not Jo's, that creates
this 'confused city'. As Jarndyce says of the bailiff Coavinces,

'we make such men necessary by our faults and follies, or by our want of worldly knowledge' (259). The inquest into Nemo's death—at which Jo, who knew Nemo, was supposed to testify—is reduced to nonsense as the 'Inkwhich' (276). Rejecting Jo—his 'terrible depravity' disqualifies him (200)—the closest the 'Inkwhich' can come to substantial under-standing is personified in the 'potboy at the corner' who is touted as 'possessing official knowledge of life' from 'having to deal with drunken men occasionally' (195).

There is no formal protest against this ignorance, however, from society itself. Indeed, society prefers ignorance: the 'fashionable intelligence' is not intelligence, and has no inten-tion of knowing the world. They have 'agreed to put a smooth glaze on the world, and keep down all its realities'. They 'have found out the perpetual stoppage', and 'are not to be disturbed by ideas' (211).

But there are ideas in the world. Even Guster 'holds certain loose atoms of an idea' (410) in her head. She can't put these pieces together, however, to make a whole thought. And those who should put things together—those who, like 'Lord Coodle and Sir Thomas Doodle, and the Duke of Foodle' were 'born expressly to do it' (273): they won't put things together. Nor will Buffy, Cuffy, Duffy, and Muffy: they are themselves but fragments. Thus in—or for—its ignorance, 'the country . . . [has] gone to pieces' (211).

When Esther is ill with the fever which accompanies her smallpox, she dreams of a 'flaming necklace, or ring, or starry circle of some kind' which is 'strung together somewhere in great black space'. She is herself 'one of the beads', and in her 'agony and misery' at being 'a part of the dreadful thing', she prays 'to be taken off from the rest' (544). But when Esther is well and healthy she doesn't want to be 'taken off'; rather, she works to relive the 'agony and misery' of 'the dreadful thing itself'. As a child Esther was a fragment: Miss Barbary—who refused to marry—insisted that Esther was 'set apart' (65). Esther determined then, in her solitary grief, 'to do some good to some one, and win some love to [her]self' (65).

Ordinarily a Dickens novel would have as its central character a young man who would 'turn to in earnest' (*Our Mutual Friend*, 885) eventually, and work in some way to save

the world. Nicholas Nickleby, for example, or Martin Chuzzlewit or Walter Gay. Or Pip, or Mortimer Lightwood. Or David.
Or Sidney Carton. But this novel's young man, Richard
Carstone, doesn't know anything, can't learn anything, and in
his 'unsettled, uncertain, and confused' state—chargeable in
part to 'that incomprehensible heap of uncertainty' called
Chancery (218)—can't make the decision to 'turn to' at anything. When it comes to choosing something to do in this world,
or 'what [he] had better be', Rick hasn't 'the least idea'. Asked
to what he is inclined, he can only answer, 'I don't know' (219).
When Rick makes a 'trial' at learning medicine he works hard
briefly, and acquires 'a considerable fund of information' (294).
Then he changes his ambition, and claims to be 'in earnest'
(295) at the law. But Rick can't 'settle' (375) at the law, either:
can't 'settle', he says, 'at anything' (376).

It is a critical commonplace to say that Allan Woodcourt
takes the place which Richard can't manage, and that his
role—as physician to this sick world—is a symbolic one. This
is true, certainly: Allan does good things, and lives a life of
'usefulness and good service' (872), and 'the people bless him'
(935). But the more significant symbolic role in *Bleak House* is
really Esther's, because what she always wants to do is 'know'.
And for this Dickens blesses her, and calls her by that made-
up, symbolic name, 'Esther Summerson'.

I call this role of Esther's symbolic rather than dramatic
because for all that she has such a large part in the action of
the novel, and is allowed to narrate better than half of it, her
'knowing' is more ambition than accomplishment. Though she
does good things—and wins a great deal of love to herself—
she remains insecure in what she knows, and is for that reason
unable to complete the novel. That she must leave to whoever
writes the other portion of the novel.

Esther doesn't unlock secrets with her keys—but she does
keep house, and in devoting her life to 'care for others',
'working and thinking . . . for all of us' (291), she becomes 'the
happiest creature in the world' (233). 'Keeping house' for
Esther is an expansive thing, and the order she creates is the
radiant order of love. She rings her housekeeping keys, and
tells herself, 'Once more, duty, duty, Esther' (592). Mrs.
Jellyby, she says, becomes 'absurd' by failing to discharge 'her

own natural duties and obligations' at home 'before she [sweeps] the horizon with a telescope in search of others' (593). Esther's principle is—as she tells Mrs. Pardiggle, that other charity-monger—'to be as useful as I could, and to render what kind services I could, to those immediately about me; and to try to let that circle gradually and naturally expand itself' (154).

Love becomes for Esther—and for Dickens—a kind of knowledge. At first love is a source of knowledge. Esther's 'comprehension is quickened when [her] affection is' (64): 'When I love a person very tenderly indeed,' she says, 'it seems to brighten' (63). As the novel progresses, we see her knowledge of the world grow through her sympathetic understanding of it; and the good that she does for others she does not by virtue of her profession, but through the power of her understanding. Ada doesn't know much, but she loves Rick; and she tells Esther, 'The greatest wisdom that ever lived in the world could scarcely know Richard better than my love does' (880). Dickens revises that line, and has Mr. Crisparkle say it in *The Mystery of Edwin Drood*: 'Love', he says, is 'the highest wisdom ever known upon this earth' (130).

The omniscient narrator in *Bleak House* begins the novel imposing his understanding of the world on us. He insists on his omniscience—forces us to see the world as he sees it, and this in no loving way. From the opening paragraphs of Chapter 1 on, he presents what he knows in the rhetoric of incontrovertibility. There is no room, no allowance, for disagreement. When he describes 'this High Court of Chancery, most persistent of hoary sinners', he says that 'the Lord High Chancellor ought to be sitting here—as here he is'; a score of lawyers and other underlings 'ought to be—as here they are— mistily engaged in one of the ten thousand stages of an endless cause'; and 'various solicitors . . . ought to be—as are they not—ranged in a line . . .' (50). When Krook dies, he dies

> true to his title in his last act . . . the death of all Lord Chancellors in all Courts, and of all authorities in all places under all names soever, where false pretences are made, and where injustice is done. Call the death by any name Your Highness will, attribute it to whom you will, or say it might have been prevented how you will, it is the same death

eternally . . . and that only: Spontaneous Combustion, and
none other of all the deaths that can be died. (511–12)

And when Jo dies, the narrator fulfils Jo's wish for large
writing, ironically, with his rhetoric. Ironically, because what
Jo wanted written 'wery large' was his apology to Allan
Woodcourt; and what the narrator writes in those 'uncommon
precious large' letters is his accusation against us:

Dead, your Majesty. Dead, my lords and gentlemen. Dead,
Right Reverends and Wrong Reverends of every order. Dead,
men and women, born with Heavenly compassion in your
hearts. And dying thus around us every day. (705)

Esther starts out in the novel knowing very little. But she is
'noticing', and observant. When she first arrives in London,
and sees 'the streets . . . so full of dense brown smoke', she asks
'whether there was a great fire anywhere?' (76). When the
omniscient narrator showed us London, he made it look like
the second day of creation, with 'the waters but newly retired
from the face of the earth' (49); and he introduced Chesney
Wold in the time of the deluge. When Esther sees London, she
guesses ahead, in time, to the end of the world.

London's streets are the 'dirtiest and darkest streets that ever
were seen in the world', she thinks, and they seem to her 'in such
a distracting state of confusion that [she] wondered how the
people kept their senses' (76). And what she sees and thinks is
again related to what the omniscient narrator showed us of this
'great (and dirty) city' of 'mud' and 'mire' and 'fog' (49).

'Although the morning was raw, and although the fog still
seemed heavy . . . for the windows were so encrusted with dirt
that they would have made Midsummer sunshine dim', Esther
is 'curious' about London, and even 'admires' the city. Again
she echoes the omniscient narrator in her observation: he
showed us the 'rawest' of afternoons and the 'densest' of fogs in
Chapter 1, 'crust upon crust of mud', and 'snowflakes—gone
into mourning, one might imagine, for the death of the sun'
(49–50).

But Esther's observation is not yet critical. In her innocence
and ignorance, 'wondering more and more at the extent of the
streets, the brilliancy of the shops, the great traffic, and the
crowds of people' (109), she can call London 'the wonderful

191

city' (110). The omniscient narrator, however, is not given to wonder. For him, the truth is that London is so crazy—the civilization it represents has so failed—that 'it would *not be wonderful* to meet a Megalosaurus, forty feet long or so, waddling like an elephantine lizard up Holborn Hill' (49; italics mine).

Esther does learn the world, however, and learn to be appropriately critical of it. As what she knows makes her more critical, her affection keeps her sympathetic; and thanks to her growing critical sympathy, there is less and less need for the omniscient narrator's protests and accusations as the novel progresses. Sometimes, indeed, Esther sounds like the omniscient narrator, as when she describes Chancery again:

> To see everything going on so smoothly, and to think of the roughness of the suitors' lives and deaths; to see all that full dress and ceremony, and to think of the waste, want, and beggared misery it represented; to consider that, while the sickness of hope deferred was raging in so many hearts, this polite show went calmly on from day to day, and year to year . . . to behold the Lord Chancellor, and the whole array of practitioners under him, looking . . . as if nobody had ever heard that all over England the name in which they were assembled was a bitter jest: was held in universal horror, contempt, and indignation; was known for something so flagrant and bad, that little short of a miracle could bring anything good out of it to anyone. . . .

But Esther's rhetoric, as narrator, is not as strong as the omniscient narrator's, and her conclusion reflects not what she now knows about Chancery, but that what she saw then she didn't understand:

> This was so curious and self-contradictory to me, who had no experience of it, that it was at first incredible, and I could not comprehend it. (400)

Sometimes Esther quotes John Jarndyce as sounding a great deal like the omniscient narrator, too. His description of Tom All-Alone's (146–47) is the particular realization of the omniscient narrator's generic representation, in Chapter 1, of Chancery's holdings. But that description comes early in the novel. Eventually, even the omniscient narrator quits shouting at the world and threatening us with his knowledge of its combustibility, as Esther takes over the serious task of knowing the world, and knowing what to do about it.

But Esther isn't a perfect character, and she isn't finally omniscient, and she can't save the world. The world isn't, in fact, saved—and nothing is really over—at the end of the novel. The suit of Jarndyce and Jarndyce has ended, but it was not settled. Miss Flite has released her birds, but the Day of Judgement has not come. Chapter 65, the antepenultimate chapter, is entitled 'Beginning the World'. And in the last paragraphs of the final chapter, Esther recites what she knows and doesn't know, and ends—stops—in the middle of a sentence:

> 'My dear Dame Durden,' said Allan . . . 'do you ever look in the glass?'
> 'You know I do. . . .'
> 'And don't you know that you are prettier now than you ever were?'
> I did not know that; I am not certain that I know it now. But I know that my dearest little pets are very pretty, and that my darling is very beautiful, and that my husband is very handsome, and that my guardian has the brightest and most benevolent face that was ever seen; and that they can very well do without much beauty in me—even supposing—. (935)

What do we do for a conclusion, when the novelist doesn't provide us with one? It's odd, to say the least, that *Bleak House* doesn't end. The omniscient narrator retires, with Mr. George, and Esther can't finish her 'portion'. *David Copperfield*—the novel immediately preceding *Bleak House*—was such a completed novel that at the end David could leave it behind, as his 'life'. *David Copperfield* was such a completed novel, in fact, that Dickens never really finished another novel after it. The conclusion of *David Copperfield* is mystically complete, like the conclusion of Dante's *Commedia*. But none of the rest of Dickens's characters ever gets to such a comprehensive understanding of the world as David did, and their worlds are still open at the ends of their novels, whereas David's is a closed book.

Hard Times is a fable, and concludes with a warning about how we had better act, to save the world we live in. *Little Dorrit* ends, marvellously, with Amy and Arthur going

down into the roaring streets, inseparable and blessed; and as
they passed along in sunshine and shade, the noisy and the eager,
and the arrogant and the froward and the vain, fretted and
chafed, and made their usual uproar. (895)

A Tale of Two Cities ends with Sidney Carton's love remaking
this world, through three generations; his vision of the future is
unique in Dickens's fiction, in predicting things to come beyond
the end of the novel. *Great Expectations* ends ambiguously, and
with no indication of what is to become of Pip or Estella except
that they are 'friends', and 'will continue friends apart'—and
that Pip sees in the future 'no shadow of another parting from
her' (493). *Our Mutual Friend* ends with Mortimer momentarily
triumphant—Twemlow has squelched the Voice of Society, for
this evening: but there's nothing permanent about the victory,
certainly, and Mortimer's 'gaily' faring home is the result of his
momentary satisfaction, not the world's salvation. *Edwin Drood*
is unfinished, to be sure, but it's not incomplete: everything is
there for us to make meaning of. What's unfinished is the work
of making meaning—and Dickens leaves that for us.

From *Bleak House* on, Dickens more and more leaves things
unfinished for us: leaves the conclusion up to us. And what do
we do, then? We do what we usually do with a work of art: put
all of the pieces together, and make a whole of what we have
experienced. Miss Flite names her birds 'Hope, Joy, Youth,
Peace, Rest, Life, Dust, Ashes, Waste, Want, Ruin, Despair,
Madness, Death, Cunning, Folly, Words, Wigs, Rags, Sheep-
skin, Plunder, Precedent, Jargon, Gammon, and Spinach'
(253). We have to make sense of her 'collection'—know what it
means *as* a collection. Caddy Jellyby represents her home,
similarly, as 'nothing but bills, dirt, waste, noise, tumbles
downstairs, confusion, and wretchedness' (238), and Esther
later describes the contents of the Jellby closets as a 'wonderful'
expansion of Caddy's list:

> bits of mouldy pie, sour bottles, Mrs. Jellyby's caps, letters, tea,
> forks, odd boots and shoes of children, firewood, wafers,
> saucepan-lids, damp sugar in odds and ends of paper bags,
> footstools, blacklead brushes, bread, Mrs. Jellyby's bonnets,
> books with butter sticking to the binding, guttered candle-
> ends . . . nutshells, heads and tails of shrimps, dinner-mats,
> gloves, coffee-grounds, umbrellas. . . . (476)

Caddy and Esther sort through all of these things, 'attempting to establish some order among all this waste and ruin' (476). And that, again, is what we must do.

There is indeed a 'portion' of *Bleak House* that Esther didn't write, and that the omniscient narrator didn't write, either. It is the portion that you and I, as Esther's 'unknown friend', have to write. All of the words are there: Hope, Joy, Youth, Peace, caps, letters, heads and tails of shrimp, a Megalosaurus forty feet long or so, mud, Tangle, Allegory, Terewth. We have to put them all together, into meaning.

Esther can't finish the novel—'even supposing' is where she stops—because she is only writing a portion of it, and because she is not secure enough in her self-knowledge to come to a conclusion. But she has given us a great deal of information about the world, and has taught us what she knows about it. Together, she and the omniscient narrator have provided evidence enough for us to reach our own conclusion about how to live in the world.

Grandfather Smallweed names reading 'Stuff. Idleness. Folly' (351). But he is wrong. It's good to read books: from cover to cover, beginning to end. In *Bleak House*, though the Day of Judgement hasn't come yet, still at the end there is a localized version of the same: and we must evaluate all the evidence, put all the pieces together, make our own judgement, and act upon it.

10

Dickens and Dostoyevsky: The Technique of Reverse Influence

by LORALEE MacPIKE

The idea of analysing an author's work based on what was borrowed by another author is not new. Mark Spilka's *Dickens and Kafka* (1963) established the idea of 'mutual interpretation' as a way of re-seeing through an artist's eyes aspects of a work not available through normal critical channels.[1] Dickens's influence upon Dostoyevsky was so great that it is possible to see Dostoyevsky as a reinterpreter of Dickens in much the way Spilka sees Kafka as such a reinterpreter. Dostoyevsky borrowed characters, plots, and ideas from Dickens almost wholesale, then transformed them by his unique vision of the nature of human beings in such a way that students of Dickens can, as it were, turn Dostoyevsky's transformations back upon Dickens to re-see the Dickens Dostoyevsky re-created in his own fictions.

Two brief examples will clarify how this reinterpretation can work. Little Nell's unsettling goodness and Dickens's unwillingness to allow her any of the possible salvations the book extends (Kit's offer of a home, Mrs. Jarley's acceptance of life as it is, even the single gentleman's potential to provide a genuine, as opposed to a 'casual', family) are mirrored in Dostoyevsky's Nellie Valkovsky from *The Insulted and Injured*, who is modelled explicitly after Nell. Nellie is Nell's double in age, provenance, and sexual victimization, but otherwise she seems very different—self-punishing, vengeful, seeking control of others through love and kindness. A close parallel reading of the two novels, however, shows that cloaked under Little Nell's Victorian innocence lies an unwillingness to admit the (humanly) evil side of her nature which emerges in her dream about her grandfather's death and is subsequently repudiated by her insistence on saving him, at whatever cost to him. The need to control her inadmissible evil drives her to suffer and even die rather than succumb to external definitions of herself—Quilp's view of her as sexual, her grandfather's need to make her wealthy—that would control her. Dostoyevsky's Nellie, born directly from the Russian author's reading of Dickens, helps to explain Nell's otherwise random and senseless flight from the very sorts of succour that would save her but whose salvation would control her (much as the Garlands' insistence on goodness makes of gloriously free Kit a pious automaton, in direct opposition to Dick Swiveller's unregenerate participation in the good *and* the evil of the human soul, which proves in the end the only power capable of finding humane solutions).

Likewise, Dostoyevsky's re-creation of Steerforth in Stavrogin of *The Possessed* shows Steerforth as a double of decomposition, whose fullness of life is parcelled out among David and his fellows as each shapes himself (or is shaped by Dickens) on a portion of Steerforth's wholeness, which contains both the good and the evil of human nature. David's question, asked in the opening lines of the novel, about whether he will be the hero of his own life can be answered by viewing David as Dostoyevsky did—a partial recreation, shaped self-wilfully, from the human wholeness that Steerforth represented. The limitations critics have castigated David for can be understood more clearly in the light of Dostoyevsky's re-vision of the development of Dickens's 'favourite child'.

Dostoyevsky's differences from Dickens do not preclude our using him as this sort of critical illuminator. In his 1882 essay on Dostoyevsky, Mikhailovsky analysed what he called Dostoyevsky's 'cruel talent', his genius for showing human evil, divisions within the human soul, a craving for suffering as

197

self-definition, a need to control others in order to maintain one's own view of oneself *vis-à-vis* society. Mikhailovsky also pointed out that his was a 'talent' many writers did not share and that Dostoyevsky was in fact singular in viewing human beings primarily as tormented. It is clear that Dickens portrayed his characters as striving towards good; he appealed to the hearts rather than the souls of his readers, and whatever he shared with Dostoyevsky of the unconscious processes motivating human behaviour came out more in the energy of his presentations than in his characters' overt psychic manifestations. Nonetheless, his novels allow a depth of scrutiny and yield up an amount of interrelated meaning that would have been impossible had Dickens been merely, in Leavis's unforgettable words, 'the great entertainer'. The extent of his genius argues for an understanding of human nature in its entirety which needs only a means of entrée to uncover.

Therefore, while Dostoyevsky's differences from Dickens prevent our accepting his version of Dickens's ideas wholesale or uncritically, it is not only possible but profitable to use Dostoyevsky as an illuminator of portions of Dickens that escape our traditional means of scrutiny, because he is so largely a painter of the potential warmth and goodness of human nature. Mikhailovsky notes that despite the extreme cruelty of Dostoyevsky's talent, it moves us to understand the good in human nature by its contrast to the ineluctible sufferings Dostoyevsky finds in the human soul. Myshkin, Dostoyevsky's idiot, is a Christ figure for Dostoyevsky *because* he is able to acknowledge and accept his own violence and hatred as well as his impulses towards good; and we must remember that those good impulses were built upon Dostoyevsky's idea of Pickwick as a perfectly good man. Dickens is just the reverse of Dostoyevsky—he writes of the good, but it is part of his genius that he is unable to create cardboard characters who do not partake of what Dostoyevsky saw as the essence of humanity—evil and suffering.

We know from his letters, novels, and essays that Dostoyevsky read *Pickwick Papers, The Old Curiosity Shop, David Copperfield, Nicholas Nickelby, Bleak House,* and *Dombey and Son.* It is possible to conjecture that he had read all of Dickens's novels, for he advises a friend to have his daughter 'read through all of

Dickens without exception', and it is doubtful he would recommend so strongly books he had not himself read.[2`]

The most extensive critical linking of *The Idiot* and *Little Dorrit* occurs in N. M. Lary's *Dostoyevsky and Dickens*, although various of Lary's comparisons have been cited briefly by previous critics. I shall here only summarize Lary's comparisons of General Ivolgin in *The Idiot* with William Dorrit. Their self-conscious, comic, disconnected patterns of speech, their shared decline in fortunes, their residence in debtor's prison (the General's, it is true, for only six months during which time he 'settled in perfectly'), and their cadging of donations, are capped by almost identical relationships to their youngest children. Amy Dorrit finds her double in Nicholas Ivolgin (Kolya), whose fate is a counterpoint to hers and allows us to see both the strengths and the limitations of Dickens's conclusion to his novel, a conclusion that has been called both unequivocally pessimistic and also Dickens's most hopeful, given the dark foundation on which it is built. Lary finds Dostoyevsky's superiority to Dickens to lie in Dostoyevsky's ability to take

> both views of the General—that of the General's family, for whom he is a serious problem, and that of the outsider, who can see his humorous side—and shows that both are, in a sense, justified.[3]

By idealizing Amy Dorrit, Dickens is forced, in Lary's view, to omit an insider's realization, for that would force a re-evaluation of Amy as an ideal, which Dickens refuses to do. Lary's view, however, neglects the Dickens that Dostoyevsky's borrowings reveal. An examination of the casual family in *The Idiot*[4] provides a critical basis to substantiate the increasing recognition of *Little Dorrit*, not only as one of Dickens's most serious novels, but also as one of his most comprehensive and fully realized statements about the relationship between society and the individual. And while a number of critics have seen that the family's failure is central to society's failure and have shown how it is so, Dostoyevsky, in his re-creation of the Dorrit family in *The Idiot*, helps us to see *why*. His anatomy of the casual family allows us to look back at William Dorrit and pinpoint his failure; to trace Amy's alternative choices; and to evaluate just how satisfactory the ending of the novel really is. A close examination of *The Idiot*'s family structures will allow a new look at the family dynamic of *Little Dorrit*.

The 'casual' father like Djunkovsky who evades his duty of passing on an 'idea' to his children becomes an egoist:

> It should be borne in mind that this continual and passionate craving to avoid any duty almost always generates and fosters in the egoist the conviction that, contrariwise, everyone with whom he is in contact is to be charged as regards him with some obligation, tax or liability . . . This peevish feeling extends also to his own children—oh, to the children par excellence. Children are the predestined victims of this whimsical selfishness; besides, they are the nearest at hand, and what is most important—there is no control: 'They are my own children!' (*Diary* II, July–August 1877, I, iii, 768)

General Ivolgin is Dostoyevsky's clearest example of such a father. He avoids his obligations in two ways: by spending irresponsibly, and by lying. He signs I.O.U.s with no concern for the people he does not intend to pay (like Skimpole in *Bleak House*) and is genuinely surprised when he is imprisoned for debt, although he rapidly settles comfortably into prison life. His lies, like William Dorrit's, create a social fabric within which he has a place. Like prison, his self-created world is comfortable for him. He focuses upon himself as an individual, becoming the egoist Dostoyevsky describes, a victim of 'whimsical selfishness' and indolence who cannot pass on advice or values to his children because he requires their services (particularly Kolya's) to support his sense of dignity. By disavowing responsibility for his children and focusing instead upon their debts to him, he imposes upon them a factitious sense of relatedness that includes him in the fabric of their lives without causing him the trouble of creating his own.

What General Ivolgin is trying to create is, of course, a meaning which will bespeak his worth as a human being. But his own need to gain comfort and to blind others to his failures makes him a slave to the same sort of luxury Mrs. Djunkovsky sought when she forced her children to scratch her heels. It is not, therefore, ironic that his attempts at factitious dignity decrease rather than increase his comfort. The best example of this is his habit of acknowledging introductions to new people by claiming he dandled them on his knees when they were children. He greets Myshkin this way; after a long separation, he greets Aglaya Epanchin similarly and is shocked to learn that his pleasant fiction is the truth. The fact that at one time he had genuine dignity and a real relationship with the Epanchins has been obliterated (in the same way that William Dorrit's tiny bit of gentility is obliterated during his fateful dinner at Mrs. Merdle's in Rome) by the lies he must tell to create the appearance of dignity. His loss of real memories forces him (and the reader) to see his low social status not as a mere chance of life but in stark contrast to his pretences, which are all the more shameful when seen as bald self-interest.

Once trapped in such a behaviour pattern, General Ivolgin is unable to help his family at all. Erratically, 'he would suddenly remember that he was "the father of a family", and he would make it up with his wife and shed genuine tears' followed by bouts of irritability and 'violent attacks of self-glorification'.[5] He attempts to cut off Ganya's match with Nastasya Filippovna by a similar assertion:

> Now, sir, a different kind of father is about to appear on the scene and then we shall see, sir, whether an honourable old soldier, sir, will scotch this intrigue or whether a shameless whore will force her way into a most honourable family. (I, 12, 156)

(William Dorrit's posturing over John Chivery is just such an attempt to manipulate the children's feelings for the father's sake.) Ivolgin indulges in the rhetoric of fatherliness without possibility of follow-through; he attempts to control but will not guide his children. He embodies perfectly the consistent pattern Edward Wasiolek notes in his edition of the notebooks for *The Idiot*, a pattern intensified by its contrast to the novel's otherwise general shapelessness: 'The horrifying prospect of a father's betrayal of his God-like trust.'[6] Ivolgin does not merely fail his children; he betrays them.

Ivolgin's final lie—his story of having been Napoleon's page in 1812—mirrors Dorrit's fiction of gentility. The enormity of such efforts requires the tacit support of the entire family, and even so the enterprise is doomed to collapse because, for Dostoyevsky, the human soul is unable to support such discrepancies between truth and desire.

The effect of the casual family on its children is even more harmful than its effect on the fathers, however, It 'produces disconsolateness', which 'in turn, increases indolence, and in hot-headed individuals cynical, angry indolence' (*Diary* II, July–August 1877, I, ii, 760). Indeed, Russia's youth in general 'is so placed that absolutely nowhere does it find advice as to the loftiest meaning of life' (*Diary* II, December 1876, I, iv, 544). For children such as Ganya and Kolya Ivolgin and Amy Dorrit,

> long after, maybe all their lives, the children are inclined blindly to accuse these men [their fathers], having derived nothing from their childhood that might mitigate that filth of their memories, and to size up truthfully, realistically, and, therefore, *acquittingly*, those now elderly people in whose midst their early years dragged out so sadly. (*Diary* II, July–August 1877, I, ii, 761)

The Ivolgin children must in effect create themselves with no foundation, no value system save appearances and social status. Ganya, like Fanny Dorrit, can see no way to gain selfhood but through social position. The greed for money and status becomes his Idea, and it supersedes all duty to others. Frank Seeley has characterized the Dostoyevsky hero's Idea as 'a theory of man's (sic) mission in the universe'.[7] In its artistic personifications it shows Dostoyevsky's idea of the duality of human nature, the pull between good and evil, the soul and the self. This is precisely what happens to Ganya. Dostoyevsky speaks at length about how Ganya is 'infected from head to foot with the desire of originality' (IV, i, 502) yet has 'a profound and continual realization of his own mediocrity and, at the same time, an irresistible desire to convince himself that he (is) a man of the most independent mind' (IV, i, 502–3). In everything he is the divided man of Dostoyevsky's time, unable to stifle the promptings of emotion yet driven to court social approval and the power of money at the expense of human feeling. His love for Aglaya does not prevent him from lusting after Nastasya Filippovna; yet his greed is not strong enough to allow him to lose his dignity by snatching Nastasya Filippovna's 100,000 rubles out of the fire. Because the various possible Ideas Ganya has to choose from are not rooted in any value system beyond individual desire, he is a hot-headed cynic unable to settle upon a single course of action.

The contrast between Ganya and Lebedev's son shows to the fullest the failure of Ganya's unaided search for an Idea. Lebedev, buffoon that he is, has an Idea: he interprets the Apocalypse. He lies and postures and plays malicious pranks, but his life's focus on a developing interpretation of the Apocalypse gives his son that handhold amidst the flux which Ivolgin is unable to give Ganya. When the son repeats and defends his father's interpretations, he is adopting an 'erroneous' idea, to be sure; but, as Dostoyevsky has said, even such an erroneous idea is 'the beginning of moral order'. Ganya lacks even such a beginning. His sad end, jobless and withdrawn, can be attributed to the lack of a central value or Idea which responsible fathering would have provided.

Kolya Ivolgin is, like Amy Dorrit, the youngest child. He looks after his father, takes the Prince to see him and warns the Prince about lending him money, and undertakes to provide what his father wants. He is aware that in caring for his father he creates meaning for his own life, and so he must defend his father's failings:

> You know, I can't help feeling that my general is an honest man. I'm sure he is! It's only his disorderly life and drink—I'm sure it is! I can't help feeling sorry for him. (I, xii, 164)

This sounds very much like Amy Dorrit pleading with Arthur Clennam that 'you don't know what he is . . . You don't know what he really is.'[8]

Thus, while Ganya repudiates his family and says he is 'jolly well going to do what [he likes]' (I, iii, 55), Kolya uses his father's debility to establish his own Idea of himself as socially responsible. During Ivolgin's final and most dreadful lie about being Napoleon's page, Kolya humours his father in much the same way we shall see Amy reinforcing her father's willed belief in his gentility in order to maintain her position in the family. Kolya devotes himself first to his father, and after his father's death to his mother and to the Prince, for whom he arranges asylum in Schneider's Swiss clinic where he had earlier been treated for idiocy. A caretaker career such as Kolya's requires disabled people who need care. Forced to invent their own Idea, even the best of children fall short of human potential.

Dostoyevsky sees this casual family as both the result and the cause of a collapse of social structure and social values:

> Every transitional and disintegrative state of society generates indolence and apathy, since in such epochs only very few are capable of seeing clearly what is ahead of them and of not being led astray. The majority, however, is confused, loses the thread, and, finally, gives it all up: . . . 'I wish I myself could manage to pull through life somehow, and why should I bother about duties!' (*Diary* II, July–August 1877, I, ii, 761)

Unless individuals can help shape what he calls the holy family, social upheaval and superficiality will continue to deprive fathers of their responsibilities and children of their birthrights.[9] The task is an individual one for which both fathers and children of casual families will find few guidelines:

> For the family, too, is *created*, and is not given to us ready-made; and here no obligations are made to order, but they all result one from the other. Only then is this unit solid; only then— holy. (*Diary* I, February 1876, II, i, 234)

Only by assuming responsibility and eschewing indolence and personal luxury can the fathers resume their position as leaders of the new generations that will shape the nation. No less than Dickens, Dostoyevsky feared the collapse of society should the fathers abandon their mission as parents. People like Ivolgin, focusing upon themselves and so unable to maintain any Idea, are doomed to a peevish, myopic sense of their own needs and comforts. Their children are abandoned to their own slender resources. Most, like Ganya, will become as self-centred as their parents. Even the few who, like Kolya or Lebedev's son, inherit or develop an inchoate Idea often do so at the expense of others. Lacking the strength that comes from shared inter-generational valuing, they use their powers to control others rather than to develop their society. For Dostoyevsky as for Dickens, the family is the nucleus without which no society can long survive. Its failure in *The Idiot* gives us a way of looking at its similar failure in *Little Dorrit* to explain the unduly muted tone of the conclusion and our critical uneasi-ness with Amy Dorrit's goodness.

Since the birth of modern Dickens criticism with Edmund Wilson's 'Dickens: The Two Scrooges', critics have seen a link between *Little Dorrit*'s overarching prison metaphor and the collapse of the family. The Dorrit family's dynamic is not merely a matter 'of simple exploitation', as George Holoch concludes,[10] nor does the novel merely show Peter Christmas's contention that 'each family represents a class' and 'a group of families is intended to represent society as a whole.'[11] Like *David Copperfield*, *Little Dorrit* is also more than 'something in the nature of a justification of John [Dickens]', as Wilson noted,[12] although the working-out in Micawber and Dorrit of what Freud has called the 'family romance'[13] allows for what is positive in Amy Dorrit's final act of marriage, her commitment to maintain an Idea, however erroneous, in the face of the general collapse of the family.

In fact, family relations in *Little Dorrit* are 'subject to a more disquieting and more radical distortion than ever before'.[14] We must remember that even Micawber finally grasps something that has 'turned up' and becomes a man of social substance, thus nearly validating his earlier comic irresponsibility, which is externally no less pernicious than William Dorrit's but which Dickens does not allow to destroy him as it destroys Dorrit. Even such psychically complex portraits as Micawber, then, are more simplistic than the scrutiny Dickens gives the Dorrit family. As John Lucas has said, the theme of the family is 'explored in ways that make [it] utterly unfamiliar'.[15] In fact, 'every relationship' within the novel 'is, potentially or actually, familial', in the words of John Wain.[16] If, as is generally acknowledged, Dickens seems in *Little Dorrit* to be abandoning his belief in the possibility of solutions to the problems he so artfully pictures for his readers, then his concept of the family, which has been one of the primary solutions throughout his earlier fiction, is likely to be restructured in ways that will not become apparent from a chronological or thematic study of his works but which must be approached from a different angle, one as 'utterly unfamiliar' as the solutions he is proposing.

William Dorrit is Dickens's clearest example of the abdication of parental responsibility. Dorrit's imprisonment, caused by some such careless improvidence as General Ivolgin's, both allows and requires an abdication of responsibility. Dorrit has no Idea that would allow him to assert himself, and so he must accept others' assertions (as, for instance, his wife must have done) by creating a self from the superficial models his culture offers. The connection between Dorrit's degradation and the prison metaphor is integral. The injustice-hunting and laziness which Dostoyevsky notes in his casual parents and which he almost certainly borrowed from William Dorrit are almost inevitable products of prisons, whether states of mind or actual institutions. 'The prison image is especially apt as a representation of the injustice-collecting tendency, and hence the masochistic conflict . . .; what could be better than a prison as a symbol of complete psychic extinction of the conscious self?' says psychiatrist and critic Edmund Bergler.[17] Once the Idea which constitutes the basis for an individual's connection with the world (i.e., identity as a social being) is lost, the individual becomes prey to the insatiable demands of the self for satisfaction. Through Dorrit's conscious masochism to sustain a sense of self, it is possible to avoid entirely having an Idea. Once this happens, the individual no longer has any intrinsic connection with society, and society becomes fragmented in the many ways Dickens pictures in *Little Dorrit*. Amy Dorrit is born into the fragmentation; so too, perhaps, was William Dorrit; or perhaps Dickens wishes us to believe that the Marshalsea—as representative of the fragmenting institutions he saw society forcing on its members—left Dorrit no choice but to create a reality based solely on himself.

Dorrit's failure, of course, mirrors Dickens's own view of his father's failure. The 'family romance' of the bad father/good child dramatized the child's working free from dependence on the parent in such a way that the dependence can be reversed, so that the child gains power without sacrificing the submission required by fear of the potentially castrating parent. The result in all of Dickens's novels dealing with the family romance is that 'his ideal children love their fathers without cause or judgement, as Little Dorrit [does].'[18] The parent is placated, just in case he turns out to have the feared power, and the child's independence from potential parental betrayal or desertion (as Dorrit emotionally betrays and financially deserts his children) takes such shape as will render the parent dependent upon the child.

With no 'strength of purpose to fight [his] troubles' (I, vi, 63), Dorrit can give Amy only the knowledge that 'a man so broken as to be the Father of the Marshalsea, could be no father to his own children' (I, vii, 72). Dorrit's occasional recognition of his failure, as when he tries to convince Amy to lead John Chivery on or when he recognizes his jealousy of Amy's love for brother Frederick, is never carried through. When he gains his fortune, his only goal is to spend money in ways that will visibly attest to the fiction of gentility he must maintain in order to avoid acknowledging reality. Ultimately, as A. E. Dyson has noted, 'there is no possibility of self-knowledge leading, through crisis, to renewal',[19] because Dorrit has no Idea, no 'mission in the universe', which would sustain him through the crisis of self-recognition. He must, as Dickens noted in his plans for the novel, focus on 'the family gentility—always the gentility'.[20] Dorrit's success in this precarious venture depends on the active collaboration of the rest of his family in maintaining the fiction. Primary in this collaboration is Amy.

Amy cannot inherit and reproduce her father's Idea because he has none. She must create her own. She does so by becoming the person who allows him to create the fiction that serves in place of an Idea. Frederick Dorrit praises Amy by saying ' "she does her duty" ' (I, ix, 94); Meagles points Amy out to Tattycoram as the epitome of duty (II, xxxiii, 813). She never complains and in fact makes a virtue out of not complaining, so that outsiders like Clennam learn to value her family not in themselves but as they relate to Amy. (This, of course, prevents him from seeing, for instance, Fanny's remarkable singleness of purpose as one of the novel's positive statements against society.) The virtue of doing one's duty, however, is shown in its true light by Pancks, whose 'whole duty of Man' is to collect rents (I, xiii, 160) and to be the willing agent of oppression. The duality of Pancks's character has not been adequately dealt with. It is true that he ferrets out the information that obtains Dorrit's release, but all his subsequent goodness does not quite counterbalance the suffering he superimposes upon the hardships of Bleeding Heart Yard's residents. And so the value of Amy doing her duty is undercut by Dickens's primary advocate of duty, a strangely divided soul.

Amy's virtues are well known. She keeps her father in some

comfort and provides opportunities for both her siblings. She cares for Maggy. She inspires Mrs. Clennam to restitution. She saves Arthur and, with him, goes forward to create whatever values the world of the novel will be able to salvage from the collapse of the factitious gentility Dorrit represents and the ephemeral social and economic structure Merdle represents. Yet these virtues are exercised not for the benefit of the recipients but for the maintenance of Amy's self-created Idea, which requires for its execution others' needs and her ministrations to those needs.

Amy gains personal power from her own vulnerability and her family's dishonour, and it is to her advantage to retain both, which she does to the end of the novel. She gains power from being small and unprotected: she seeks out her nickname and insists, sometimes not so gently, on its consistent use. She uses her apparent weakness to control John Chivery's advances and to keep Arthur from questioning her sacrifices (children must do what their parents require). Because she is small and powerless, it is easy to see her as having no choice but complicity in Dorrit's self-deception, but this is not true. In fact she manipulates their life together for her own ends as much as for his. She forces Tip to hide the truth of his imprisonment, for example, because that fact might change their circumstances— Dorrit might no longer be able to maintain the pretensions that allow her to be his caretaker, or, even worse, he might possibly take actions that would establish him as a real father and eventually get him out of the Marshalsea. In either case, Amy would be forced into a different position and have to find moral justification on her own rather than through her efforts for her unfortunate father.

Similarly, she doesn't want her father released and discourages Arthur from trying, just as she advises him to ignore her father's bid for Testimonials; not in order to prevent the old man from making those bids, for she knows he will only redouble his efforts if he believes he is misunderstood, but precisely *in order to* maintain his ordinary behaviour which, however offensive, is nonetheless necessary if she is to gain her Idea through her devotion to him. Not only does she not protest his mistreatment of her and his maudlin self-pity, she purposely prolongs scenes of degradation. There are many opportunities for her to show her father his responsibility for himself, but she chooses not to because, like Little Nell, her subjection is her means to power. Amy's Idea, born and nourished on her father's failure, is the Idea of the good child in the family romance. She takes over the parental role, becoming what Geoffrey Thurley has called '*die schreckliche Mutter*', the Jungian archetype of the perfectly caring, all-giving mother who demands—and will accept—nothing in return.[21] But of course her success in this role requires her father's failure as a parent and his inability as a human being to develop an Idea of his own outside social conventions. The success of Amy Dorrit's Idea requires that her father be a failure as a human being.

Thus it is understandable that she is unwilling to change when her father comes into his fortune. She refuses to buy new clothes, to Fanny's despair, and she feels she has 'glided into a corner where she had no one to think for, nothing to plan and contrive, no cares of others to load herself with' (II, iii, 463). She continues to choose to see her father as 'deserted, and in want of me' beneath all his social posturing (II, iv, 470). Both of her letters to Clennam are sad ones, filled with bad news under a patently artificial veneer of cheer. The first letter is a plea for the old ways and the old times, when she can be the same 'little shabby girl' (she is now 23) instead of Miss Amy (II, vi, 471). The second recounts her dream of herself as a child learning needlework, suggesting a psychic desire to return to the times when she was in control of the family. With Fanny's open scorn and William Dorrit's refusal to acknowledge the existence of the past which gave her life meaning, it is no surprise that Amy turns to Arthur (through letters) and to her uncle Frederick (in person). Each retains a vision of her as Little Dorrit; each values her according to her self-chosen standards. Her union with Arthur is the ultimate logical outcome of her Idea.

The family's reaction to Amy after their change of fortune indicates their sense of being manipulated for Amy's purposes. Fanny complains that with Amy 'she was always being placed in the position of being forgiven, whether she liked it or not' (II, xiv, 588). One cannot be an all-forgiving Mother without errant children to forgive. By insisting that Amy conform to ordinary standards of dress and behaviour, Fanny is making a first step towards breaking the cycle of dependence and forgiveness which gives Amy her sense of self at Fanny's expense. Even while Dorrit is in prison, the family must assert itself against her encroaching Idea—Dorrit by refusing to admit that she works, Tip by evading the responsible occupations she finds for him, Fanny by encouraging Edmund Sparkler against Amy's reservations—in order to retain any independence at all. Fanny's fury at Amy after the sisters' visit to Mrs. Merdle juxtaposes the validity of her Idea against Amy's. But Amy will not admit that Fanny too ' "may have been thinking, you know, of the family" ' (I, xxi, 245), because it diminishes their dependence on her.

Fanny's Idea is of particular interest here because it has some possibility for bringing about genuine changes. By marrying Edmund Sparkler, Fanny becomes empowered to compete with Mrs. Merdle. ' "I would make [that competition] the business of my life" ', she avows to Amy when trying (in vain, of course, because it opposes Amy's Idea) to convince Amy of the utility of the marriage. Nothing Amy could do would have any effect on the Circumlocution Office's power to thwart Doyce and the financial world created by people like Merdle to destroy Arthur; she merely staves off despair. But by competing with and besting Mrs. Merdle, Fanny might be able to mitigate the power of the Merdles of the world. Her own social aspirations are competitive rather than malicious and have as little potential for general harm as Edmund has for altering the Circumlocution Office. By remaining a victim, Amy feeds rather than destroys the Merdles of the world. In a world of casual families, where each child must create an Idea and then try to superimpose it upon an unwilling world, Fanny's Idea may actually be more useful and more humane than Amy's.

What all this makes of Amy is a psychic masochist, what Edmund Bergler calls a 'nice masochist',[22] who chooses suffering in order to prove that she is good and worthwhile. Thus, while Leavis is right in saying that Amy 'needs collaboration in creating the reality she can grasp' and finds it 'in the responsive human needs of her father and his other children',[23] he is evaluating Amy exactly as she would have herself evaluated. But to evaluate Amy so is to accept her Idea not merely as hers but as the truth. If we move beyond Amy's view, or even the novel's view, we can see Amy's Idea as an expression of 'energy that keeps a self real self in the sense of a center of willing set up in opposition to one's milieu', as Richard Stang has put it.[24] She wills her Idea into reality by making a positive value of her father's 'casualness'. The validity—even the laudable success, from Amy's point of view—of her Idea can be acknowledged without moving, as Leavis dangerously does, to belief in its ultimate truth. What Leavis's uncritical acceptance causes him to miss is that Amy's celebrated collaboration is a neurotically dependent one which requires the others—Dorrit, Fanny, Tip—to be 'bad children' so that Amy can rescue them. But in the end, such 'nice masochism' is as powerless as Miss Wade's more direct masochism to make the world better.[25]

And making the world better is what Dickens is all about. Like Dostoyevsky, he sought approximations to the 'perfectly beautiful man'. His task was perhaps more difficult because he did not have direct access to that cruel talent which saw into the evil of the human heart and loved it because it was human. But even without this direct vision, Dickens was unable to create, in his later books at least, undimensional characters of unrelieved and unbelievable goodness. Amy Dorrit has upon her a 'speck . . . of the prison atmosphere' (I, xxxv, 422) which allows the reader to evaluate her actions as Dostoyevsky did when he created Kolya and Ganya Ivolgin. Kolya's devotion is transferred from his father to the Prince, and it is possible that to the Prince's example of genuine love and goodness Kolya will be able to join his helpfulness to effect genuine improvement in the world. So too, joined with Arthur in marriage, Amy Dorrit may be able to pass on to her children (and Fanny's, the story implies, giving Amy a wider scope for future action that she had during her first twenty-two years) a less erroneous, more humane Idea that might be the beginning of a mutually inter-dependent, mutually responsible society.

This chance is only hinted at in *Little Dorrit*. Amy insists on being for Arthur (even against his will) what she was for her father: a 'domesticated fairy' (I, xxii, 258), an image of truth that verifies his guilt. She returns to him wearing her old dress; she nurses him in prison and brings him his release. All her actions are designed to establish them in the old father-daughter relationship, where the archetypical mother figure gains by her smallness and poverty and need the unchanging love and dependence of her child-father. This psychic pact is cemented by Amy's complicity with Mrs. Clennam in suppressing Arthur's history and fortune. Either an identity or independent wealth would remove Amy's function, and so in suppressing both she recreates her relationship with her father and becomes Arthur's surrogate mother. 'As the difference in their ages implies, their marriage represents a child's conception of the ideal family, the union of parent and child', says Randolph Splitter.[26]

It is only through Arthur that Amy can realize a larger Idea. He has not succumbed to or mirrored his mother's vindictive repressiveness but has tried to empower good people by allowing them freedom of action in their areas of strength (Daniel Doyce, Mr. Pancks). His weakness lies in the area of personal relationships. Peter Scott has said that Arthur chooses to avoid hurt (as when he decides not to woo Pet Meagles) rather than risking the possibility of good.[27] If he had wooed Pet and won, he could have saved her from a dreadful marriage and helped her realize her potential as a good woman. By avoiding the risk of hurt, he becomes partly responsible for her fate. He would have acted the same way with Amy had she not offered herself to him (another 'sacrifice'). Arthur's Idea is the most hopeful in the book, but it is doomed to die with him unless he is saved from his fear of risk. This is the one thing Amy, in her chosen persona of Little Dorrit, can do for him. Together, they offer the only hope the book puts forward. Their marriage

> means not some renewal of their society as a whole, but the possibility in the individual life of escaping from the maze of delusion imposed or inculcated by the social matrix, by a fallen culture, by family life depraved in not only the theological but also possibly the most literal sense. The delinquency of the earlier home environments, in both Amy's and Arthur's respective cases, signifies the general human inheritance.[28]

They are forming a new family that has a possibility of being more than casual. Amy's goodness, shaped by Arthur's ability to allow others to work for good in their own ways, may help to enrich the general human inheritance.

To see the Dorrit family interaction as Dostoyevsky saw it makes it impossible to say any longer, as Leavis did, that

Amy's 'genius is to be always beyond question genuine—real'.[29] The Amy she lets us see is, without the anchor of Dostoyevsky's holy family, as little real as any of the other characters, because she has nothing upon which to make herself real, to realize herself. Amy's most real achievement is to make the connection—with Arthur Clennam—that can help her create a new Idea which may become the basis for a future holy family. They must 'try to create a new social reality', a task which causes a genuine 'terror of freedom', in the words of Richard Barickman[30] precisely because of Amy's unreality, her lack of an Idea. This may not be what Dickens *meant* to say or how he intended his readers to view life. But it is what he could not escape saying. It is the real fear underlying the hopeful family restructurings that come to naught; it is the substance of life which only hope can erode, the rock of human reality which Dickens's genius could not fail to acknowledge and to which Dostoyevsky gives credit when he creates General Ivolgin on the pattern of William Dorrit.

Dostoyevsky's recreation of William Dorrit and his family in General Ivolgin's 'casual family' can thus be seen to give the critic a way not only of describing but also of evaluating the family structure in *Little Dorrit*. The technique of reverse influence offers insights difficult to arrive at in other ways. Indeed, in his subsequent novels, *Great Expectations* and *Our Mutual Friend*, Dickens tries to establish other family structures (without blood ties, like Pip and Magwitch, or across class structures like Lizzie and Eugene) which form a basis for individual responsibility that can in turn shape the new societies that these families will create.

NOTES

1. Mark Spilka, *Dickens and Kafka* (Bloomington: Indiana University Press, 1963), and see also Loralee MacPike, *Dostoyevsky's Dickens* (London: George Prior, 1981).
2. *Pis'ma*, ed. A. S. Dolinin (Moscow: Goslitizdat, 1928–30), IV, p. 196.
3. Lary, op. cit., p. 104.
4. The casual family is also shown in detail in *A Raw Youth*, which Dostoyevsky wrote in order to show how a youth could become 'polluted

with the dreadful possibility of depravity, early hate, because of his nothingness and "accidentalness" ["sluchainost", or "casualness"]'— *Diary* I, i, 2, p. 160 (January 1876).

5. *The Idiot*, trans. David Magarshack (Baltimore: Penguin Books, 1961), IV, iii, pp. 520, 521. Future references, to be included in the text, will be from this edition.

6. Edward Wasiolek (ed.), *Notebooks for the Idiot*, trans. K. Strelsky (Chicago: University of Chicago Press, 1967), p. 149 (emphasis mine).

7. Frank Friedeberg Seeley, 'Dostoyevsky's Women', *Slavonic and East European Review*, Vol. 39 (1961), 305.

8. *Little Dorrit* (London: Oxford University Press, 1953), I, xiv, p. 172. Future references, to be included in the text, will be from this edition.

9. See Elizabeth Dalton, *Unconscious Structure in 'The Idiot'* (Princeton: Princeton University Press, 1981).

10. George Holoch, 'Consciousness and Society in *Little Dorrit*', *Victorian Studies*, 21, No. 3 (Spring 1978), 343.

11. Peter Christmas, '*Little Dorrit*: The End of Good and Evil', *Dickens Studies Annual*, ed. Robert B. Partlow Jr. (Carbondale: Southern Illinois University Press, 1977), Vol. 6, 135.

12. Edmund Wilson, 'Dickens: The Two Scrooges', *The Wound and the Bow* (Boston, 1941), p. 52.

13. Sigmund Freud, 'Family Romances', *The Works of Sigmund Freud*, Standard Edition (London: Hogarth Press, 1959), IX, pp. 235–44. See also Branwen Bailey Pratt, 'Dickens and Father: Notes on the Family Romance', *Hartford Studies in Literature*, 8, No. 1 (1976), 4–22.

14. A. O. J. Cockshut, *The Imagination of Charles Dickens* (New York: New York University Press, 1962), p. 154.

15. John Lucas, *The Melancholy Man: A Study of Dickens's Novels* (London: Methuen, 1970), p. 255.

16. John Wain, '*Little Dorrit*', in *Dickens and the Twentieth Century*, ed. John Gross and Gabriel Pearson (Toronto: University of Toronto Press, 1962), p. 183.

17. Edmund Bergler, '*Little Dorrit* and Dickens' Intuitive Knowledge of Psychic Masochism', *American Imago*, 14, No. 4 (Winter 1957), 372.

18. Pratt, op. cit., 17.

19. A. E. Dyson, *The Inimitable Dickens* (London: Macmillan, 1970), p. 210.

20. See Paul D. Herring, 'Dickens' Monthly Number Plans for *Little Dorrit*', *Modern Philology*, 64, No. 1 (August 1966), 32, 42. Herring's analysis of Dickens's number plans has not received the recognition it deserves.

21. Geoffrey Thurley, *The Dickens Myth: Its Genesis and Structure* (London: Routledge & Kegan Paul, 1976), p. 232.

22. Bergler, op. cit., 380.

23. F. R. Leavis, *Dickens the Novelist*, p. 256.

24. Richard Stang, '*Little Dorrit*: A World in Reverse', in *Dickens the Craftsman*, ed. Robert B. Partlow Jr. (Carbondale: Southern Illinois University Press, 1970), p. 156.

25. Such a view of Amy Dorrit in relation to her father is not new. Both Peter Scott (*Reality and Comic Confidence in Charles Dickens* (New York:

Barnes and Noble, 1979)) and Randolph Splitter ('Guilt and the Trappings of Melodrama in *Little Dorrit*', *Dickens Studies Annual*, 6 (1977), 119–33) explicitly see that Amy chooses her prison and does so in conjunction with her father's elaborate self-deception.

26. Splitter, op. cit., 130.
27. Scott's is one of the best analyses of the Amy-Arthur relationship.
28. Scott, op. cit., p. 191.
29. F. R. Leavis, op. cit., p. 226.
30. Richard Barickman, 'The Spiritual Journey of Amy Dorrit and Arthur Clennam', *Dickens Studies Annual*, 7 (1978), ed. Robert B. Partlow, Jr. (Carbondale, Ill.: Southern Illinois University Press), pp. 165, 172.

11

Hidden Rivalries in Victorian Fiction: The Case of the Two Esthers

by JEROME MECKIER

Hitherto undetected internal divisions of the sort deconstruc-
tionists currently ponder are not really present in Victorian
multiplot novels. Even if they were, they still would not be the
most important instances of the internecine that Victorian
fiction contains. This distinction should be reserved for the
onslaughts major nineteenth-century novelists direct against
each other. Structuralism to the contrary, the interesting
rivalries are between Victorian novels, not within them. Entire
works, not plots within each, persistently revalue one another
in a counterpoint that is genre-wide.

Many Victorian novels, it appears, were written not just for
their own sakes but to restate a competitor's views. Often, the
recipient of such treatment turns out to be Dickens. Thackeray's
declaration of war against 'Boz' could have been proclaimed
even more justifiably by George Eliot, Trollope, or Mrs.
Gaskell: Dickens 'knows', Thackeray wrote, 'that my books
are a protest against his—that if one set are true, the other
must be false.'[1]

In *Oliver Twist* Dickens announced his arrival as a serious
novelist by redoing the Newgate novels of Ainsworth and
Bulwer. Instead of offering an outlaw's life-style as an escapist

216

fantasy, he captured the actual squalor of the criminal world others romanticized. Usually, however, Dickens is the primary target of competitive revaluation and thus remains one's best index to the breadth and intensity of this Victorian phenomenon. A modern such as Waugh accuses Dickens of underestimating the negative impact secularization would have on the social fabric. But Victorian novelists considered his melodramatic realism overly severe for a social critic. They thought of him as an exaggerator, an alarmist who would give the era a bad name.

Gerald Graff believes that the New Criticism, unwisely following Blake, assigned art a different kind of truth from practical, scientific knowledge. This made art irrelevant. Artists, Graff contends, were condemned to fabricate a formal order impossible to duplicate in politics, economics, or external nature.[2] Yet Dickens, George Eliot, Thackeray, Trollope *et al.* fought among themselves to determine whose version of the truth most closely reflected the actual world. At stake in these pitched battles was a licence to be the age's foremost social analyst, its presiding sage, a position moderns later contend for under the title of salvationary philosopher. The most persuasive realist, the writer whose depictions of contemporary social conditions were judged most convincing, would have his admonishments heeded. Whenever variables begin to replace absolutes, as happened during the Victorian period, a novelist has to convince readers he possesses the necessary grasp before presuming to prescribe. Inaccurate description, the implied rule goes, precludes effective prescription. Conclusions, it becomes clear, develop more pragmatically than ever before from the assembled circumstances. Hence the obsessive concern with establishing the sheer physical reality of the novelist's chosen scene, whether it be Tom-all-Alone's in *Bleak House* or a workingman's home in *North and South*.

Society in modern fiction often disappears altogether in favour of contradictory individual perspectives. Victorian novelists play a role in this ill-fated unravelling and facilitate post-modern elaborations of it by disowning one another. Competition between the perspectives of disputatious novelists, each striving to furnish society with a new overview, calls nineteenth-century realism into question and foreshadows the modern world. Victorian novelists, by challenging each other's claims to truthful representation, contribute to the current disenchantment with creative endeavour. The progression is from the Victorian novel as a competition, a struggle between opposing interpretive realisms, to the contemporary theory that everything is subjective, that realism—artistic and analytic statements about the so-called real world—is itself a fiction. Unparalleled questioning of the veracity of someone else's art, the key to relationships between many Victorian novels, leads to an equally unexampled questioning of art *per se*.

To encompass a secular world that seems ever more complex, Victorian novelists begin multiplying story-lines: they invent the multiplot novel. But these novels disagree with one another about the nature and extent of society's problems. Victorian novelists cannot sustain the Romantic conception of objectivity as intersubjectivity or concensus. Moderns deplore the shapeless diversity that results. Without intersubjectivity, multiplicity is a secularist's nightmare. Aldous Huxley eventually finds reassurance in the mutually corroborative accounts of spiritual experience written by unrelated mystics. Joyce and Virginia Woolf invent experimental techniques that assume common internal psychological processes. Exploring the subjectiveness of several individuals, they say, shows that intersubjectivity still operates out of daylight's reach. In Virginia Woolf, this entails a collective subconscious: moments of coherence (Wordsworthian spots-in-time) exist in a general memory bank and can be recollected in tranquillity by those who shared them; saintly figures like Mrs. Ramsay achieve immortality—i.e. self-fulfilment—as benevolent connective influences in the subconsciousness of all who knew them.

Victorian novelists repeatedly borrow a competitor's themes, scenes, characters, or situations and deliberately refashion them to say something different. Major writers consolidate—sometimes first discern—their own positions by revising a rival's work. The novelist wants to substitute a truer rendition of the way people behave or things happen for another author's misconceptions. The undercutting of the false, the exaggerated, or the improbable by an account held to be of greater validity should be seen as a kind of parody.

Thus the Victorian period, especially in the novel, is not the wholly earnest, non-satiric age literary historians once accepted.[3] On the contrary, earnestness regularly expresses itself in the clearing away of descriptions and occurrences deemed irresponsible, misleading, or unscientific. Dickens's work is consistently dismissed as too inflammatory. Another way to revalue the Victorians is to observe them revaluing each other. Whenever one novelist recycles another's materials, his actions underscore fundamental disagreements in their philosophies.

The intention behind reuse of character and theme is always contradiction. Permutations are reconstructive as well as deconstructive, however; they are never plagiarisms. Rivalries between Victorian novels have remained hidden because critics generally ignore them. To some extent, Victorian novelists concealed them too. A Victorian novel always does its own job first, while less directly—one could say surreptitiously—it undoes someone else's. Even when respondent or revaluative, the Victorian novel makes sense on its own. One can appreciate *Felix Holt*, for example, without connecting it with *Bleak House*. Antipathy between these novels resembles the hostility *Brave New World* has for *Men Like Gods* rather than the symbiosis that demands *Pamela* be mentioned in every discussion of *Joseph Andrews*. Competing multiplot novels are assertions as well as rebuttals: their proposals are simultaneously counter-proposals (and *vice versa*). To the critic with double vision, *Felix Holt* is both a statement in its own right and a counterstatement, a restructuring of *Bleak House*. Every time George Eliot reshapes Dickens towards her own ends, the reformulations always become sufficiently engrossing to stand alone by virtue of their internal logic. Restatements hide, in effect erase, the novels they reformulate.

Although Victorian novelists regularly write against one another, each remains unshakably confident as a realist; so Dickens is everywhere in his prefaces. Victorian realism needs redefining as the attempted installation of one author's views in place of aberrations he finds in his contemporaries. 'The novel', John Fowles notes, has always been 'a kind of self-feeding form, a cannibal form . . .', so that one 'cannot conceive of a writer not breaking down the material he admires in past novelists and reusing it in his own work'.[4] Victorian fictions are cannibalistic, but seldom out of admiration: they break down material to subvert and replace it. To the degree Victorian novelists feed on the effusions of their rivals, they write the first anti-novels. A novelist hopes to displace a work he distrusts by redoing it more honestly in one of his own.

This pugnacious sharpening of one another's perceptions should not be confused with the improving influence Dorothea and Lydgate exert on each other's character in *Middlemarch*. On the other hand, it is less cacophonous than a discussion scene in a Huxley novel, where each egoist tries to drown out all the others. Competition between conflicting Victorian realisms is Victorian in content and context, yet modern and post-modern by anticipation. For onlookers, if not for participants, Victorian revaluation (novelists revaluing novelists) seems a healthier state of affairs than the breakdowns it has culminated in for post-modern art and post-structuralist criticism (deconstructionism). From one point of view, Victorians reconsidering Victorians results from the collapse of orthodoxy, the loss of consensus, and is a harbinger of worse disagreements. From another, it becomes the new norm; by comparison with it, subsequent departures appear increasingly parodic and soon prove self-defeating.

No one rewrote Dickens more diligently than George Eliot. This major novelist made a second career out of parodying his novels to promulgate her own ideas. More so than *Middlemarch*, which also contains parodies of *Bleak House*, *Felix Holt* is the classic instance of Victorian revaluation: a systematic revision, a complete redoing, of Dickens's masterpiece. The point of overhauling his novel with her own is to reuse the same matter to reach different conclusions. George Eliot wants her more optimistic conception of existing social conditions to supersede Dickens's. Tensions develop between his bleak perspective and a revised forecast reaffirming life's organic soundness. Every readjustment of a character, incident, or theme from Dickens results in a satiric counterpoint between her book and his.

Dickens's masterwork is a stumbling block for the would-be

Victorian sibyl. She has to neutralize its anti-evolutionary satire before her own more hopeful vision of England's prospects for gradual improvement can gain acceptance. She insists that Dickens's brand of radicalism is destructive rather than ameliorative. Even though she shares Dickens's contempt for most existing political and economic procedures, she is not as equivocal about fresh starts. An exasperated Dickens invokes spontaneous combustion as a veiled metaphor for revolution and seems half in love with his own scare tactic. But George Eliot fears that a clean sweep, a disruptive upheaval, will carry with it ideals better preserved. The more painstaking task for a radical, she cautions Dickens, is to sift the outmoded and cumbersome in order to isolate the perennially valuable. One must guarantee, in addition to eradicating abuses, that worthwhile tradition will be passed on.

Felix Holt is the first of three principal examinations of society's evolutionary potential. Along with *Middlemarch* and *Daniel Deronda*, it explores the reformer's calling as a secular apostolate, the supreme individual response to energies already at work in life's flow but in need of expert direction. None of this makes sense if Esther Summerson's maturation is as perilous as Dickens contends or as limited. The reformer's vocation seems quixotic as long as the third-person narrator's Juvenalian satire remains the accredited estimate of the human situation. *Felix Holt* is George Eliot's most anti-Dickensian novel because it must create room for itself and two subsequent studies of reformist endeavour.[5]

The plot of *Felix Holt* teems with Dickensian importations employed slightly askew. For instance, George Eliot parodies the device of hidden parentage. First she doubles Dickens's reliance upon it, then she decides that being the progeny of sexual transgression, a melodramatic metaphor for the restraining power of the past, cannot be taken seriously as divine punishment; it does not predetermine one's fate. Rufus Lyon initially lacks courage to inform his daughter that he is not her real father, but Matthew Jermyn avoids prosecution from the Transomes by telling Harold that he is his. Unlike in other ways, Esther and Harold resemble each other in that the identity crisis each undergoes in the novel is not caused or resolved by sensational disclosures. Harold realizes on his own that he is not truly an English radical, in fact, by inclination not English at all. Esther Lyon learns her status depends on the mission she and the man she decides to marry choose to undertake, not on who her father was or how much money he left her.

Both novels feature an interminable law case: for Jarndyce versus Jarndyce, read Bycliffe versus Transome as its parody. In *Felix Holt*, the law suit is not quite so endless; lawyers still work things out. Bycliffe versus Transome is not self-consuming in the way Dickens finds typical of antiquated systems and corrupt institutions. Nevertheless, Esther Lyon, rightful heir to Transome Court, declines to inherit. A labyrinthine law case, one of Dickens's depressing images for life, turns out to be as inconsequential in George Eliot's novel as belated discovery of one's true parentage. The enlightened individual in this revisionary perception of Victorian England already is an heir. Contrary to the tenets of sensation novels, legacies are not essential for social salvation. Esther Lyon's birthright and, later, Dorothea Brooke's, is, to paraphrase Arnold, the best ideas that men have thought and said.

Having inherited the ongoing cultural process in the world's foremost country, Esther can bequeath as well as receive, a feat seemingly beyond Oliver Twist or David Copperfield. She is fortunately positioned in the advance guard of nineteenth-century civilization and can disseminate its strengths. In her place, one cannot help but feel legitimate, indeed, chosen. Thanks to Felix's advice, Esther need only commit herself to the evolutionary flux, the forward march of life and mind, in order to save and be saved. Thus she must avoid the deathly fixity that comes from desiring position and a legally certified but unearned identity. She could make the same mistakes as either Richard Carstone or Lady Dedlock but emulates neither. She puts monetary inheritance out of mind. She does not wed Harold Transome, the novel's equivalent for Sir Leicester's aristocratic inutility. The outcome of Jarndyce versus Jarndyce, George Eliot suggests, is highly improbable, grossly unfair to the legal profession. In addition, it is more immaterial to any reasonable person's welfare than Dickens realized.

Mrs. Transome, like Lady Dedlock, has a sexual sin in her past to conceal. Guiltily she paces the corridors of Transome Court as if it were the walk at Chesney Wold and she its ghost.

Mrs. Transome, however, is no Gothic figment; in George Eliot's novel she is required to survive revelation of her shame. Only if a community is not continually advancing can the lives of individuals, like law cases and governing bodies, reach false climaxes or come to dead ends. Otherwise, life goes on.

Another survivor is Job Tudge. For this sickly, neglected child, Felix makes, without fanfare, the sensible provision George Eliot believes Woodcourt ought to have hit upon for Jo. Truth again discredits fantasy when Jermyn replaces Tulkinghorn, whose misogyny George Eliot thinks is unmotivated. Jermyn has had the sexual encounters with Mrs. Transome that Dickens's lawyer only approximates by toppling Lady Dedlock. Both villains excel at keeping secrets for profit. Yet Jermyn, again more realistically says George Eliot, discloses a major secret to preserve himself, not to destroy another person.

One finds almost as many secrets in *Felix Holt* as in *Bleak House* and *The Woman in White* combined. George Eliot despises secrecy more vehemently than her more sensational rivals did. She deprives these melodramatic materials of the social significance Dickens taught Collins to give them. Characters maintain secrets in *Bleak House* to avoid responsibility, just as society keeps secrets and shuns responsibility by prolonging a law case or driving its unfortunates into out-of-the-way places. Collins maintains that oppressive moral codes compel individuals to lead secret lives. For both novelists, secrecy results from and satirically mirrors larger societal failures. A more sanguine George Eliot cannot allow this if her thesis that social process is an often invisible but generally orderly progression is to prevail. She revalues Dickens's position by defining secrets as a wedge a person unwisely drives between his private life and the ongoing public good.

Secrets in *Felix Holt* are counter-evolutionary and therefore of shorter duration than in Dickens. They are futile attempts to put self before community, to interrupt life's incessant unfolding by a folding in of the self. Secrets impede that beneficial interaction through which George Eliot's characters overcome egotism and exchange the personality traits each needs to acquire new abilities. They prevent the improving world displayed in her novel from reaching forward to the least partial good. As a consequence, George Eliot portrays secretives as exceptions to life's rule, not extensions of it as in Dickens and Collins. She downplays secrets as individual aberrations, entertaining to read about yet tangential in any scientific analysis of the way life moves forward.

Whenever the moral order is sufficiently outraged, revelations in Dickens and Collins come with Old Testament ferocity to shake an entire society. By contrast, disclosure invariably saves in *Felix Holt*. The character testifying or most affected thereby celebrates the life process if the secret is benign, rejoins it if a confession of guilt is involved. This holds true when Esther nobly reveals her love for Felix at his trial and Jermyn basely saves himself from criminal proceedings by telling Harold: '*I am your father*.'[6] As character witness for Felix, Esther cannot avoid realizing his superiority to Harold Transome. Jermyn, by saving his own skin, lifts a burden from Mrs. Transome. This prepares the way for a stronger bond between her and her son. For the first time, a considerate Harold puts another's feelings before his own.

Esther Lyon's 'inward revolution' (591) is of greater consequence in *Felix Holt* than the election riot at Treby Magna. The revolution takes her from idle young lady to a full life as Felix's wife and co-partner in educating England's workers. Similarly, Holt's decision to become a worker-teacher, a cultural missionary to his own class, is a more significant event for George Eliot than the resolution of a long-standing law case. She borrows incidents from Dickens to help her put things in proper perspective.

Revelations of parentage, resolutions of a legal matter, and the outcome of an election are crucial in some theories of what constitutes history and in most melodrama. But, says George Eliot, they generally do not improve society. That Esther and Felix are authentic in ways Harold Transome is not amounts to a realization one comes to on grounds unrelated to law, votes, or finance. The unimportance of pyrotechnics stolen from Dickens is the assertion George Eliot's multiplot novel is carefully designed to emphasize at his expense.

Felix and Esther risk forfeiting the reader's sympathies only when they become entangled in the novel's Dickensian apparatus. Esther's involvement in Bycliffe versus Transome is a trap. So is her stay at Transome Court, during which she recognizes that she can possess it and Harold too. Felix unwisely gets caught up in a mob scene that could have originated in *Barnaby Rudge*. Although he participates in confusion to head off greater disaster, he seems out of his element throughout the disturbance. He is later justly punished, one feels, not for inadvertent manslaughter but for endangering his leadership abilities in a pointless mêlée.

Complaints about gratuitous complications in the plotting of *Felix Holt* miss the point of George Eliot's parody. Her novel is said to be 'unlike *Little Dorrit* or *Bleak House*' because its 'complexity' is 'unrelated to the central areas of what the novel is saying. There is nothing being said *through* the complexity.'[7] This argument, which pits the novel's convolutions against its central areas, sounds fashionably deconstructionist. Garrett seems at fault for neglecting to expound it.[8] But it is Dickens whom George Eliot is deconstructing so that she can substitute the missing centre, the vital point, she thinks his complications lack.

George Eliot reuses events dear to melodramatic realism to turn them against themselves, to defuse them and prevent further employment. At the same time, of course, they enhance her chances for a popular success. Dickens's complexities, George Eliot contends, falsify the social process; they divert attention from events that may appear less exciting but are truly momentous. In *Felix Holt* she tries to reverse this effect. She decentres Dickensian material, driving out his sort of sensational irrelevancies with really significant occurrences she believes will both reflect and influence the actual world. Displacement, revaluative substitution of the real and the desirable for the unreal and the meretricious—that is what is being said *through* the novel's complexity.

The union of Felix and Esther gradually emerges to replace all else as the novel's climax and goal. That it does so in spite of the book's complex irrelevancies enhances the moral argument. When Esther and Felix consecrate themselves to one another and to a better future for society, they substantiate George Eliot's conception of progressive evolution, a programme which the real or central plot opposes to the ultimately peripheral histrionics lifted from Dickens. A host of lesser

revisions—Jermyn for Tulkinghorn, Mrs. Transome for Lady
Dedlock, Job Tudge for Jo—smooth the way for grander, more
philosophical revaluations. Esther's maturation, her
marriage to a social reformer as intelligent as Felix, attests to
'the wonderful slow-growing system of things', which Holt
himself celebrates as a major theme in his 'Address to Working
Men' (616).[9] Growth, slow but wondrous, is life's first principle,
George Eliot claims, for individual lives, culture in England,
and all societies.

At first Esther confuses elegant social surfaces at Transome
Court with a moral content, a vitality, found only in Felix.
Similarly, George Eliot charges, admirers and practitioners of
Dickens's kind of novel invariably mistake life's superficial
confusion, 'the abuses of society', for the 'natural order' that
Felix insists still lies 'beneath' (609). To clarify the difference
between basic integrity and surface malfunctions, George
Eliot offers her rural novel in place of Dickens's metropolitan
nightmare. The implication is that a Londoner's realism mis-
apprehends urban blight, which is superimposed, for the real
order of things, which is Romantic and organic, agricultural
rather than municipal, more like a crop or slowly ageing tree
than a clogged sewer.

Dickens, one might object, parallels the Chancellor in
London with Sir Leicester in the country, Chancery with
Chesney Wold, as complementary obstacles to progress.
George Eliot re-creates Chesney Wold at Transome Court to
rewrite Dickens's parallelism. As the first part of the name
implies, Transome Court is an illusion, readily seen through,
rather than an immovable object. True parallelism renders it a
holdover, as negligible to the future of society as the law case
determining its ownership. This relic from the dead past is
outmoded politically, like a sovereign's retinue, which the
second half of its name suggests. George Eliot renames Sir
Leicester's estate to deny it any connection with a forest,
which, like society, is an extension of the living past and an
illustration of a 'slow-growing system'. Transome Court anticipates Wells' Bladesover, not E. M. Forster's Howard's End.
Unlike Lady Dedlock, who dies attempting to escape from
Chesney Wold, Esther Lyon simply walks away from the
prison Transome Court represents. The house is not connected

to life's core the way Dickens says Sir Leicester's country seat is.

Perpetual stoppages and suppressed human relationships in *Bleak House* anger George Eliot. She parodies Dickens's novel as a false perspective on social problems, a pessimistic misreading of the evolving nature of things. The realism of *Felix Holt* opposes that of *Bleak House*. Each purports to explain the world, but the result is a debate between a modern Juvenal and the modern Lucretius. Their novels become philosophical poems in disguise. As did the Greek scientist and epic poet, George Eliot calms fears. Despite Dickens's epic indictment, life is not deteriorating; divine punishments, she insists, are not imminent; mankind, like Esther Lyon, is in charge of his own development, a situation which continues to offer an exciting challenge.

In both *Felix Holt* and *Bleak House* the heroine is named Esther and her parentage is obscured. Garrett invents a competition between the narrators in *Bleak House* that seems contrived when compared with the rivalry between these two Esthers. George Eliot asks readers to decide that Esther Lyon better represents a maturity to model oneself upon. Her Esther's life story is meant to seem truer and hold out more promise for everyone's future. The point is to replace Dickens's idea of a secular saint with George Eliot's version. Both novelists rewrite *The Book of Esther* for Victorian audiences, but George Eliot considers her heroine more entitled to an illustrious name. Esther Summerson is not the saviour of her race. Esther Lyon, by contrast, could be.

George Eliot's Esther is middle-class with the pretensions of an aristocrat. Felix, resorting to the novel's abundant animal imagery, initially portrays her as a 'squirrel-headed thing' (153), a 'long-necked peacock' (151). When this would-be lady marries into a class beneath hers, she combines her new-found strengths and her inherent grace with an intellectual working man's indomitable spirit. More than Connie Chatterley, Esther Lyon will have a social as well as a sexual role to play. She will help to save the classes she and Felix represent from falling upon each other in upcoming labour disputes or on future election days.

The improved Esther of *Felix Holt* is provided with a spacious arena for reformist activity and a profounder helpmate than Alan Woodcourt. Harold Transome, for a time a dangerously attractive suitor, regards public matters in terms of his own private needs. Fortunately, Holt schools Esther to regulate her personal life so as to serve the general necessity, to redeem the future. Esther Lyon's mission as cultural ambassador to England's workers brings opportunities which George Eliot, revising Dickens, points out are absent from the narrower round of primarily domestic duties reserved for the Esther in *Bleak House.*

Dickens's Esther reports that she never walks out with her husband without hearing the people 'bless' him. 'I never lie down at night,' she continues, 'but I know that in the course of that day he has alleviated pain.'[10] 'The people even praise Me as the doctor's wife,' she adds; 'they like me for his sake. . . .' No doubt Dickens's heroine modestly omits her own good deeds. Nevertheless, hers is largely a reflected glory as 'the doctor's wife'. By contrast, Esther Lyon, as Felix's ideological ally as well as the mother of his children, enjoys a fuller partnership. Not surprisingly, Transome's son behaves like an untutored savage; his father is not a conduit for civilization's values. But Esther Lyon's progeny, one presumes, will be splendid hybrids in the front rank of an organic process of cultural and biological evolution, the syllabus for which would read like a blend of Darwin, Arnold, and Marx.

Together, Felix and Esther will begin to educate the masses so that, besides getting the vote eventually, their minds will be enfranchised with England's cultural tradition, the richness men can only carry in their heads. The 'current of ideas' Arnold found essential among the intelligentsia for the appearance of great poets must be made to flow towards the illiterate and poorly educated, George Eliot believes. They pose the biggest threat to the cultural transmission they also stand to gain from most.

As an apostle of culture to the amorphous consciousness of the workers, Esther Lyon will participate in what her father calls 'the transmission of an improved heritage' (341). This utopian undertaking is parental in the broadest sense and seems an appropriate task for a heroine whose parentage was once confused. The poorly instructed, George Eliot argues, are the only true illegitimates. Esther Summerson, after all, was properly schooled by a mysterious guardian who turns out to be Jarndyce. But the workers to whom Felix is drawn have been cut off from their country's finest things. Transmitting 'an improved heritage' to working men and their children is George Eliot's answer in advance to Carlyle's 1867 anxieties that new reform measures will speed up life's flow until it turns into Niagara's rapids.[11]

The process of cultural transmission is described, fittingly, by a clergyman, Esther's stepfather, for it is a question of passing on the new religion. More so than Rufus Lyon realizes, George Eliot implies that an operation previously spiritual and sacred has become physical and secular, although it retains its religious aura. Felix Holt is the successor to men like Mr. Lyon. The eloquence of this good-natured clergyman is far superior to Chadband's oily locomotions but tellingly archaic in syntax and substance. Esther's father's religion seems to have made a minimal impression upon her. It remains for Felix to put her in touch with her 'best self' (366), to awaken 'the finest part of her nature' (418). As tutelage leads to betrothal, it becomes virtually a religious experience. Although Esther Lyon is a clergyman's daughter, she is Felix's first convert.

George Eliot projects for her Esther the 'difficult blessedness' found only in 'beings who are conscious of painfully growing into the possession of higher powers' (327). Esther Lyon is commissioned as a preserver of traditions and a veritable agent of the life force. Such 'higher powers' combine the political and the progenitive, the sacred and the sociological. They are clearly beyond Esther Summerson's reach or desire. Esther Lyon's growth is more arduous than Esther Summerson's because it takes her further. It apparently designates George Eliot's heroine the superior life form. Esther Lyon is designed to replace Esther Summerson in the reader's mind and on life's biological scale, just as Felix usurps Byron's place in Esther Lyon's dreams. Woodcourt and Esther Summerson form a saving remnant, whereas Holt and Esther Lyon, seemingly left behind by the political whirl of 'the memorable year 1832', are actually in the vanguard. A sign of new beginnings, they are 'a little leaven spread within us' (327).

Consequently, disdain for *Exodus* 34:7 in *Felix Holt* reads like a parody of Dickens's exegesis in *Bleak House* and Collins's subsequent use of the same text in *The Woman in White*. The moral arguments carried by the plots of these three novels are firmly at odds. Dickens rewrites the passage about 'the sins of the fathers' to warn that each generation pays for the inadequate reforms instituted by its predecessors. The text gives Collins another pretext for denigrating overly strict moral codes. He takes it to mean that new improprieties are often commited as the only way of keeping the father's original trespass secret. George Eliot tries to disprove the Biblical admonition each of her rivals modifies to suit his own social concerns.

George Eliot rejects the anti-progressive contention that individuals suffer directly a revenge life exacts for actions not their own. Events, she maintains, do not happen the way a misguided reformer like Dickens claims. By the time Jermyn declares himself, Harold Transome has already lost the election and Esther's decision not to marry him has been made in her heart. Jermyn's disclosure in Chapter 47, just four from the end, is therefore climax and anti-climax (a parody of climax). It is almost as exciting as Chapter 59 of *Bleak House*, where Esther finds Lady Dedlock's body, but far less relevant.

More so than Harold Transome's case, Esther Lyon's proves that the enlightened individual is absolved of the dead past as a restriction, a determinant, or a source of guilt and punishment. The deconstructive past is definitely not part of the heritage one must improve and transmit. The message of George Eliot's novel, contrary to that of *Bleak House*, is that secularized Victorian life is liberation, not imprisonment. One is free to disregard the Old Testament rumblings hyperbolic novelists rely on to bolster their authority. In fact, George Eliot implies that the Old Testament itself is a sensationalist document whose principle of inexorability, a relentless providence, must be replaced by a sense of continuity that is more of a marvel yet scientifically—that is, biologically—verifiable.

Walter Hartright's retrospective on events in *The Woman in White* will rely heavily on 'Scripture denunciations'. Following Dickens, Collins has Walter reflect:

> But for the fatal resemblance between the two daughters of one father, the conspiracy of which Anne had been the innocent instrument and Laura the innocent victim could never have been planned. With what unerring and terrible directness the long chain of circumstances led down from the thoughtless wrong committed by the father to the heartless injury inflicted on the child![12]

Like Felix Holt, George Eliot puts her trust in 'the wonderful slow-growing system of things' rather than in something as punitive as 'the unerring and terrible directness' of a 'long chain of circumstances' over which individuals have slight control. It takes Esther Summerson thirty-six chapters to realize she is as 'innocent' of her birth, though illegitimate, as a queen is of hers. Coincidentally, Esther Lyon's true identity and her right to the Transome estates are discovered in Chapter 35. But she beats her rival to self-realization and beyond by more than a chapter. By Chapter 35, she has already been 'growing into the possession of higher powers' for over 100 pages.

Esther Summerson, in the course of surviving her trials, develops a fuller appreciation for providence: 'I saw very well how many things had worked together, for my welfare.'[13] Dickens decides that the warning 'about the father's sins being visited upon the children' applies to irresponsible societies. Nevertheless, Esther helps to keep secret for a time her mother's sin, which gives Collins his cue for interpreting *Exodus* 34:7 in relation to the proprieties. Esther must accept some of the punishment, if not the guilt, for her parents' clandestine love. To varying degrees, she will always be Esther Hawdon or Esther Dedlock as well as Esther Woodcourt. This multiple identity, rather than her many nicknames, is a sign of imperfect maturation.

On the other hand, Esther Lyon realizes that becoming Esther Bycliffe or Esther Transome (as Harold's wife) would be 'to abandon her own past' (496), that is, to downgrade those acts and decisions of her own which have made her who she is. Thus she rebuts Esther Summerson when she discerns 'no illumination' in her stepfather's theory of a 'providential arrangement' behind her sudden inheritance (505). For a passive Esther Summerson, 'reserved' by providence 'for a happy life', George Eliot substitutes an activist Esther Lyon, committed to influencing the future. George Eliot's Esther is made conscious of her only real self, Esther Holt, the way the novelist insists such things actually happen: not by providential intervention but by social interaction. Esther Lyon matures through formative, progressive contact with another evolving human being. The exchange of love and ideas between Felix and Esther demonstrates that George Eliot has not misplaced her confidence in 'the efficacy of one personality on another' (327).

George Eliot writes *Felix Holt: The Radical*, as the subtitle indicates, to explain true radicalism and, in the process, revise Dickens's faulty concept of it. She redefines this phenomenon to mean change continuing organically via careful evolution *from the root*, centre, or fundamental source of life, which is an energy perceived as positive and good. Radicalism does not mean sudden or sweeping reform and therefore is not the stark opposite of conservatism Dickens would designate it. George Eliot identifies continuity, orderly transition, as the concern both conservatives and radicals can profitably adopt. If society is an organic continuum, as George Eliot's supposedly scientific assessment says it is, only culture, knowledge and wisdom transmitted from one era to the next, keeps it so.

When Harold Transome is defeated in an election for Parliament as was Sir Leicester, George Eliot evens the score by bringing in a conservative for the one Dickens tossed out. In her opinion, however, it hardly matters who represents the Trebians in London. Conservatism and radicalism in *Felix Holt*—or Tory and Benthamite—become the real Coodle and Doodle; they are two equally disruptive misconstruings of the life process, which must be encouraged to flow steadily without long-term stoppages or sudden uncloggings. The immovable Dedlocks are hopelessly reactionary, as are the Trollopian Sir Maximus Debarry and his adherents; but the opportunism in the radical sentiments of a rootless Harold Transome is transparent. Dickens's Tories are self-serving protectors of privilege. In reply, George Eliot cautions against unprincipled reformers who either see a chance for power in the advocacy of quick change, as Transome does; or, more likely, will throw out good with bad from a lack of education.

Felix Holt, who, unlike Trollope or Dickens, would never think of standing for Parliament, has the only feasible social agenda in George Eliot's novel. Moreover, he personifies the prospectus he recommends. George Eliot's model radical aspires to become a learned artisan, a practical man of the people, equipped for the future as a self-supporting craftsman but with an intelligent appreciation of the past, a sense of 'the wealth that is carried in men's minds' (602). He wants to be

> a demogogue of a new sort, an honest one, if possible, who will tell the people they are blind and foolish, and neither flatter them nor fatten on them. (366)

Long before Shaw, Wells, or C. P. Snow, George Eliot has a clear idea of what the new man should be like.

In the person of Felix Holt George Eliot offers her paradigm: 'a man of this generation' who 'will try to make life less bitter for a few within [his] reach' (367), chiefly by broadening their minds. The phrase 'less bitter' indicates how modest a radicalism George Eliot prefers. Holt's programme, she contends, is more realistic than 'the formulas of [Esther's] father's beliefs' (369) and thus provides Esther with 'the first religious experience of her life'. It is also more practical than the master plans of England's rival political parties and thus gives the workers Felix addresses, in an appendix to the novel, their first taste of sensible reform. Parties think in terms of leaps, George Eliot implies, because they do not know how to take the first steps. More so than charity or benevolence in Dickens's early novels, it is reform, George Eliot argues, that can only be entrusted to enlightened, public-minded individuals who forego all connection with officialdom.

Holt is a compromise between Mr. Rouncewell and Sir Leicester. Consequently, he is also an alternative to Dickens's juxtapositioning of new man and old. George Eliot finds both as unbelievable as they are undesirable: the ironmaster is an impossible ideal, too Carlylean to be of real service to the masses; the baronet is a mere caricature, whereas the civility and refinement of a well-educated aristocracy is too valuable to discard. One can also interpret Felix as a reply to such epitomes, respectively, of compliancy and cunning as Stephen Blackpool and Slackbridge in *Hard Times* and to Mrs. Gaskell's portrait of Nicholas Higgins in *North and South*. Eventually, Holt will be qualified to supervise the transference of authority from a moribund élite, the world of Transome Court and Chesney Wold, to the as yet uncouth proletariat to be found not so much in Tom-all-alone's as in places like Sproxton.

In the workable world George Eliot both describes and forsees, individuals complete one another by exchanging needed characteristics. The patient tutorial Felix administers for Esther awakens her to the beauties of a life of purposefulness. At the same time, however, Esther modifies Felix's resolution never to marry by teaching him, as Adam Bede did for Dinah, that purposiveness increases in power when suffused with love. Felix's cultivation of Esther forms the first part of what he terms his difficult 'knighthood' (419). Before opening any night-schools for workers, he gives Esther a course in broad daylight. It is an upgrading of Mr. Knightly's attempts to improve Emma in that the education of Esther by Felix not only deals with matters George Eliot considers more important than Jane Austen's but proves reciprocal. The 'inward revolution' Felix stirs up in Esther revalues—parodies and eclipses—the elaborate seminar in values John Harmon arranges for Bella Wilfer in *Our Mutual Friend* a year before George Eliot's novel.

Throughout *Felix Holt*, George Eliot advances her claim always to have been a fomenter of internal, moral revolutions seismically superior to the changes of heart for which Dickens's novels were famous. Modifications of character are more extensive in *Felix Holt* than in the misleading sensationalism of *Bleak House*. No transformation in Esther Summerson quite matches the rapid improvement in Esther Lyon once she begins to think like George Eliot. She develops a missionary zeal more level-headed and far-reaching than Mrs. Jellyby's. George Eliot deflates Dickens's excesses and disarms his caricatures to remind readers that the most meaningful kind of social change begins quietly and internally, though not without prodding from an outside agent. She submits Esther Lyon's 'inward revolution' to de-sensationalize Krook's incredible travesty of it.

Dickens uses Krook's spontaneous combustion to stand for the inevitable demolition of Chancery by its irate victims if reforms are not forthcoming. George Eliot's sensible parody of Dickens replaces the satirical but grotesquely improbable with an internal revolution both positive and more plausible. Revolution from within, Dickens warns, is what society must at all costs avoid. 'Inward revolution', as in the case of Esther Lyon, is what individual members of society need most, George Eliot counters. Above all, the novelist wants to show that reciprocity, the mutual exchange of character traits, works politically for classes as well as it supposedly does personally between individuals. If one personality can be efficacious for another in a manner beneficial to society, then Felix, the learned artisan, and Esther, the genteel middle-class lady, will create an intermediary class of cultured workmen as hypothetical, unfortunately, as Carlyle's captains of industry.

The competing realisms of Dickens and George Eliot are thus simultaneously competing idealisms. Arguments over what is realistic or accurately depicted lead to disagreements about the way things should be if they were to change for the better. Rivalries between Victorian multiplot novels extend to conceptions as well as perceptions, to the half-created as well as the half-seen. George Eliot subverts the exemplary characters Dickens looked to for redress. She feels his remedial figures, unlike his exaggerations of society's ills, seldom go far enough. As a consequence, the limited powers of Esther Summerson and Amy Dorrit seem to comment in advance on George Eliot's more ambitious creations, deflating them as idealizations. Amy and Arthur Clennam are lost in the roar of the crowd, but Felix and Esther combine in one couple the best of the Webbs and the Leavises. Esther Summerson, though a much maligned heroine, is not impossibly good, Dickens might argue, when compared with Esther Lyon; nor is Rouncewell wishful thinking if placed alongside Holt.

Is the real world an organic continuity that sifts itself as it evolves and improves? Or is it discontinuous, a labyrinthine parody of interconnectedness, a place torn between darkness and light, so that upheavals become necessary periodically to get the recalcitrant reform process back on course? The argument on this score is by no means over. Julian Huxley updates the case for secular evolutionary humanism in *Religion Without Revelation* and *Man in the Modern World*. A religious perspective is re-introduced by Teilhard de Chardin in *The Phenomenon of Man*, and a more sophisticated scientific approach to an organic vision of life informs Fritjof Capra's *The Tao of Physics*. Bleaker elements in Dickens's dystopian vision cater to anti-linear theories of history. They excite moderns like Kafka and are carried to metaphysical extremes in post-moderns like Beckett.

In 1866 George Eliot tries to influence the reader's decision by having the unfolding that unites Felix and Esther transpire inevitably, despite such volcanic plot eruptions as the election riot. Melodramatic events crowd the novel's surface but, says George Eliot, never touch its essence. An allegedly truer rendition of life as an underlying process of gradual growth, for communities as well as individuals, is substituted for dramatic surface events. According to George Eliot, melodramatic but superficial events make radicalism and sensationalism in many Victorian fictions, especially Dickens's, roughly equivalent and equally unreal.

Felix Holt is the classic instance of hidden rivalries in Victorian fiction because, although less subtle in rewriting *Bleak House* than *Middlemarch* would be, revaluation is both subject and technique. Revaluative substitutions characters make throughout the novel re-enforce those George Eliot introduces out of disdain for Dickens. Esther Lyon, for example, refuses to take the place of the Transomes at Transome Court but willingly substitutes England's cultural heritage for Harold's wealth, social service for private comfort, and Felix Holt for idle fantasies about Byron. Similarly, Felix elects marriage to Esther instead of the celibate apostolate he originally planned, and the novel endorses his ideas about radicalism in place of Harold Transome's and Dickens's. In *Middlemarch* the rewriting of Dickens has already been done, so that one confronts finished reconsiderations.[14] But in *Felix Holt*, once one is alerted to the practice, one seems to be observing George Eliot as she inserts her revisions. One watches revaluative substitution actually in progress.

Although the argument that Dickens reincorporates into Victorian fiction everything Jane Austen threw out explains the need for another purging, *Felix Holt* is more than George Eliot's *Northanger Abbey*. Austen openly satirizes the cult of the

Gothic for having little bearing upon real life. But neither she nor the Gothicists believe life resembles *Vathek* or *The Romance of the Forest*. The quarrel is not over whose novels better represent reality; it is about the novelist's obligation invariably to do so. Dickens is always prepared to defend the fidelity of his melodramatic realism, its capacity to isolate and emphasize existing abuses, if not flaws in the nature of life itself. He is more dangerous to George Eliot than Walpole or Mrs. Radcliffe to Jane Austen because his stories, even when they use far-fetched incidents, are never escapist. He mimics popular diversions, including the Gothic mode, but invests them with skilfully constructed moral judgements designed to make a verifiable point about society.

Austen's protest in *Northanger Abbey*, like a Peacock novel, is primarily literary parody. George Eliot's strategy is to give the impression hers is too.[15] But the scope of her attack and the seriousness with which he presses it indicate otherwise. She realizes that she is obliged to discredit an accomplished social satirist whose less cheerful world view seems to be a pre-meditated barrier to her own. *The Castle of Otranto*, an easy target, does not preclude *Pride and Prejudice* as effectively as *Bleak House* stands in the way of *Middlemarch*.

George Eliot's novel engages Dickens in a mid-century dialogue. At stake is not just the way the world works but whether it can be said to work for good or ill. The double logic that *Felix Holt* manifests is a matter of George Eliot's philo-sophical perspective overtaking, correcting, and finally dis-placing Dickens's. A plot George Eliot considers reflective of the 'slow-growing system of things' proves its validity by gradually dislodging melodramatic plot devices from Dickens, which are judged false to the life process.

NOTES

1. Quoted by Walter C. Phillips, *Dickens, Reade, and Collins: Sensation Novelists* (New York: Columbia University Press, 1919), p. 22.
2. Gerald Graff, *Literature Against Itself* (Chicago: University of Chicago Press, 1979), p. 35.

237

3. James Sutherland's pioneering chapter on satire in the Victorian novel treats Dickens, Thackeray, and others as occasional satirists whose targets did not include each other. See *English Satire* (Cambridge: University of Cambridge Press, 1962), pp. 122–32.

4. See the interview with Fowles in *The Saturday Review* (October, 1981), 39.

5. Catherine Gallagher accounts for the novel's Dickensian elements with the improbable thesis that George Eliot's theory of realism had changed since *The Mill on the Floss*. See 'The Failure of Realism: *Felix Holt*', *Nineteenth Century Fiction*, 35 (December, 1980), 372–84.

6. George Eliot, *Felix Holt* (Penguin Books: Harmondsworth, Middlesex, England, 1977), p. 581. Subsequent quotation from this edition is by page numbers included in the text within parentheses.

7. Peter Coveney summarizes this argument in Appendix B to the Penguin edition of *Felix Holt*: 'A Note on the Law of Entail in the Plot of *Felix Holt*', p. 629.

8. Peter K. Garrett ignores *Felix Holt* in favour of *Middlemarch* and *Daniel Deronda*. See *The Victorian Multiplot Novel: Studies in Dialogical Form* (New Haven: Yale University Press, 1980), Ch. 4.

9. See Appendix A to the Penguin edition for 'Address to Working Men by Felix Holt', p. 609. One should regard the Address as part of the novel.

10. Charles Dickens, *Bleak House*, ed. Duane DeVries (New York: Crowell Critical Library, 1971), p. 824.

11. See 'Shooting Niagara: And After?' in Frederick William Roe (ed.), *Victorian Prose* (New York: The Ronald Press Co., 1947), p. 73.

12. Wilkie Collins, *The Woman in White* (Penguin Books: Harmondsworth, Middlesex, England, 1977), p. 575.

13. *Bleak House*, p. 486.

14. See Jerome Meckier, ' "That Arduous Invention": *Middlemarch* Versus the Modern Satirical Novel', *Ariel*, 9 (October, 1978), 31–63.

15. Robert L. Caesario agrees. He calls *Felix Holt* a conscious critique of Dickens's kind of plot. See *Plot, Story, and the Novel: From Dickens and Poe to the Modern Period* (Princeton: Princeton University Press, 1979), p. 97.

Index

240